Kinship, Descent and Alliance among the Karo Batak

Kinship, Descent and Alliance among the Karo Batak

MASRI SINGARIMBUN

UNIVERSITY OF CALIFORNIA PRESS
Berkeley, Los Angeles, London

University of California Press
Berkeley and Los Angeles, California

University of California Press, Ltd.
London, England

ISBN 0-520-02692-6
Library of Congress Catalog Card Number: 73-93061
Printed in the United States of America

Contents

Tables

Figures

Maps

Foreword

Kinship systems have long held a central place in the attention of anthropologists and of all those concerned with the common and distinctive features of our human social life. It is easy to see why this should be so. Human beings, everywhere and always, with only minor exceptions, have lived in families. We have developed our wider social institutions in conformity with, and sometimes in direct articulation with, our patterns of family living. In particular, some of the most complex intellectual achievements of human communities are the various symbolic systems which they have evolved for describing relations between kinsfolk and for specifying what the content of these relations should be. The development and perpetuation of these intricate schemes has scarcely been correlated with the attainment of technical mastery over the natural environment, for some of the societies most advanced technically manage with quite unimpressive systems of kinship.

Sporadic excursions into the comparative study of kinship go back a long way, but just over a hundred years ago, with the publication of Morgan's *Systems of consanguinity and affinity,* scholars were provided for the first time with a substantial corpus of data on kinship systems throughout the world. Ever since then, questions of kinship have remained matters of active debate among anthropologists and comparative sociologists. The questions have changed as one phase in the debate has given way to the next but the same body of data, continually augmented by the results of fresh field research, has been under sustained scrutiny.

During the 1950s this debate had several foci or storm centers. One of them was what interpretation should be given to the evidence from various societies in several different parts of the world where, so it was reported, every man is typically required to marry either a daughter of one of his mother's brothers, or else some other woman whom he refers to by the same kin term as his mother's brothers' daughters, and where he is also forbidden to marry any of the daughters of any of his father's sisters, or any of the women he classifies with them. Some protagonists in the debate took the view that if these rules are present, the kinship system of the society concerned is rightly described as an asymmetric prescriptive alliance system. In societies with these systems, they asserted, marriages, although arranged as occasion demands between individual men and women, are nevertheless determined by enduring relations of alliance between corporate groups; these alliances are asymmetric, in the sense that if group A has an enduring relation with group B which is manifest in group A providing brides for men of group B, then women of group B never marry men of group A; and the kin terms of reference which members of one group apply to their relatives in the other are the names of social categories of persons, into which various relatives may happen to fall, rather than the names of genealogically-specified person-to-person links. The literature of the debate between those anthropologists who made these assertions during the '50s and '60s and their colleagues who attacked them on one or other ground is voluminous indeed and cannot be summarized here. The interested reader fresh to the controversy might begin by looking at the divergent critiques provided by Needham (1971) and Scheffler (1972) and by following up the references they give.

On the basis of the ethnographic evidence then available, advocates of the existence of asymmetric prescriptive alliance systems included in their roster of societies the Karo Batak of North Sumatra. This is the society described by Dr. Singarimbun in this book and to which he belongs by birth. The theoretical axe that Dr. Singarimbun grinds consists of a denial that the Karo Batak belong to this analytic category of societies, and this denial is taken further in the appendix contributed by Dr. Scheffler, where he queries the validity of the concept itself. It is not for me to comment in detail on the arguments they bring forward, but I do wish to draw attention to a wider aspect of the debate. Elsewhere, Scheffler (1972:323) remarks that "Anyone who ventures for the first time into the contemporary literature on systems of kin classification may be excused for wondering if he should take any of it seriously." One of the reasons for this is that the ethnographic data available for many of the societies under discussion were often meager and inadequate. Indeed, the poorer the ethnographic account of a society, the more controversial its analytic status was likely to be. The debate was conducted in an epistemic limbo, neither adequately rooted in empirical reality nor liberated from the contingent constraints of time and place. Dr. Singarimbun now supplies just the evidence needed to show why questions of kinship are still serious, and how they can and should be lively and interesting as well. Unlike so many of the societies which have served as pawns in the debate between theorists, the Karo Batak are, thanks to Dr. Singarimbun's work, well documented and very much alive.

It is sometimes said that anthropology needs not more fieldwork, yielding only more monotonous data, but more critical ideas. Like most dichotomous assertions, this proposition may have heuristic value but is plainly false. Both ongoing fieldwork and careful imaginative analysis are essential for any cumulative scientific study of human society and culture. The debate that lies behind the presentation of Dr. Singarimbun's account of Karo kinship was, in my view, particularly plagued by dichotomous polarization: descent versus alliance, categories versus genealogical links, and so on. Uncompromising dichotomies are useful, perhaps even unavoidable, in periods where an established mode of analysis has ceased to be fruitful; but once a new analytic stance has achieved recognition, they should be replaced, wherever possible, by more sensitive measures. Yet even the dogmatic assertions and counter-assertions of the '50s and '60s may, in the long run, prove to have been less sterile than they seemed to be at the time if they stimulate empirical inquiry of the high quality shown in Dr. Singarimbun's work. With the full evidence before us, set out here with a degree of clarity that I can only envy, we see that the real world of Karoland is much more complicated, and very much more interesting, than the rival simplistic models between which we were supposed to choose. Despite the existence of a few self-reciprocal kin terms, Karo kinship is characterized by a remarkable profusion of asymmetric relations. Institutionalized reciprocity is absent from the domain of kinship to an extent that contrasts strongly with other aspects of Karo culture, as well as with many well-known kinship systems. But if in this respect the Karo Batak approximate to the paradigm of an asymmetric prescriptive alliance system, Dr. Singarimbun demonstrates convincingly that by other criteria their kinship system departs radically from the requirements of this paradigm.

The opportunity to introduce Dr. Singarimbun's book to a wider public gives me great personal pleasure. I have known the author for many years and have followed his work with much interest. I once had the singular good fortune to spend a few days in his company living in an adat house in Kuta Gamber, one of the villages described in this book. I still recall the impression I gained of a lively and vigorous local community, confident in the appropriateness and moral worth of its distinctive way of life, ready to adapt to changing external and internal conditions but determined never to surrender to them. The Karo Batak have been well served by their first own ethnographer, and rightly so.

J. A. Barnes

Churchill College, Cambridge
20 December 1973

Preface

This study is the result of a long-standing interest. I am a Karo Batak; I was reared in Tiganderket village about one kilometer from Temburun village where I was born. I am a member of Temburun lineage, Singarimbun subclan, Perangin-angin clan. My schooling began in Tiganderket but was interrupted by the Second World War. I was forced to leave school in 1942, and during the unsettled years that followed – years of occupation by the Japanese and then of revolution against the Dutch – I became, often in difficult circumstances, a tobacco and cattle trader, a butcher, a refugee and finally a "smuggler." With two Karo companions I engaged in the hazardous task of carrying medical supplies through the jungle from Republican to Dutch-occupied areas, there to collect illegal Republican currency. Then, for security reasons – I had fled from Dutch soldiers attempting to arrest me in a village where my mother was then living – I had to leave my homeland in 1948 and seek shelter in Medan where I entered a private middle school.

Soon after this I became interested in the study of the customs of my own people. My teacher in adat (custom) was my classificatory "father" (my father's half-brother), Nini Satria, who instructed me when I spent my school vacations in Tiganderket. From Nini Satria I learned a number of myths, the history of our lineage and subclan, and tales of ancient warfare and of supernatural beings.

In high school I learned that there was a branch of knowledge that dealt with the adat of preliterate peoples and I received my first lessons in ethnology. Our textbook was based on Duyvendak's *Inleiding tot de ethnologie van de Indische Archipel* (1940) in which the subject matter of ethnology is defined as the cultures of primitive or "nature" peoples. Duyvendak's book contains a long account of the Mentawai, the natives of an island off the western coast of southern Sumatra; our textbook carried this emphasis even further, the major part of it being devoted to a description of Mentawai custom. Thus for us students the Mentawai came to represent primitive peoples in general. Although I found the subject fascinating, it did not occur to me at that time that the customs of my own people might be part of the subject matter of ethnology, for we Batak have our own script.

I left Sumatra for Java in 1955 to continue my studies in the Faculty of Education, Gajah Mada University. By that time I had learned something of Karo dance and music and had compiled about 1500 Karo proverbs. At Gajah Mada, my interest in anthropology found new ground because, in addition to our normal courses in anthropology and sociology, I was fortunate to have the opportunity to join weekly seminars concerning these subjects which were held by the Social Research Committee. I also had the opportunity to join one of my teachers, Professor M. A. Jaspan, on two brief field trips (in 1956 and 1957) to Karoland, and thereafter to become one of his research assistants.

The opportunity to undertake an intensive ethnographic study of the Karo arose when I was awarded a research scholarship in the Department of Anthropology and Sociology at the Australian National University in 1959.

The fieldwork on which this monograph is based was carried out in two neighboring Karo Batak villages, Kuta Gamber and Liren, in the district of Taneh Pinem. My wife and I arrived in the area in September 1960 and remained there until April 1962. The first twelve months were spent in Kuta Gamber and the final seven months in nearby Liren. Our main reason for selecting these villages was that they were then fairly conservative in their adherence to traditional Karo culture. At first we had planned to work in another area, Liang Melas in the Kutabuluh district, which was more isolated from roads and markets. However, a brief tour of the area revealed considerable depopulation; many villages had recently been deserted and in others up to fifty percent of the inhabitants had migrated to the more fertile valleys or to market towns.

In contrast to the situation in most other Karo villages, the peoples of Kuta Gamber and Liren are still largely dependent on shifting cultivation, and more than two-thirds of them still live in adat houses. Also, adherence to traditional Perbegu religious beliefs and practices is stronger than in many parts of Karoland. There are seven spirit mediums (*guru si baso*) and three medicine men (*guru*) in Kuta Gamber alone. With the single exception of one Moslem family in which the husband was converted to the religion of his in-marrying wife, all the inhabitants of these two villages practice the traditional religion. There were no converts to Christianity in 1960-1962.

Being a Karo gave me a number of advantages. Most importantly, the language is my mother tongue, so I was able to mix freely with people and had no difficulty in understanding their use of idioms and proverbs, of which I had already made a special study. In addition, I already knew a great deal about adat, the kinship system, and the culture in general. This enabled me to begin immediately to work on the research project I had conceived in Australia.

A potential danger, of which I was aware from the outset, was that distortion could result from my strong identification with my own people. I think, however, that my experience of life in other societies with other cultures – at different stages in my life I have lived among Alas, Malays, Javanese and Australians – and my anthropological training have helped me to guard against the dangers of subjectivity and ethnocentrism. Also, while in the field I had the benefit of my wife's perspective as a non-Karo observer of village life.

Another potential danger was that my own kinship rights and duties might interfere with and unduly complicate my social relations with the people of Kuta Gamber and Liren. But this turned out not to be a problem. Kuta Gamber and Liren are quite far away from my natal village, so far in fact that few people in my natal village knew where Kuta Gamber was. Partly as a consequence of this, I had no close relatives in Kuta Gamber or Liren and I was not obliged to take sides in disputes or even to participate in ritual activities if I did not wish to do so. Also, I was far removed from my own relatives; they understood and sympathized with my situation, and they refrained from pressing my adat obligations as though I were not in Karoland.

The topic of this monograph is kinship and affinal relations among the Karo Batak. My reason for selecting this topic is my belief that an understanding of the Karo system of social relations between kin and relatives by marriage is the necessary starting point for an understanding of most other aspects of Karo culture and society. Moreover, the Karo kinship system is similar to the kinship systems of numerous other peoples – including other Batak – which have become the focus of considerable anthropological interest and much theoretical debate. The Karo practice matrilateral cross-cousin marriage and they regard each and every marriage, whether or not it is between cross-cousins, as establishing a special kind of social relationship between the relatives of the spouses, a relationship they call *anakberu-kalimbubu.* In this relationship, the wife's people (the *kalimbubu,* who may be also the husband's mother's people) are jurally superior to the husband and his people (the *anakberu*). This asymmetrical social relationship is perpetual; it endures in subsequent generations (but in an attenuated form) whether or not the immediate descendants of the original intermarrying families also intermarry. However, these descendants may intermarry, provided they do so in accord with the rule that the *anakberu-kalimbubu* relationship established by their marriage is consistent with the previously established *anakberu-kalimbubu* relationship between the spouses and their families of origin. Of course, this implies that a man may not marry his FZD[1] or a woman her MBS, but that a man may marry his MBD and a woman her FZS. Indeed, such marriages, when they occur, are strongly approved by Karo in general.

These institutions have been much discussed in the ethnographic literature on the peoples of Indonesia generally and in the literature on the Batak in particular. But in my opinion, the hitherto published accounts of Batak societies contain no adequately detailed ethnographic accounts of these institutions or of the relations among them. In the Dutch literature, interest

[1] In this notation, which is used throughout this study, English kinship terms are represented by their capitalized first letter, except for "sister" which is represented by Z. In addition, C is sometimes used for "child" or "children". Thus:

F = father	S = son	B = brother	H = husband
M = mother	D = daughter	Z = sister	W = wife

Chains of such expressions are to be read as follows: FZD = father's sister's daughter; MBS = mother's brother's son; WBC = wife's brother's child; and so on.

has tended to focus on the concept of "circulating connubium" or asymmetrical exchange of women in marriage between patrilineal descent groups. There has been a correlative tendency to interpret the institution of matrilateral cross-cousin marriage as nothing more than a means of perpetuating or maintaining such intergroup marital alliances (see, e.g., Fischer 1935:288-89; 1936; and van Wouden 1935 [1968]; also Lévi-Strauss 1969 [1949]). In addition, some Dutch scholars have been concerned to demonstrate the essential unity of social organization, myth, and ritual in Indonesian societies. Thus, Needham has recently argued that the Dutch literature on the Batak confirms his theory of "asymmetric prescriptive alliance systems" by demonstrating beyond any reasonable doubt that societies of that type do exist (Needham 1962:53-54; 1966a:1266-68; 1971:lxii-lxiv). This model of Batak society does seem to be supported by many statements of fact and of interpretations in this literature, especially if one approaches it with the aim of confirming the prevailing Dutch interpretation. Yet the Dutch literature, though massive and often quite thorough in its coverage of certain topics, provides a somewhat incomplete and misleading basis for an understanding of these institutions.

This is not the place to review the Dutch ethnographic and theoretical literature in detail, but it should be noted that the attempt to understand Indonesian societies holistically, though admirable and successful in some respects, has gone too far in others. There is much of value in this rather extreme form of functionalism, but applied dogmatically it can obscure rather than enlighten our understanding of Batak (or any other) societies. For example, these scholars have strongly tended to conceive of the essential elements of Batak social structure as lineal descent groups linked in a system of asymmetrical connubium, with jural-status differentials based on wife-giving and wife-taking relationships. Consistent with this, individual, interpersonal relations of kinship are reduced to, or interpreted as, relations between persons as members of descent groups or as members of different descent groups which happen to be allied in marriage in some particular way.

I hope to show in this monograph that the actual state of affairs in Karo Batak society is precisely the opposite. Relations between persons as members of different descent groups which happen to be related as *anakberu-kalimbubu* are in fact reflections of and are structurally dependent on social relations ascribed between those close relatives who are the structurally primary *anakberu* and *kalimbubu*. There are many reasons, I think, to suppose that Karo society is not unique or aberrant in this respect. The tendency of Dutch and other anthropologists to interpret Batak kinship terms as the names of "social categories" is responsible, in large part, for this failure to perceive the actual structural priorities between the Batak kinship and descent systems.

It should be noted, too, that Dutch ethnographers and theorists, though strongly influenced by Durkheimian sociology, have sometimes confused "historical" and structural description and analysis. Perhaps because so much of traditional society was disappearing or being greatly modified before their very eyes, and perhaps also because of the predominance of "historicism" as the theoretical orientation in the early years of ethnographic inquiry, the Dutch have been much concerned to discover the basic structural elements of old or original Indonesian culture.

The theory that early or original Indonesian society was holistically organized around unilineal descent groups related by rules of prescriptive intergroup marriage was, quite early, accepted as established fact. Subsequent ethnographic studies were often concerned with the degree to which the original social structure and its associated cultural expressions still existed in the societies under study. Unfortunately, failure to find much direct contemporary evidence for the existence of such a social and cultural system was explained away as the consequence of recent or not-so-recent social and cultural change. Various elements of folklore, religious beliefs, etc., were interpreted as remnants of this hypothetical original form of the society. Not surprisingly, it is sometimes difficult in dealing with this literature to distinguish between statements of ethnographic fact and conjectures about what might have existed at another time in the more or less remote past.

It is not my intention to minimize the contributions of the many dedicated Dutch scholars who compiled and preserved an ethnographic record which, as a Batak and an anthropologist, I have found invaluable. Indeed, it is not so much with the ethnography that I find I have to disagree, but with the theory that the Batak social and cultural systems constitute a unitary whole which is best comprehended by the theory of asymmetric prescriptive alliance systems.

Finally, those anthropologists who may have had occasion to read my doctoral dissertation (*Kinship and Affinal Relations Among the Karo Batak,* Australian National University, 1965), will note that, although there are no inconsistencies in statements of ethnographic fact between that account of Karo social structure and the present account, there are some differences of interpretation. In 1965 my knowledge and understanding of the anthropological theoretical controversies about the nature of Batak and similar societies was not as extensive as I hope it is now, and I was then somewhat too willing to accommodate my understanding of Karo society to the model of asymmetric prescriptive alliance systems. In particular, I did not then realize the degree to which the theory reverses the actual structural priorities between the Batak kinship and descent systems. Consequently, in my dissertation the interpretations I presented did not always accord with the facts. Part of the reason for the long delay in publication of the results of my study was my dissatisfaction with the earlier analysis, which should now be regarded as superseded.

Acknowledgments

I am greatly indebted to Dr. H. W. Scheffler for his keen interest, encouragement and his valuable contribution on Karo kin classification in Appendix III. Without his help this monograph would not have been published. I am indebted also to Professors M. A. Jaspan, J. D. Freeman and J. A. Barnes for the training I received from them and their assistance to my work over the years. In addition, I would like to thank Professor Barnes for the generous foreword he has written to the book.

I wish to thank my wife for her assistance at all times. She helped me obtain information from Karo women during the course of our fieldwork, and she drew the diagrams for this monograph. I am grateful for the help given by many Indonesian officials, by my landlords, and by informants during my fieldwork. Their names need not be mentioned here individually. "Mention all their names or none at all," a Karo would say in this context, and I have decided to follow the latter course.

Finally, I wish to express my gratitude to the Australian National University for the scholarship which made my research possible.

A note on spelling and terminology

The new orthography for Bahasa Indonesia, notably "c" for the English equivalent "ch", has been adopted throughout the monograph in writing Karo and Indonesian words, including place names. Karo and Indonesian words are underlined. Indonesian words, excluding those which have become spoken Karo, are followed by (I).

Chapter One

Introduction: Karoland and Its People

KAROLAND

The area of Karo settlement, Karoland (Taneh Karo), is approximately 5,000 square kilometers, stretching between 3° and $3^{o}30'$ north latitude and $1^{o}30'$ and $2^{o}30'$ western longitude. Broadly speaking, Karoland may be divided into two main areas, the Karo highlands and the Karo lowlands or Dusun. These two areas merge into one another; there is no sharp escarpment dividing the lowlands from the highlands. The lowlands proper (Lower Dusun) lie at an altitude of approximately 40 to 200 meters; the transitional country (Upper Dusun) – included in the Karo lowlands – lies between 200 and 700 meters, and the highland villages are at an altitude of 700 to 1,400 meters. The seven highest peaks in the Karo highlands range from 1,815 to 2,417 meters. Two of these, Sibajak (2,070 m.) and Sinabun (2,417 m.), are active volcanos.

The geographic neighbors of the Karo are the East Coast Malays to the north, Simelungun to the east, Pakpak to the south and Alas to the west (see Map 1). With the latter three peoples, the Karo have close bonds of language, culture and clanship. Traditionally there was no common boundary between Karoland and Tobaland.

Karoland is not a single unit in the modern administrative system. Since Independence (1945) it has contained one regency (*kabupaten*) and parts of three other neighboring regencies. These four areas are: (1) Kabupaten Karo, in the Karo highlands, regarded as the original homeland and main cultural center of the Karo people; (2) Kabupaten Langkat, a plantation area to the west of Medan, consisting of alluvial coastal plains and rising foothills; (3) Kabupaten Deli-Serdang, which is ecologically and demographically similar to Langkat, in that the Karo population of these two regencies is concentrated in the interior and the

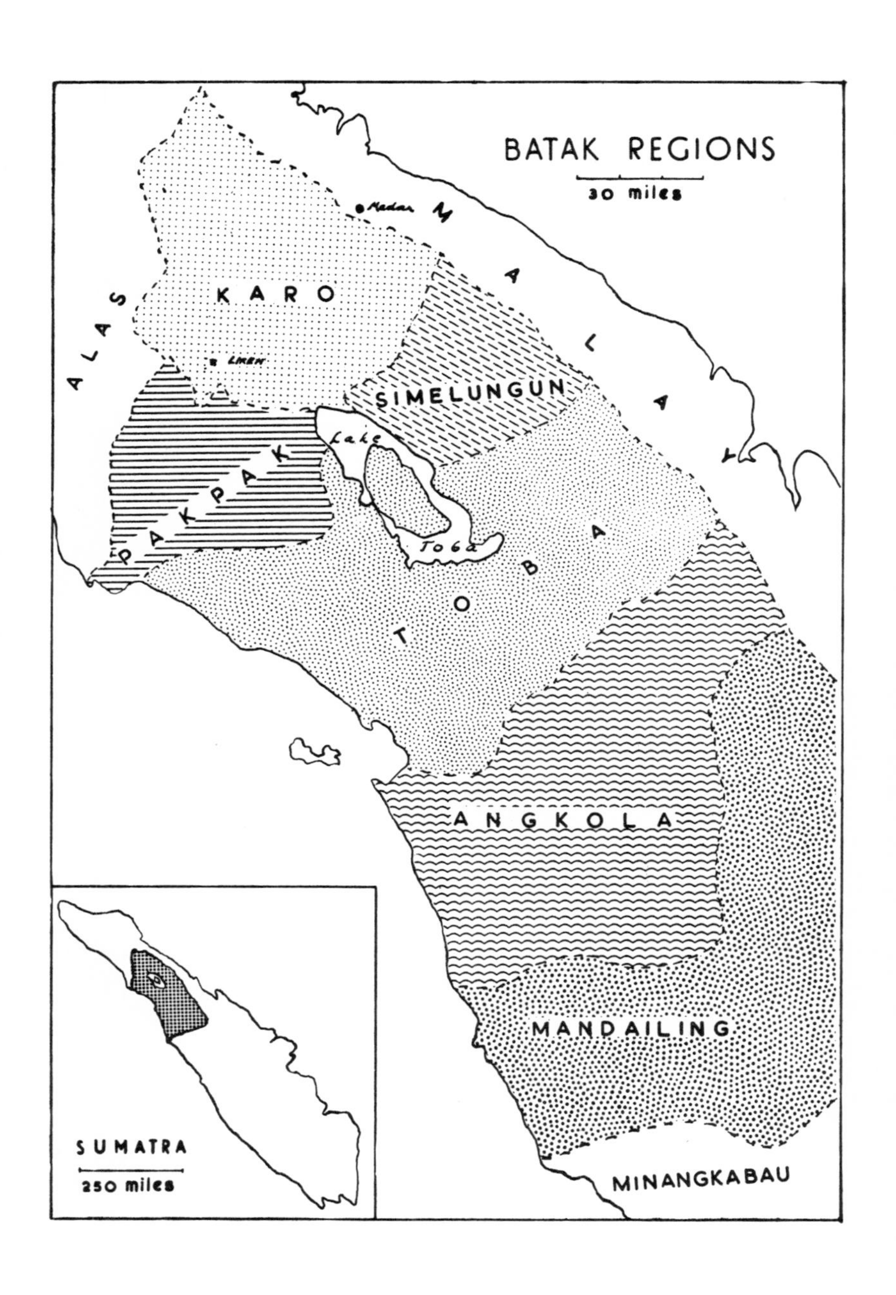
BATAK REGIONS
30 miles
Medan
MALAY
KARO
ALAS
SIMELUNGUN
Lake
Toba
PAKPAK
TOBA
ANGKOLA
MANDAILING
MINANGKABAU
SUMATRA
250 miles

coastal strip is inhabited largely by Malays; (4) a small part of the highland Karo reside in the Pinemland district (*Kecamatan*) of Kabupaten Tapanuli Utara. This district is geographically contiguous with Kabupaten Karo to the north and east. Since the PRRI [1] rebellion of 1958, the Pinemland district, together with the northeastern part of North Tapanuli (Dairi), has been declared a special area called Wilayah Koordinator Dairi (Dairi Co-ordination Region) and is subject to the direct rule of the provincial governor in Medan. As noted in the Preface, the intensive fieldwork for this study was conducted in this area, i.e. in Kuta Gamber and Liren villages in Kecamatan Taneh Pinem.

The climate and rainfall vary from one part of Karo country to another. The average daytime temperature in the Lower Dusun is about 80°F.; inland it is lower because of the higher altitude. Buluh Awar village in the Upper Dusun, at an altitude of 400 m., has an average daytime temperature of 75°F., minimum 61°F., maximum 88°F. In the highlands the range of temperatures is greater; in Kabanjahe (1,300 m.) the average minimum and maximum temperatures are 50° and 85°F. In the highlands people distinguish two seasons of the year: the dry and the wet. Roughly speaking, the first half of the year is dry and the second wet. In the lowlands there are two dry and two wet seasons. April to May is the "little," and August to December the "big" rainy season. Rainfall is heavier in the lowlands than in the highlands. In the Lower Dusun it averages about 2,200 mm.; in the Upper Dusun about 4,000 mm.; in the highlands it varies between 1,500 and 1,900 mm.

THE PEOPLE

The Karo are one of the so-called Batak, a collective name for several linguistically and culturally related peoples – Toba, Karo, Simelungun, Pakpak, Angkola and Mandailing – of North Sumatra. They call themselves Karo or Batak Karo, but seldom Batak. Only the Toba now strongly identify themselves with

[1] Pemerintah Revolusioner Republik Indonesia – the Revolutionary Government of the Republic of Indonesia.

the name Batak; perhaps "the least" Batak are the Angkola and Mandailing (cf. Keuning 1958: 3-4), the only two wholly Moslem societies among the Batak.

The reason the Moslems dislike being called Batak is that the name is stigmatic, though it was more so in the past than it is now. According to Loeb,

> The origin of the name Batak is not certain, but it was already in use in the seventeenth century. It was probably an abusive nickname given by the Mohammedans and signifying pig-eater. The Bataks have taken up this nickname as an honorary title, thus distinguishing themselves from the Djawi, the Mohammedans, and Malays (Loeb 1935: 20).

Moreover, the term is associated with barbarism because in the past the people practiced cannibalism. Even today one may hear the expression *Batak makan orang* (I), "Batak eat people," in many parts of Indonesia.

Joustra (1926: 15) pointed out that the practice of cannibalism was indeed an important feature which distinguished the Batak from neighboring peoples. This practice, however, was more or less terminated before the beginning of this century. Until 1904 there were still some sporadic occurrences of cannibalism in some parts of Simelungun and Pakpakland. Among the Toba cannibalism was given up about half a century earlier, and there has been no cannibalism among the Karo since the beginning of the nineteenth century. Joustra says also that reports of cannibalism among the Batak were often highly exaggerated and sometimes baseless, as for instance when it was reported that old people were eaten.

Independence brought drastic social and economic changes for the Batak. Many Batak hold important economic, military and political positions both inside and outside their homeland and this has tended to lessen the stigmatic connotations of the name Batak. Even Moslem Batak are no longer ashamed of being called Batak.

Because the 1961 and 1971 censuses do not include information on ethnic affiliation, the exact number of the Karo is not known. According to the 1930 census, the total number of Karo in East Sumatra and Tapanuli was then 154,350. [2]

[2] Departement van Landbouw, Nijverheid en Handel, *Volkstelling 1930*, vol. 4, Batavia, 1935.

Assuming a natural annual rate of population growth of 2 percent since 1930, the total number of Karo would have been about 300,000 in 1962 and 370,000 in 1972.

Karo ordinary dress is much the same as that of neighboring peoples. The essential garments for a man are a pair of trousers and a shirt; a woman wears a sarong and *kebaya*, a long-sleeved blouse reaching below the waist. It is also customary for a man to wear a sarong in addition to his trousers. On formal occasions a man wears a black velvet cap (*songkok*) and a coat. Additional garments for a woman are a stole, which she hangs over her shoulder, and occasionally a folded cloth headdress (*tudong*).

On ceremonial occasions everyone wears colorful ceremonial attire called *paken adat*, adat (customary) attire. Unlike everyday clothing, the material for which is either imported from overseas or manufactured in Java, adat attire is the product of local industry. The adat attire of a man consists of a long black cloth with geometrical decorations, which covers the lower part of his body from his waist to his ankles, a red sarong with starlike decorations, which he uses as a stole, and a headdress of cloth decorated with golden threads. Women wear heavy colorful headdresses, stoles on their shoulders and long cloths covering their sarongs. On special occasions both men and women wear golden bracelets and necklaces.

HISTORY

Not much can be said about the pre-colonial history of the Karo. Despite the existence of an indigenous script (*surat Batak*), there are, to my knowledge, no chronicles written in that script. Such texts as do exist deal mainly with divination and spells written by priests (*guru*) on bark, bamboo and, more recently, on paper. The practical value of the script in everyday life is virtually nil.

Hindu influence in Batak culture is remarkable. Loeb writes:

> Direct Hindu influence is said by the natives themselves to have come from the east (Timur).[3] They state that this country was the starting

[3] Timur or Timor is a classic name for Simelungun; Loeb's observation (1935:20) that "The Toba Bataks who live east of the Toba Lake (sic) are called Timur (east)" is mistaken (cf. Tideman 1935).

> point of indigenous 'science' (divination books, magic staves, and magic preparations). The more important Hindu traits imported into the Batak country were wet rice culture, the horse, the plough, the peculiar style of dwelling, chess, cotton and the spinning wheel, Hindu vocabulary, system of writing and religious ideas. Some of the colonies from India were Dravidian, as had been shown by the presence of Dravidian sib names among the Pak-pak, Karo, and even the Gajo and Alas. Even the Batak term for sib (Toba, *marga;* Karo, *merga*) is Sanskrit in origin. Mohammedan influence came to Sumatra earlier than Java and had the effect of stopping Hindu influence on the Bataks, thus isolating them from contact with higher civilizations (Loeb 1935:20-21).

Barus, Pansur and Lubuktua, the three important commercial centers on the southern coast of Batakland, undoubtedly played an important role in channeling these foreign influences. Barus or Baros has long been known to the outside world for its camphor and benzoin. This is evident from the term – used both in Malay and many local languages – *kapur* Barus (literally, Barus lime) for camphor. In about 150 A.D. Ptolemaeus had already referred to North Sumatra and its surrounding islands as the Barus islands (Joustra 1926: 20).

Available data indicate that, for political and religious reasons, the Batak people, including the Karo, were never on good terms with the Achehnese. The latter made several attempts to establish political control over the Batak and to convert them to Islam. The Batak reacted strongly against this. Moslem proselytizers from Acheh frequently visited Karoland but did not have much success. One of them, Tengku Sheikh Lau Bahun, was opposed by the Karo and killed. His grave is at a place about five kilometers from Kabanjahe. The only notable success for Islam was at Tigabinanga, which now has approximately 250 Karo Moslems.

There are many accounts in Karo folklore of conflict with the Achehnese. Most important is the story of Puteri Ijo. The Indonesian version, which is slightly different from the Karo, is called Puteri Hijau and has been published in verse form (see Rahman: Sja'ir Puteri Hidjau, Djakarta, 1955). The Karo version has not been written but it is a popular story in their oral literature. A summary follows.

> There was a beautiful princess in Deli Tua named Puteri Ijo who belonged to the Sembiring clan by birth and originated from Seberay

village in the Karo Highlands. She had two brothers – a cannon and a huge snake.

One morning the king of Acheh saw a brilliant blue light in the east and sent a number of officials in his court to inquire what it was. The officials returned to Acheh saying that the blue light was the radiance of a beautiful princess, Puteri Ijo, the daughter of the king of Deli Tua.

The king of Acheh fell in love with her and sent an envoy to make a proposal of marriage but this was refused by the princess. He decided to marry her without her consent and sent his troops to capture her.

There followed a bitter war in which the Achehnese were beaten. Later the Achehnese renewed their attack, this time employing new tactics. They used silver coins as bullets and the Deli Tua troops, instead of defending their country, busied themselves collecting the precious coins. However, the cannon, who was Puteri Ijo's brother, fought violently. Eventually his body became aglow and got thirsty. He asked Puteri Ijo for some water. His sister refused saying: "You won't get a drop of water before the Achehnese are defeated." When someone served the cannon some water, it fell to pieces, one part in the vicinity of Sukanalu village in Karo highland and the other part near Medan. (There is a broken piece of a cannon near Sukanalu and the other one at the front yard of Sultan Deli palace; both are believed to be the broken pieces of Puteri Ijo's brother and have been treated as sacred objects.) Deli Tua was defeated. After conversing with his sister, the snake left Deli Tua and went to the ocean.

At her own request Puteri Ijo was placed in a glass container on board the ship which brought her to Acheh. Another request of the princess was that every Achehnese family should give her a handful of *cimpa* (uncooked rice flour mixed with brown sugar) and a chicken egg and these should be placed in a heap at the harbor at which she landed. When she set foot in Acheh it was indeed near the heaps of *cimpa* and eggs and looked out to the sea. Thereupon a storm broke out and a huge snake, the brother of Puteri Ijo, emerged from the rough sea and landed near his sister. The snake consumed all the heaped *cimpa* and eggs. Then Puteri Ijo climbed onto the snake who carried her out to sea where they disappeared.

Despite this and other legends, the Karo may have conceded a degree of political authority to the Achehnese prior to the coming of the Dutch. It is remembered that a representative of the Sultan of Acheh – who was called *tuan kita* (our lord) – came to Karoland and appointed four Karo *rajas* called *sibayak* (literally, the rich) to govern Karoland. According to Tamboen (1952: 25-6), the king of Acheh summoned the Karo chiefs to a place near the Bahun river between Lingga and Surbakti villages. Here the appointment of a *sibayak* was based on an ordeal. Only a chief who was endowed with supernatural power could be a *sibayak* and, to test this, each chief in turn drove a legendary buffalo called *si nangga lutu*. It is said that when a qualified chief drove the buffalo the animal felt heavy and its back caved in. Through this procedure the king of Acheh nominated four Karo *sibayaks*: the *sibayaks* of Lingga, Barusjahe, Sarinembah and Suka. Each *sibayak* received a knife called *bawar* as a symbol of office from the king of Acheh.

However, the effective authority of the four *sibayaks* was very limited because the Karo had no tradition of kingship. Political organization hitherto had been based on a non-centralized segmentary lineage system and there is no tradition of Karo ever having paid homage to foreign peoples or their kings, not even to the king of Acheh.

A turning point in the history of the Karo people was the annexation of their country by the Dutch in 1906 without significant opposition from Karo. The Dutch troops met with some opposition when they arrived in Kabanjahe in 1904, but the Karo were comparatively backward in military organization and equipment and their attempts at resistance were overcome without much difficulty. Pa Tiram, an old man of Lau Perimbon, said: "It was useless to fight against the *tuan* (Dutch). They could shoot in any direction and were able to reload their guns in such a short time. Their guns were much more powerful than ours and could kill a man across a paddyfield. We could not shoot downhill because our round bullets would roll out of the barrel. Powder and bullets were loaded separately and so loading took a long time. When it rained we were in a hopeless situation. We could not load our guns in the rain."

The only local chief who refused to cooperate with the Dutch government was the renowned Pa Tolong, the *sibayak* of Kuta Buluh. Pa Tolong, according to my informants, prevented his people from performing statute labor in building a main road to and through the highlands. Further, Pa Tolong claimed that what he meant by "my people" was "those who grew bamboo" (*buluh*). It is said that when the Dutch admitted that they grew bamboo, Pa Tolong said, "You also are my people." This expression became very popular among the Karo. Pa Tolong was captured and brought to Seribu Dolok in Simelungun, then the capital of the subdivision of Simelungun and Karoland. He did not return and what happened to him is not known. Today the Karo regard Pa Tolong as a hero; recently there has been an attempt to have him declared a national hero by the national government in Djakarta.

The coming of the Dutch brought drastic changes in many aspects of Karo social life. The tribal political organization which lacked central authority was incorporated into the colonial government. Traditional institutions, such as intervillage warfare and slavery, were abolished and Christianity was introduced. A number of new regulations were issued by the Dutch including the prohibition of abortion, which had been a common practice in the pre-Dutch period, the restriction and later prohibition of opium trading, and the segregation of lepers to a newly-founded asylum at Lau Simomo; finally, vaccination became obligatory.

In the Dutch administrative system Karoland was divided into a number of administrative units. The political implication of this fragmentation of Karoland was that, under the prevailing policy of indirect rule, some Karo became subject to non-Karo native chiefs. Thus, the Dusun Karo were administratively separated from the Karo highlands which they regard as their place of origin. They were included in the sultanates of Langkat, Deli and Serdang, each of which was ruled by a Malay sultan. Part of Karoland was included in the Dairi of Batakland district, whose capital was Tarutung. Although Dairiland is indeed another name for Pakpakland, economically and politically the Pakpak and their country were subject to Toba hegemony.

Karoland, in administrative and therefore political terms, was restricted by the Dutch to a confined area of the highlands. It became the "onderafdeeling Karolanden" (Karoland subdistrict), administered by a Dutch "controleur" whose office and residence were in Kabanjahe, the newly-built capital town. Together the Karoland subdistricts constituted the "afdeeling Simelungun en de Karolanden," headed by a Dutch assistant resident at Pematang Siantar. This "afdeeling" was included in the province[4] of the East Coast of Sumatra, whose chief administrator was a Dutch governor in Medan.

4 Since August 1915, the status of the East Coast of Sumatra as an administrative unit was raised from *gewest* to *gouvernement (Encyclopaedie van Nederlandsch-Indie*, vol. III, 1919:148).

The Dutch appointed the existing four *sibayaks* as subdistrict chiefs. In addition, the Dutch government nominated one other *sibayak*, the *sibayak* Kuta Buluh, so that the Karo highlands or the Karoland subdistrict was then subdivided into five smaller administrative units. Each unit was called a *kerajan* (I, literally, kingdom) and was headed by a *sibayak*.

Each *kerajan* was divided into several *urung*. The number of *urung* in a *kerajan* ranged from two to six and the total number of *urung* in the highlands was eighteen, each administered by a *raja urung*. Each *urung* contained several villages, each with a village chief called *pengulu* (from *ulu*, head). The offices of these native chiefs, from *pengulu* to *sibayak*, were transmitted to their descendants following the rule of male primogeniture.

This administrative system remained in force until the end of the Japanese occupation in 1945. After Independence, however, various modifications were introduced, including the elimination of the perogatives of the traditional chiefs. Now the chief administrator at each administrative level is elected to his office. At the village level the headman is elected by the villagers and at the higher levels by a body of local representatives. The administrative divisions above the village level are the district (*kecamatan*), regency (*kabupaten*) and province (*propinsi*) respectively, the first two terms being Javanese in origin and the last Dutch.

The development of a network of roads in Karoland after Dutch annexation, the establishment of new market places, the introduction of industrial goods, the demand for wage laborers in various fields, and the obligation to pay annual taxes, all were significant factors in changing the Karo economy. Another important factor in the economic development of the Karo highlands has been the geographical proximity of Medan, a boom town on the east coast about sixty kilometers from the Karo highlands. The cool climate of the highlands makes this area the main source of fruit and European vegetables for Medan; it is also important as a tourist and recreation area.

The Bataksch Instituut, established in 1908 in Leiden, played an important part in this economic development, although the primary aim of the Institute was to promote scholarly studies of the Batak. The Institute had an irregular publication called "Uitgaven van het Bataksch instituut." Of the twelve numbers published before 1916 two deserve special mention: "Batakspiegel"

("A Mirror of Batak Society") (1910) and "van Medan naar Padang en terug" ("From Medan to Padang and Back") (1915), both by M. Joustra. In addition to its scholarly activities, the Institute conducted experiments in practical fields and these have subsequently been of great importance in the economic development of the Karo. Under the leadership of Mr. Botje, an agriculturist, the Institute sponsored an experimental garden near Berastagi in 1911 (since 1915 located in Kuta Gadung between Kabanjahe and Berastagi). There Botje demonstrated scientific methods of growing European vegetables and emphasized the considerable demand for these goods in Medan. Botje's first experiment with tomato-growing proved successful and this had a great influence on the people around Berastagi. The Karo highlands soon became an important vegetable and fruit producer for Medan and other cities in East Sumatra and later for Penang and Singapore.

The development of the Karo lowlands followed a different course, however. In the highlands there are no foreign plantations, but Langkat, Deli and Serdang in the lowlands became important centers of foreign plantations in Netherlands East Indies; this shaped, to a large extent, the economic life of both the rural and the urban population of the area.

The highland Karo enjoyed a better political and economic position than the lowland Karo; this fact is widely recognized. It is also acknowledged that "adat is stronger" in the highlands. Malay influence is strongly felt among the lowland Karo, particularly in music, dancing and religion. In the past many Karo families became Malays as Karo were then at the lowest level of the regional ethnic pyramid. There were advantages to be gained from identification with the culture of the Malay sultans. Another reason for "Malayanization" was that this offered an escape and refuge for Karo who were banished from their own society for one reason or another.

Since Independence, however, conditions have changed radically. The sultans and their followers are no longer in power. They were victims of the social revolution (*revolusi sosial*, I) of 1946 in East Sumatra, which ended the political and economic hegemony of the Malay chiefs in the area. Also the Karo have made substantial advances in various fields and now hold many key positions as army officers and higher government officials in North Sumatra. The lowland Karo and other peasants in the area have repossessed the land that had been alienated by the plantations, although in many instances they are still illegal squatters.

Chapter Two

The Village

The Karo village is not only a collection of houses and the families that reside in them. It is also a complex community with a distinctive social structure, albeit a structure shared with other Batak communities.

Each village has its own name which is frequently based on a geographical, floral or other feature of the locality. Kuala, for example, means an estuary or a place of confluence of two rivers; Kuta Gamber means the village of gambier; Kempawa is a kind of palmtree; Kuta Mbaru means a new place or new village, and so on. Other villages are named after their alleged founders.

Surrounding the village is the village land (*taneh kuta*) used for agriculture and pasture. The inhabitants of the village constitute a land-owning unit and non-residents may not use village land for economic purposes. The only exception to this rule is hunting, provided that one foreleg of the quarry is given to the *pengulu*, the village chief, and fishing, for which no such gift is required. After Independence, however, the headman's right to the foreleg was abolished. The perogative was deemed feudalistic.

Village communities vary greatly in size, from ten or fewer to several hundred families. Juhar, the largest Karo village, has a population of about 4,000 or about 800 families.

There is a strong correlation between village population size and political structure. Large villages are usually divided into several wards (*kesain*) and in the past (before Independence), each ward was a political unit with its own chief (*pengulu kesain*) and land (*taneh kesain*); the chief of the senior (first-established) ward was recognized as the senior chief. The number of wards in large villages varies; in Juhar there are twelve wards.

Kuta Gamber and Liren, with which I am concerned, are villages of medium size – their populations are 372 and 189 respectively – and they are not divided into wards. Indeed, the great majority of Karo villages (about 95 percent) may be classified as medium or small and are not divided into wards. Following the people's own classification, I classify a village as small if it is occupied by fewer than 25 families, medium if occupied by 25-100 families, and large if occupied by more than 100 families. Kecamatan Taneh Pinem, the administrative district (kecamatan) to which Kuta Gamber and Liren belong, contains 43 villages and only one of them, Lau Perimbon, has ward subdivisions.

LOCATION AND PHYSICAL ENVIRONMENT

To reach Kuta Gamber and Liren from Medan, the capital of the province, one travels by motor road to Kabanjahe, the capital of Karo regency (see Map 2). The distance between Medan and Kabanjahe is seventy-seven kilometers and the condition of the road, in 1961, was good; but the journey usually took about three hours, partly because the bus stopped several times on the way. The journey is continued by bus from Kabanjahe to Tiga Binanga, about twenty-eight kilometers to the west, and this takes another two hours. From there one may continue by bus for another hour on a bad road to Kuta Buluh, but the majority of people prefer to walk from Tiga Binanga to Kuta Gamber or Liren. It is cheaper, of course, and continuing the journey by bus to Kuta Buluh does not speed up the journey. The journey by foot from Tiga Binanga to Kuta Gamber covers about twelve kilometers and takes about three hours; from Kuta Buluh to Kuta Gamber the distance is about eight kilometers and it takes about two hours.

The terrain around Kuta Gamber and Liren is mountainous. Both villages lie on the slope of a mountain, Deleng Kempawa, about 650 meters above sea level. This slope is the main agricultural land of the two villages. The Lau Rimbon river marks the end of the slope and it was the bathing place for Kuta Gamber in the past. Across the Lau Rimbon is part of the Bukit Barisan range which has to be crossed by people walking from Tiga Binanga to Kuta Gamber or Liren. The western slope of this part of Bukit Barisan serves as grazing land for both villages.

The land is bare except for a grass known as *lalang* or *alang-alang* (I: *Imperata cylindrica*) and small trees growing in the

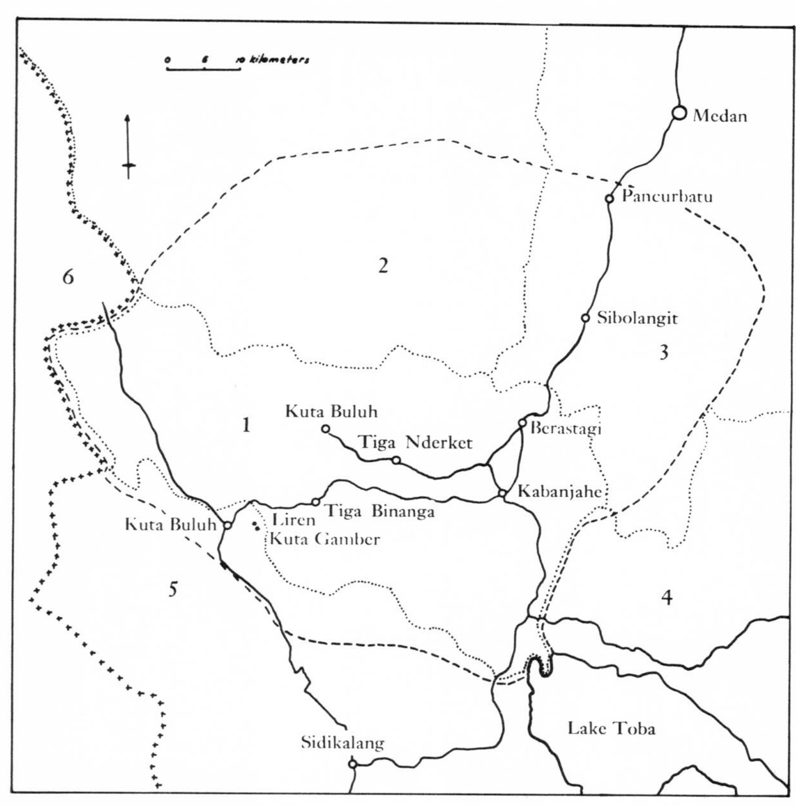

Map 2. KAROLAND

--- Rough area of Karoland

... Regencies

+ + + Provincial boundary

1. Karo Regency
2. Langkat Regency
3. Deli-Serdang Regency
4. Simelungun Regency
5. Dairi
6. Alas

ravines. The people regret that, because of extensive use of the land for shifting cultivation and an increasingly short fallow period, the once extensive forest has disappeared. In the past the fallow period ranged from ten to fifteen years; at present it has been drastically reduced to three or four years. Also, the period of cultivation has increased; instead of having one or two crops of rice within one or two agricultural years before the land is allowed to lie fallow, it is now a common practice to cultivate a plot of land for six to eight crops – rice and cash – in three or four successive years. The condition of the soil has been described by a geologist[1] who made a survey of this area.

> Lateric soils of different kinds depending upon the percentage of Fe203 and Fe304 which changes with the location; this is because of the more or less intense weathering of original rocks which could be encountered in the sub-surface, e.g. limestone, marls and metamorphic rocks like schists and shales. Also apparently the existence of pegmatites is present with Si02 percentage which is relatively high in the petrographical sense.
>
> So, from agricultural standpoint, it could be said that in general the soil in this area is poor and will not give satisfactory yields. Besides, the influence of erosion (as the result of shifting cultivation) is great and special measures have to be taken for conservation of the soil.

THE LAY-OUT OF THE VILLAGE

In stories and love songs a village is always described as sheltering under coconut palms. Indeed, looking at a village from some distance, it looks like a coconut grove. It seems that coconut palms are planted when a village is founded; when speaking about the history of a village, it is frequently said that certain coconut palms are as old as the village itself. A number of villages have been abandoned but their sites are still marked by coconut palms.

In the past every village was encircled by a strong fence six feet high, and the people who owned the gardens around the village were responsible for its upkeep. There was a gate for the entrance of cattle and carts but people entered the village by

[1] This is a personal communication from the geologist concerned, but at his request I have not given his name.

climbing one ladder and descending another. There was thus a clear demarcation of the village site, and when people said "in the village" they were referring to the area "inside the village fence and gate." The fence and gate were built primarily for defense in the olden days but also to prevent pigs from leaving the village and damaging the fields. During the dutch occupation, intervillage warfare ceased and keeping the pigs in check became the primary function of the village fence and gate. Since Independance, as part of the national cleanliness movement (*Gerakan Kebersihan Nasional,* I) pigs are not allowed to roam in the village. Villagers must keep their pigs in pens, and those who disregard this instruction run the risk of a police patrol killing their pigs. This has resulted in village fences being neglected and gates have practically disappeared. Instead, pig pens surround a village.

Map 3 shows the lay-out of Liren village which is a typical or average Karo village. I choose Liren rather than Kuta Gamber for this description because, unlike Kuta Gamber, it has a *sembahen,* traditional shrine.

There are two types of dwelling place: the adat house and the modern house. In Liren there are six adat houses, one of which is of the small type with only four apartments; the rest are of the larger and more representative type, each with eight apartments (see Chapter 4). The divisions of the houses in Map 3, however, represent the number of families occupying the houses, rather than the number of apartments. In three of the six adat houses there are as many families as there are apartments (*jabu* or *sencepik,* see Chapter 4). In three houses some families each occupy one apartment and other families each occupy two adjacent apartments. In one case a single family occupies four apartments. This house is comparatively small, however, about the size of two apartments in a large adat house.

In Liren there are nine modern houses. These are architecturally distinct from the adat houses and resemble modern houses in a town. One of these houses looks more like a hut than a modern house. Compared with an adat house, a modern house is smaller in size and is occupied by a smaller number of families. An adat house is occupied ideally by eight families and a modern house by one. As shown in Map 3, some modern houses are occupied by more than one family. One of the six modern houses in Liren was occupied by two families, another by three.

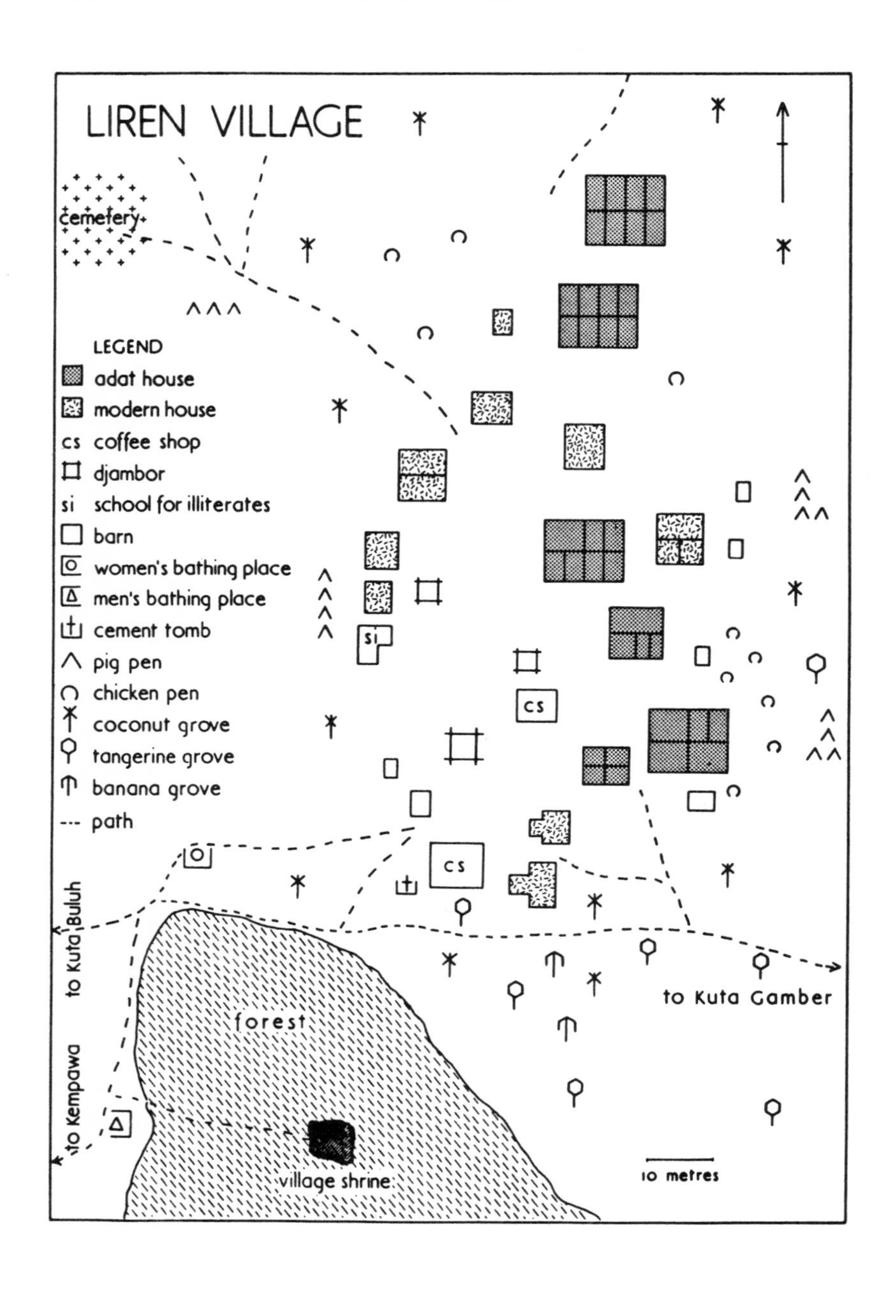
LIREN VILLAGE
cemetery
LEGEND
adat house
modern house
cs coffee shop
djambor
si school for illiterates
barn
women's bathing place
men's bathing place
cement tomb
pig pen
chicken pen
coconut grove
tangerine grove
banana grove
--- path
si
cs
cs
to Kuta Buluh
to Kempawa
forest
village shrine
to Kuta Gamber
10 metres

There are nine barns in Liren village. Five of these barns serve as sleeping places for young boys, unmarried men, and male travellers. They sleep in the attics of the barns. Again, two types of barns may be distinguished: one with an open platform and the other without. There are six barns with platforms in Liren. This type of barn has potentially three functions: it is a storehouse for paddy, its attic may be used as a sleeping place, and the open platform of its lower part as a meeting place or sort of community center.

The barns located in the center of the village and fulfilling the three functions mentioned above are called *jambor*. This expression is used when speaking of the building's use as a dormitory for unmarried men or as a meeting place. When people say, "He sleeps in the *jambor*," reference is to the attic, but when they say "He is chatting in the *jambor*," the reference is to the open platform beneath the granary. One does not say that the paddy is stored in the *jambor*. In that context the building is called *sapo pagé*, the paddy hut.

Of the six store-houses with open platforms in Liren, only three are called *jambor*: "the big *jambor*" (*jambor mbelin*), "the small *jambor*" (*jambor kitik*), and "the *jambor* of women" (*jambor diberu*). The names of the first two *jambor* are based on their size but the third name is based on its function as a meeting place.

In general, the *jambor*, as a meeting place, is used exclusively by men. It is the place for a man to spend his leisure time, to talk there with friends, or to do some minor task such as making a bamboo spoon or repairing a fishing net. When coming back from the fields in the afternoon, a man usually goes to the *jambor* and "there he waits for the food to be cooked." He goes home only after the meal is ready, and it is common practice to return to the *jambor* after having a meal, and later to return home again to sleep. The same thing happens in the morning: a man gets up around six o'clock, goes to the bathing place to perform his toilet and have a bath, and then goes to the *jambor* to smoke a cigarette and have a chat before breakfast.

That there is a "*jambor* of women" in Liren is indeed exceptional. Although this *jambor* is not as extensively used by women as the other *jambor* are by men, it is, nevertheless, frequently filled with women. However, unlike the other *jambor*, which are exclusively for men, this *jambor* is not exclusively for women. Every morning a number of men sit there but at noon it is sometimes occupied exclusively by women while they dry their paddy in the sun before taking it to the rice mill. Women may go there to plait their mats or pandanus containers, or to delouse one another.

The "big *jambor*" is also called *bale'* (courthouse). In the traditional judicial system, the lowest judicial body in the hierarchy was at the village level where councils were held on the *bale'*, i.e., the platform of the *jambor*. After Independence the judicial system was simplified and the village court was abolished. At present the lowest court in the hierarchy is at the regency level. Even so, minor disputes are occasionally adjudicated by both the village chief and village elders so the function of "the big *jambor*" as a courthouse still survives.

Liren and Kuta Gamber each have two coffee houses. The coffee house is a recent but important institution in Karo village life. Every village of medium size has at least one coffee house. Like the *jambor*, the coffee house is exclusively for men. Men drink tea or coffee there but lemonade, beer, and wine also are available.

In addition, miscellaneous domestic needs such as kerosene, small kerosene lamps, salt, dried fish, needles, buttons, medicine, etc., are sold in the coffee shop.

Indeed, the coffee shop manifests the changing economic and social patterns of village life. In the shop, village people, like those who live in towns, sit on chairs, read the daily newspaper and listen to the transistor radio. The coffee shop is therefore an important source of information. Travellers usually stop at the shop, drink a cup of coffee and exchange news. Similarly, villagers who have visited other places, when returning home, spread news in the shop. At night it is the only place which is well-lit in the village. For that purpose each coffee shop has at least one kerosene pressure lamp.

There are two separate bathing places, one for men and the other for women. Water is channeled through a bamboo pipe under which people shower. The place is sacred because it is believed to be the dwelling place of spirits. A bathing place has therefore an important religious function. In rites of passage, for example, a newborn child is taken there and various cleansing rites are performed.

Near the spring is the *sembahen*, the village shrine, located in a small sacred grove. The shrine itself is an area about five meters square covered with the traditional sacred plants: *kalinjuhang* (*Cordyline fruticosa Backer*), *besi-besi* (fam. *Acanthaceae*) and *sangka sempilet* (*Justicia gendarusa*). This is the place of the guardian spirits of the village. In times of distress, such as epidemics and war, people go in procession to the shrine and ask for protection. The ceremony is conducted by the ruling lineage because it is believed that only a member of the ruling lineage can communicate with the guardian spirits of the shrine. The village is thus a ritual unit.

The chief spirits of every village shrine are Pa Megoh and Nandě Megoh who, according to a myth, are husband and wife but also brother and sister. They were twins and because they were born on an inauspicious day their parents deserted them under a pandanus tree downstream from the bathing place. A civet cat took them away to the forest where they grew up as spirits and got married. One day a traveller passed the forest in which they lived and through him they sent a message to their parents telling them about their dwelling place. The parents were astonished to hear this news and went to the forest to visit their children. A voice came from a tree saying that they, the twins, were now husband and wife, the husband called Pa Megoh and the wife Nandě Megoh. They would become guardian spirits, they said, and would guard the village on the condition that a special ceremony were held and offerings made upstream from the bathing place. The villagers performed the ceremony as directed and the shrine was created upstream from the bathing place.

The graveyard, situated outside the village, is believed to be a wandering place of spirits. A graveyard is always a wilderness. A new grave has a bamboo fence but after a couple of years have passed the fence decays and the grave is no longer distinguishable. There is no custom of cleaning the cemetery. In fact, cleaning a grave is taboo because it is believed to invite death. "Let the grave be a wilderness so that people are reluctant to stay there (i.e., to die)," said Pa Jiman.

In the Perběgu, the traditional religion, there is no account of the abode of the dead. It is believed that the spirits of the deceased (*běgu*) visit the graveyard frequently and for this reason offerings are frequently placed there. The spirits live somewhere else. The spirit is believed to join his or her relatives; a deceased man joins his agnates (patrilineal kin) and a married woman her deceased husband and his agnates.

In the mortuary rite a spirit medium presents offerings to *si mada pateken*, the founder or head of the graveyard, the spirit of the first man buried there. The spirit medium says to the head of the graveyard: "Here I am making offerings to you in order to let you know that your grandchild so-and-so [the name of the deceased] is coming to you. Please send him to his relatives. If you cannot find his relatives pretty soon, please take care of him in the meantime; he can tap palm wine for you." The rite is called *sehken ku kade'kade'na,* sending (the deceased) to his or her relatives.

It is believed that, in general, the way of life of the spirits is the same as that of the living. They live in houses and villages, have joys and sorrows and engage in various occupations for their living. No one knows where they live.

The skull of a distinguished person is kept in a skull house (*geriten*). There is one such house in Kuta Gamber in which the skulls of Pa Tingger and his wife are kept. Pa Tingger was the chief of Kuta Gamber and a wealthy man. His son Tingger succeeded him as chief and erected a skull-house for his parents. The skulls are placed in a wooden box and kept in the attic of the skull-house. In the first two years the corpse is buried in a grave; after the skull is dry it is removed to the skull-house in a major ceremony.

In recent years the cement tomb has become more popular than the skull-house. There is one such tomb in Liren and one in Kuta Gamber; the former is the tomb of a chief and the latter of a well-known priest. Like a skull-house, a cement tomb is a status symbol. It reflects the economic status of the children of the deceased because only well-to-do people can afford to build a cement tomb; dedication of such a tomb, or a skull-house, requires a large mortuary feast. Only a member of the ruling lineage, a priest, a spirit medium, a smith, or a player in the traditional orchestra has the right to a skull-house or cement tomb.

In the past, there was always a pounding house in the village where women pounded paddy. Today pounding houses have all but disappeared and rice mills with hullers have taken their place. There is no pounding house in Liren or Kuta Gamber. The people send their paddy to a rice mill near Kuta Gamber which is cooperatively owned by the two villages.

There is no school in Liren or Kuta Gamber. Children of both villages go to school in Lau Perimbon, the nearest elementary school. To reach Lau Perimbon takes about forty-five minutes on foot from Kuta Gamber and one hour from Liren. School commencement age is about seven or eight years and almost all children of that age go to school. For further education children are sent to Kuta Buluh, Tiga Binanga and Kabanjahe.

In both villages, however, there is a P.B.H. (*Pemberantasan Buta Huruf*, I, anti-illiteracy) school. A hut was cooperatively built for this school in Liren and in Kuta Gamber an empty hut was made available. Attendance is obligatory and the school operates in the evenings for the benefit of adults.

SOCIAL COMPOSITION

According to adat (customary law), a single agnatic group, no matter how large, may not found a village. For a settlement to be regarded as a structurally complete village, it must be occupied not only by members of the ruling lineage (*bangsa taneh* or *anak taneh*, people of the land), but by members of at least three other lineages as well. These are the *anakberu* of the ruling lineage, the *kalimbubu* of the ruling lineage, and the *senina* of the ruling lineage. The *anakberu* are married women of the ruling lineage plus their husbands and their husbands' agnatic kin or descendants. The *kalimbubu* are the parents and brothers and other agnatic kin of wives of men of the ruling lineage. The *senina* in this instance are men (and their wives and children) of other lineages of the same clan, but not the same subclan, as the ruling lineage.

The lineage whose members were the *anakberu* of the village founder, and who founded the village with him, is known as the *anakberu tua* of the ruling lineage; similarly, the lineage whose members were the *kalimbubu* of the founder of the village, and who founded the village with him, is known as the *kalimbubu tua* of the ruling lineage. Since the subsequent marriages of members of the ruling lineage were not confined to taking wives from the *kalimbubu tua* or giving lineage women as wives to the *anakberu tua*, the *kalimbubu* or *anakberu* inhabitants of a modern village may belong to a large number of different lineages, subclans and clans. The clan and subclan affiliations of the residents of Liren and Kuta Gamber are listed in Tables 1 and 2. These tables show that all five Karo clans are represented in both villages. Fifteen subclans are represented in Liren and twenty-one in Kuta Gamber. In smaller villages fewer clans and subclans may be represented.

Table 1

Descent Groups Represented in Liren

Clan	Subclan	Male	Female[a]	Total
1. Perangin-angin	a. Pinem	25	22	
	b. Sebayang	1	2	
		3	-	
		29	24	53
2. Ginting	a. Munte	6	-	
	b. Sugihen	-	5	
	c. Babo	8	7	
	d. Suka	-	2	
		14	14	28
3. Sembiring	a. Busuk	-	1	
	b. Milala	35	30	
	c. Keloko	-	1	
	d. Gurukinayan	-	1	
		35	33	68
4. Tarigan	a. Gersang	7	7	
	b. Sibero	8	5	
	c. Tua	3	3	
	d. Jambor Lateng	-	2	
		18	17	35
5. Karo-karo	a. Kaciribu	2	3	5
Total		98	91	189

[a] Membership by birth.

Table 2

Descent Groups Represented in Kuta Gamber

Clan	Subclan	Male	Female[a]	Total
1. Perangin-angin	a. Pinem	53	44	
	b. Sebayang	5	-	
	c. Bangun	5	5	
		63	49	112
2. Ginting	a. Munte	35	36	
	b. Sugihen	7	12	
	c. Ajartambun	2	1	
	d. Tumangger	-	1	
		44	50	94
3. Sembiring	a. Busuk	20	19	
	b. Milala	19	7	
	c. Sinulaki	-	4	
	d. Keloko	-	4	
	e. Berahmana	-	1	
	f. Depari	-	1	
		39	36	75
4. Tarigan	a. Gersang	15	13	
	b. Sibero	21	25	
	c. Tua	-	1	
		36	39	75
5. Karo-karo	a. Kaciribu	5	6	
	b. Sinulingga	-	2	
	c. Surbakti	-	1	
	d. Kaban	-	1	
	e. Purba	-	1	16
Total		187	185	372

[a] Membership by birth.

In the traditional political structure of the village, the chief is assisted by one of his *anakberu* (a ZH or DH, for example), who is his deputy, and by one of his *senina*. His *kalimbubu* also have important roles to play in the religious and ceremonial activities of the village. Again, these *anakberu* and *kalimbubu* are not necessarily members of the *anakberu tua* and *kalimbubu tua* of the ruling lineage. But, again, members of the *anakberu tua* and *kalimbubu tua* lineages have important ritual and ceremonial rights and duties in respect of members of the ruling lineage (see Chapters 6 and 7), especially if they happen to reside in the village. When I inquired how Derpih, for example, became a resident of Kuta Gamber, he said: "My ancestors and I were born in this village. My great grandfather married into this village and his descendants have continued to live here. Moreover, we are the traditional *anakberu* of this village."

Almost all the inhabitants of any Karo village are related in one way or another to members of the ruling lineage of the village, and the three principal kinds of relationship to members of the ruling lineage are *anakberu, kalimbubu* and *senina* . I was frequently told "There are no others in the village."

Wage laborers, however, may reside temporarily in a village. Nowadays these men are Toba, Pakpak, Singkel, Gayo and Javanese. Sometimes there are as many as seventy or eighty such men in Liren and Kuta Gamber. They come in groups of three to five, each group consisting exclusively of men of one ethnic category. Some are newcomers but some have been to the village several times before. The presence of the wage laborers in the village is closely related to the agricultural cycle. There is much work to be done after the harvest in January because this is the time for planting tobacco and onions, two of the most important cash crops in the area. So from January to March there are many wage laborers in the village. Additional labor is required also in July and August when the tobacco is processed.

The daily wage of a laborer in 1961 was 50 Rupes excluding meals. The employer provides food either by serving the laborer a meal at his house, or by giving him one liter (=Rp 14) of rice daily, some salt, tobacco and *bulung ipah* (pandanus for smoking) and lending him a cooking pot. The second arrangement is most commonly adopted. Laborers may sleep in huts in the village or huts in the fields; occasionally groups of workers sleep in unoccupied rice barns in the village.

Wage laborers are treated as strangers by the villagers. They do not take part in the social activities of the village and are not invited to attend meetings or festivities. The lingua franca is Karo or Bahasa Indonesia but some villagers speak Pakpak and Toba as well. Without exception the laborers are males, married or unmarried. None are Karo. There is no intermarriage between them and village girls. The villagers look down on the laborers partly because of their social position as laborers, but principally because of ethnic prejudice.

HISTORICAL BACKGROUND

Each Karo village has a traditional history, the story of its foundation. The history of Kuta Gamber and Liren usually begins with Raja Enggang, a mythical ancestor whose natal village was Jambu in central Pakpakland. He went to Karo and founded Pinem village. One of his descendants from Pinem founded Mbacang village and the founding ancestor of Liren came from this village. He lived with his first wife in Liren and placed his second wife in Kuta Gamber. The alleged genealogical depth, from the present youngest generation to the founding ancestor of Liren and Kuta Gamber, is eight generations. (For further details, see Chapter 5, pp. 89-90.)

There are no written records of this history and in the people's oral accounts of the past – when speaking about the "past," reference is always to the period before Dutch occupation – emphasis is laid on intervillage war. Despite the fact that the principal lineages of Liren and Kuta Gamber are said to be agnatically related, social relations between the two groups were marked by serious antagonism and a number of wars. The last war occurred not long before the coming of the Dutch; under Dutch rule intervillage warfare was strictly prohibited.

The Dutch appointed the chief of Liren as subdistrict chief (*kepala negeri,* I); his office was in Liren. This appointment was consistent with a traditional rule. According to custom, Liren is the village-of-origin of a number of neighboring villages including Kuta Gamber because, as we have seen, the ruling lineage of Kuta

Gamber is said to descend from a younger son, the child of the second wife of the founding ancestor of Liren. Similarly, the founding ancestors of Kuta Buluh and Kempawa came from Kuta Gamber and those villages are therefore junior to Kuta Gamber. Normally such alleged agnatic relationships between the founding lineages of different villages have little political significance.

Some people outside Liren explain that the lack of solidarity between Liren and Kuta Gamber is due to the fact that those who now claim the status of members of the ruling lineage of Liren are not in fact agnatic descendants of its founder – and so the Kuta Gamber people owe them no loyalty or allegiance. Those who say this claim that the present members of the Liren lineage are in fact descendants of a man who came to live with the chief of the Liren lineage some time in the past. He was a member of the Sukatendel subclan of Perangin-angin clan, the clan to which Pinem (subclan) Liren (lineage) belongs; but he later changed his subclan to Pinem. He happened to be a clever man and was much more intelligent and able than the chief himself. He was a great help to the chief and the chief gave him one of his wives who was thought to be barren. However, after she married this man, she had a number of children by him. This man gradually gained power in the community and was eventually recognized as its chief. According to this story, the descendants of this man claim to be descendants of the chief who was his sponsor, but they are only the descendants of one of the chief's ex-wives and their blood is not genuine Liren blood.

For strategic reasons the Dutch removed the capital of the subdistrict from Liren to a new place, Taneh Pinem, in 1919. Disturbances were still being caused by some disloyal Achehnese around Taneh Pinem and the government decided to shift the capital to that area so that troops could be stationed there permanently. More than half the population of Liren shifted to this place. It is estimated that the population of Liren was about ninety families at that time and that about fifty families moved to Taneh Pinem. Thereafter, Kuta Gamber, with a population of about eighty-five families, was larger than Liren. As a consequence, Kuta Gamber has become politically more important than Liren.

People in Kuta Gamber and Liren were pleased to talk about the revolution of 1945 because the general feeling is that they contributed much to the struggle for independence. They were proud that most families possessed guns at that time. This was in response to a proposal of the Indonesian government. They purchased the guns through agents and, when the situation became critical, the government collected their weapons for the army. So it is still fresh in the memory of the people that Pa Linap contributed a Japanese rifle, Pa Rido a British rifle, Pa Sora, a well-to-do man in the village, two guns, and so on. There was a rumor in 1950 that the government would pay full compensation for the weapons but compensation still had not been paid in 1962.

During 1947 and 1948 Kuta Gamber and Liren were crowded with refugees. In late 1947 the Dutch army seized control of the Karo highlands and people from the area fled to isolated places. The refugees built huts in small forests around the villages. As the situation worsened, the villagers themselves moved to huts in the forests. It was considered likely that the Dutch would launch an attack on these remote villages particularly because Kuta Gamber was the headquarters of a regiment of guerillas. The Dutch had already fired two mortars which exploded about 200 meters from Liren. Selamat Ginting, the then chief of the Third Sector, led his troops from Kuta Gamber.

Political parties were established soon after Independence and almost everyone in Liren and Kuta Gamber joined the P.N.I. (the National Party) which has since been the strongest party in Karo. In 1961, however, some villagers felt that they were being neglected by their political leaders in the towns.

In 1958 Kuta Gamber and Liren became *kampung gabungan* (I), a joint village, which meant that the two villages were to be administered by one village headman. This was the result of a new regulation that a village headman should have at least 100 families or 500 people under his jurisdiction. Small villages were thus combined to form joint villages, and the former village chief of the largest village was appointed joint-village headman (*kepala kampung gabungan,* I); the village chiefs of the smaller villages became the deputies of the joint-village chief. Thus, the village headman of Kuta Gamber became the joint-village chief and the headman of Liren became his deputy.

THE LAND

All inhabitants of Liren and Kuta Gamber, without exception, are farmers. In the two villages there were three schoolteachers, four shopkeepers, one tobacco trader, and a number of spirit mediums, each with a cash income but all of them engaged in agricultural activities. Those who are well-off own a number of cattle, but cattle-breeding is not an important source of income. Buying cattle is instead a means of saving money. Because of the continuous inflation since the Japanese occupation, people are reluctant to keep their savings in the form of cash.

The primary economic resource is the land on which shifting cultivation is still practiced. Wet-field cultivation (*sabah*) is of little economic importance in this area, though more so in others. In Kuta Gamber only ten of the eighty-eight families owned small irrigated plots with a total area of about two hectare.

There is a conventional classification of village land into two categories: "inside the *kajang*" (*ibagasen kajang*) and "outside the *kajang*" (*iluar kajang*). The meaning of *kajang* is obscure but the people associate the term with the rule concerning domestic animals in the village. According to Pa Ngajam, an adat elder in Kuta Gamber, the area "within the *kajang*" is the potential wandering place of the domestic animals, particularly pigs. This area encircling the village has a radius of about 500 meters.

The area inside the *kajang* is planted in coconut, tangerine and banana groves which are individually owned by villagers. These groves belong to the descendants of the early settlers of the village, that is, to the members of the ruling lineage and their relatives, especially their traditional *anakberu* and *kalimbubu*. In order to prevent pigs from destroying the fields, the owners of gardens within the *kajang* are obliged to fence their gardens. According to the adat rule, a pig is regarded as a domestic animal inside the *kajang*; the implication is that one may not kill a pig there even though it has destroyed a garden. In this case, it is not the pig but the owner of the garden who gets the blame because he has not kept his fence in good order. There is, however, an exception with regard to unruly pigs. If the fence is in good order but a pig enters the garden by digging a hole under the fence, then the owner of the animal is fined.

The main agricultural land of the village is the area outside the *kajang*. Here a pig is regarded as a wild animal and, should a farmer kill a pig in his garden, the owner of the animal may not claim compensation. In 1948 a group of hunters in Kuta Gamber killed a pig by mistake outside the *kajang*. They shared the meat among themselves but gave the head to the owner.

Thus we find the application of two methods of cultivation side by side: sedentary cultivation inside the *kajang* where people grow perennial trees like durian, coconut and tangerine, and shifting cultivation outside the *kajang* where people grow the staple (paddy) and cash crops.

In shifting cultivation, *ngumbung* is the first step in opening a plot of land. *Ngumbung* refers to the act of fixing a bamboo pole in the center of a proposed field. A bundle of shrubs is hung from the top of the pole and this serves as a sign that someone is about to open the land. The gardener then reports his action to his village chief.

Ngumbung is a series of ritual actions. The gardener undertakes *ngumbung* on an auspicious day and clears the land about one meter square in which he fixes the pole. He grows a number of special plants there. Then he brings home a handful of the soil, wraps it in a piece of cloth and puts it near his pillow. For four nights he watches his dreams for signs through which he, with the help of a priest, will know whether or not the proposed land is suitable.

Having opened the land for cultivation, he enjoys a usufructuary right over it. This is best described by Pelzer:

> The person who clears the land and plants the crop gets the produce. Nobody has the right to plant a plot that has been cleared by someone else. As soon as the land is abandoned all rights are forfeited, except the right of the community. However, if trees have been planted, the ownership of the trees and their produce remains with the person who planted them (Pelzer 1945: 18).

In general this holds true for the Karo. When a person clears secondary forest or a wilderness for cultivation, he enjoys no special residual right over it. The land is regarded as abandoned when the stalks of the paddy of the cultivator have disappeared and his hut has collapsed. Then anyone who wishes to claim and clear this land can perform the *ngumbung* without giving notice to the former occupant.

There is an exception for those who clear virgin forest for cultivation. They enjoy the right of second cultivation of the same plot of land. Since virgin forest has almost disappeared from the farming land of Liren and Kuta Gamber, only a few people enjoyed this right in 1960-61.

In the greater part of Karoland, shifting cultivation is no longer practiced. There are irrigated rice fields in many areas and the use of fertilizers is increasing. The availability of land has become a serious problem in Kuta Gamber and Liren, and we may assume that shifting cultivation will disappear in the near future. Extensive use of land for cash-crops has resulted in a shortage of land for this and ordinary agricultural needs. Conflicts over land are rife, the short fallow period results in degradation of the land and in poor crops. Three people in Kuta Gamber introduced fertilizer to their fields during 1960-61 and this will accelerate the adoption of sedentary cultivation.

Chapter Three

The Karo Family

The Karo expression *jabu* has several closely related meanings – nuclear family, domestic family or household, and an apartment (also *sencepik*, section) in an adat house. Each married man is normally (and normatively) the head of his own domestic family or household, and the domestic family consists most often simply of a married man and his wife and their unmarried children. Furthermore, each domestic family normally occupies one or occasionally two apartments in an adat house – thus the designation of family and dwelling-unit as *jabu*.

The domestic family or household is usually a small group of from one to nine people (see Table 3). Ninety-nine (about 75 percent) of the 134 households in Liren and Kuta Gamber had from three to six members in 1961. The mode was 5 and the arithmetical mean 4.2. Table 4 presents detailed information on the composition of the 134 domestic families in Liren (46) and Kuta Gamber (88). Table 5 summarizes the data in Table 3. Those relatively few cases in which the domestic family is a simple nuclear or elementary family represent particular phases in the developmental cycle of the domestic group (Goody 1958). It will be useful briefly to outline this process before discussing intrafamilial social relations in detail.

Table 3

Size of Domestic Families

Number of persons in the family		1	2	3	4	5	6	7	8	9	Total
Frequency	Kuta Gamber	8	5	20	13	23	12	3	4	-	88
	Liren	4	7	6	10	8	7	2	1	1	46
Total		12	12	26	23	31	19	5	5	1	134

Table 4

Composition of Domestic Families

	Number of Jabu			Percentages		
	K.G.	L.	Total	K.G.	L.	Total
1. Elementary family	63	27	90	71.6	58.7	67.2
2. Elementary family plus children by previous marriage (of husband)	1	5	6	1.1	10.9	4.5
3. Elementary family plus HM	2	-	2	2.3	-	1.5
4. Denuded elementary family (widow plus unmarried children)	5	4	9	5.7	8.7	6.7
5. Elementary family plus spouse of one child	2	-	2	2.3	-	1.5
6. Polygynous family	1	1	2	1.1	2.2	1.5
7. Married couple (no children)	3	2	5	3.4	4.3	3.8
8. Married couple (children left parental home)	2	2	4	2.3	4.3	3.0
9. Married couple plus children by previous marriage (of husband)	-	1	1	-	2.2	0.7
10. Married couple plus HM	1	-	1	1.1	-	0.7
11. Widow (single female)	7	3	10	8.0	6.5	7.5
12. Unmarried woman (single female)	-	1	1	-	2.2	0.7
13. Widower (single male)	1	-	1	1.1	-	0.7
	88	46	134	100%	100%	100%

Legend: K.G. = Kuta Gamber
L. = Liren

Table 5

Summary of Composition of Domestic Families

Number of generations in jabu	Frequency	Approximate percentage of sample	Main type of genealogical composition
1	21	15.7	Widows and couples without children (childless or married children have left home)
2	111	82.8	A couple with children
3	2	1.5	A couple with children plus a grandparent
	134	100%	

The Developmental Cycle of the Domestic Family

Each child becomes a member of his or her father's domestic family at birth, and children normally reside with their parents. After the age of eight, however, the boys no longer sleep in the parental home but remove themselves and their belongings to a rice barn where they sleep with their age mates. The boys remain identified with their fathers' families and continue to take their meals with them. A young man, even though fully orphaned, may not set up his own household, for according to the adat the place for a young man is in the rice barn, not the dwelling house. One of the reasons for this is that household labor such as bringing water, cooking and sweeping is woman's work, and a young man cannot do these things without incurring criticism and ridicule. Another reason is that they may too easily get involved in illicit, especially adulterous, sexual relationships if they sleep in dwelling houses. An orphaned young woman, however, may continue to occupy her deceased parents' apartment (see Table 4, no. 12), but this is regarded as an unusual and inappropriate arrangement; such a girl should reside with a married sister or brother until she marries.

When a young man marries, he and his wife may reside with his (or less commonly her) father and mother for a year or so, until they have established and harvested crops from their own gardens and are economically independent of their parents. At this time the young couple, whether or not they have had a child, move into their own apartment (perhaps in another house): "they light their own hearth" and this marks the formation of a new *jabu.* Thus, a newly-formed domestic family may consist of a man and his wife; they need not have any offspring to be recognized as a *jabu* so long as they are economically independent of their parents.

The new domestic family continues to grow in size as children are born to the couple. Its size begins to decrease when their children begin to marry. The daughters marry and usually go to reside temporily with their husbands' parents, while the sons marry and usually bring their brides to reside with the family for a year or so. When all the offspring of the original couple are married, the domestic family consists once again of husband and wife. If the man dies before his wife, she maintains their household until she dies, at which point their *jabu* ceases to exist. A widower, however, may not maintain his own household; there is a customary rule against this and, furthermore, looking after a household is woman's work. Thus, a widower, all of whose children are married, will eat with the family of one of his children and sleep in one of the rice barns. Following the death of both parents, the surviving sons divide the family estate. This division marks the economic dissolution of their family of origin.

Of course, the developmental cycle of the domestic family is not always so simple; there may be contingencies to be dealt with. For example, a man's wife may die after having one or more children by him. He may sleep in their apartment for no more than four nights following her death, after which he must sleep in one of the rice barns and take his meals with a married child or some other close kinsman. His children must be fostered by, and reside with, close agnatic kin until he remarries, at which time they rejoin him and his new wife. Seven of the domestic families noted in Table 4 (nos. 2 and 9) consist of a man and his wife and their children (if any), as well as his children by a previous marriage. It is considered best for a widower to remarry immediately so that there are no cases in Table 4 of domestic families composed of a man and his wife and *her* children by a previous marriage. This is because a widow or divorcee is not entitled to custody of her children. According to Karo adat, a widow who wishes to marry a man who is not her deceased husband's brother or his close lineage "brother" must first ritually divorce her deceased husband and, in consequence, part with her children. (No such ritual is required of widowers who wish to remarry.) Thus, many widows with children do not remarry; they cannot bear to part with their children. Indeed, Karo consider that a widow who loves her children will not remarry, unless to a brother or close lineage "brother" of her deceased husband.

Polygyny, though permitted by adat, is rare. There were two polygynous families in Liren and Kuta Gamber. In one instance a man took his brother's widow as his second wife; in the other a poor man married a childless widow who was much older than his first wife, for the widow had a fair income as a spirit medium.

A major obstacle to polygyny is the negative, indeed obstructive, attitude of women toward it. "For a woman, being given a co-wife is like being given poison," said Pa Murdap. Sometimes the first wife physically attacks the second, especially in the first few weeks of the second marriage, but occasionally even before the marriage takes place. Nande Milas related that she began to keep a careful watch on her husband's outings after she heard that he would like to marry a certain woman. One day she met the woman and her husband walking together outside the village, and she beat the woman with a stick. "My heart boiled and at that moment I would have preferred to die rather than see that woman with my husband," she said emphatically.

Because of the antagonism between co-wives, they never live under the same roof. Each wife maintains her own household economically independent of the other, and sometimes in different villages. The husband alternates his residence from one household to the other, but according to no fixed or customary rules.

As noted above, the usual arrangement is for a son to bring his bride to reside with his parents for a year or so immediately after marriage. This is discussed more fully in Chapters 5 and 8, but it may be noted here that occasionally the newlyweds reside temporarily with the bride's parents (one case in Table 4, no. 5). There is no rule of patrivirilocal residence at this stage. It is rather that the new husband's father has the obligation to provide food and shelter for his son and his son's wife until they are able to harvest food from their own garden. If such support is offered by the bride's parents, the couple may reside with them.

Of the twelve old widows in Liren and Kuta Gamber (eleven of whom had children), three chose to reside with their married sons (Table 4, nos. 3 and 10) rather than to maintain their own households. All did so for the same reason: their health did not permit them to live alone. If it were not for this, they would have preferred to live alone like the other widows. In Kuta Gamber there was one widower (Table 4, no. 13) living alone and maintaining his own household. According to the other occupants of the house, an exception was made in this case because he was a kindly old man and they all felt sorry for him. As noted above, a widower may sleep in one of the rice barns; he may also live in a hut in an orchard outside the village. His eldest son has the obligation to feed him, but some widowers take their meals with the families of their married daughters.

THE HOUSEHOLD

Karo village houses (but not those in towns) have no furniture to speak of. The common room, the place where the people eat, chat and receive guests, has a mat spread permanently on the floor, and from time to time, when considered necessary, other mats are added to sit on. On relatively formal occasions three layers of mat are spread: the coarsest mat on the floor, another of medium size and texture on top of that, and a fine mat on the very top. It is an honor to be given a fine mat to sit on.

The household equipment that exhibits the greatest variety is the kitchen equipment, consisting of homemade tools and factory products. The former include rice storage bags, bamboo containers for salt, and large bamboo spoons. Earthenware pots for making curry are made in some villages and offered for sale in the local markets. Knives and pails are made by local smiths and tinworkers. Most other kitchen utensils such as plates, spoons, cups, kettles and cooking pots are factory products and are bought in towns.

Sleeping gear in the bedroom (see Figure 1, p. 58) consists of a mattress for two people, two pillows, and one or two blankets. Usually the mattress is unfolded on the floor after the floor has been covered with a mat. Only well-to-do people raise their beds on a large box as wide as the mattress and about twenty inches from the floor.

Children up to four or five years sleep with their parents in the bedroom. Older children sleep with their same-sex companions of about the same age in the common room. At the age of eight, however, the boys remove themselves to one of the rice barns. Until they reach puberty, boys may return to the family house during the day to play with their companions, but after puberty a young man may go to his family's house only for meals and must leave as soon as he has finished eating. A young man may be chastised or ridiculed if he stays any longer, for it might be thought that he had improper sexual intentions with regard to the girls or married women of the house.

Differences of age and sex are the two main criteria for the division of labor within the household. Heavy work or light work involving danger is counted as men's work, and light work that takes up a great deal of time is women's work. Thus, men wage war (or used to do so), hunt, look after the cattle, climb and cut down trees, and occupy themselves with specialized crafts. Women do all the kitchen work, carry water, plait mats and bags, and look after the children, chickens and pigs. Children do light chores appropriate to their sex. Some tasks are performed jointly by both sexes. Men and women work together clearing fields, cultivating and harvesting crops, and carrying the produce to the village. However, plowing and using the dibble-stick are men's work, while the women put the seed into the holes and cover it up.

THE FAMILY ESTATE

The domestic family is a property holding unit. Except for personal effects such as clothing and ornaments which are personal property, all other things, including immaterial property such as guardian spirits, are the corporate property of the family. Products of the labor of family members are family property. For example, a son who plants perennial fruit trees such as tangerines or coconuts cannot say that the crop belongs to him. Under the customary rule, he has no special right to the product of his labor since the energy to work, it is said, is indirectly the product of food served by the family. One proverb likens the products of the labor of family members to "the steam of the rice." Riman's case illustrates this principle. Riman and his father built an adat house and occupied two apartments in it. Riman married not long after the house was finished and wanted one of the two apartments for himself and his wife. His father refused to let him have it. At a family meeting held to consider and resolve the dispute Riman argued that one apartment belonged to him for these reasons: he had worked on both apartments occupied by his father's family and he had collected a large part of the materials for the house, in particular the palm fiber for the roof and the wood for the walls. Riman's father argued that Riman had no greater right to one of the apartments than did his brothers who had not helped to build the house, because Riman had helped to build the house when he was still a member of his father's domestic family, not as the head of his own independent domestic family. In accord with the adat, Riman's claim was not allowed, for he was claiming as his own something he had produced as a member of his father's domestic family.

Among the Karo only sons are entitled to share, more or less equally, in the family estate when it is divided. Daughters have no right of inheritance. An apparent exception to this rule is that all children, male and female alike, have equal rights to household equipment *(barang irumah,* literally, goods inside the house), particularly pandanus containers and mats. These however are non-durable items of little economic value, though they have considerable sentimental value for the daughter of the woman who used them. In general discussions of inheritence, Karo do not usually mention these items but confine their attention to items of greater economic value such as apartments, cattle, groves and the like. When asked why daughters have no right of inheritance in respect of these more valuable items, the people say that daughters are bought by "other people" and so if daughters were parceners the family property would go to "other people." Even so, should she remain a spinster, a daughter will not become a parcener.

The eldest surviving son has prior right to articles such as staffs, knives or heirloom dishes that cannot be divided, but not to the family apartment. Again, these items have no great economic value but they may have considerable sentimental and ritual value. In addition, the eldest son is also caretaker of the guardian spirits of his father's family (i.e., the spirits of his father's father and mother). Eldest surviving sons also succeed to positions of traditional chieftainship, such as village chief *(pengulu),* chief of the subdistrict *(raja urung)* and district chief *(sibayak).* If the eldest surviving son, for some reason, cannot succeed his father, the right of succession passes to the youngest son, then to the second eldest, then the second youngest, and so on.

Although daughters have no right of inheritance, a daughter may be given a gift *(pemere')* when she marries. In those areas of Karoland where sedentary agriculture and individual land tenure have become established, this gift may include lifetime rights to the use of a specified parcel of land. It is not uncommon that, at the time of partition of the family estate, a daughter is given one or two buffalo, or if there are only a few buffalo but one is pregnant she may be promised the calf. Whether or not a daughter gets anything at this point depends on the size of the estate, the economic condition of her brothers and herself, and the quality of her social relations with her brothers. If the estate is small, she may get nothing, but if so, she has no right to complain, for she has no right of inheritance and anything she receives from the family estate is a gift from her brothers. The brothers are morally, but not legally, constrained to be generous to their sisters if they can afford it.

One contingency that sometimes has to be dealt with is that some of the sons of the family may not yet be married at the time their parents die. If this is the case, the family estate cannot be divided until all the sons are married and the necessary expenses have been deducted from the estate. (No such expenses are necessary in the case of daughters. See Chapter 8.) Karo regard these expenses as a "debt" owed by fathers to their sons, and each time a son marries a man may say "one of my debts is already paid." If all sons are married while he is still alive, then all his debts are paid; if one or more sons is unmarried, then the necessary expenses must be reckoned as a debt against the father's estate, or rather against the estate of his domestic family. If the estate is insufficient, the sons who are already married must assume responsibility for marrying off the others. This responsibility usually falls on the eldest son, who also takes the younger unmarried sons into his household.

Also, the costs of burying the parents must be met from the assets of the family estate, and if these are insufficient, this cost is the collective responsibility of the sons.

In those areas of Karoland where individual land tenure has become established, sons are allocated portions of the family land when they marry and become heads of their own domestic families. These tracts are considered part of their share in the family estate and are taken into account in the final partition. A similar practice occurs in Liren and Kuta Gamber with regard to cattle, as is shown in the following example. Nisam, a widow past 80, had three married sons and five married grandsons. She had thirty-two head of cattle. Each of her sons "borrowed" buffalo from her on special occasions of financial need. Her eldest son "borrowed" three, the middle son three, and the youngest son two, eight in all. Of these, five were used to marry off the son's sons, two to cover the costs of erecting houses, and one to cover the cost of an illness. It was understood that the "loans" would not be repaid but would count against the sons' shares in the inheritance. On each occasion when the cattle were "borrowed," Nisam's two sons-in-law (her *anakberu*) were present to witness the transaction, and they would later serve as witnesses again if a dispute arose concerning the transaction.

INTERPERSONAL RELATIONS WITHIN THE DOMESTIC FAMILY

Husband and Wife

A Karo wife is described as the property of her husband. "She has been bought," say the Karo, and one expression meaning "wife" is *tukor emas,* that which is bought with the bride-price. A woman certainly is jurally inferior to her husband (as to her brothers) since, for example, she has no right to custody of her children in case of divorce. Nevertheless, Karo women enjoy a fairly high jural status in relation to their husbands. Both husband and wife have the same responsibility in management of the household, the one no less than the others. "They share the same fate." A proverb says that husband and wife "eat from the same plate and wash their hands in the same bowl." This is given symbolic expression in the marriage rite *(mukul)* when the couple eat from the same plate. As a sign of mutual respect, a man may not mention his wife's name and vice versa. Before they have children, husband and wife address each other by the second person plural pronoun *nake'*; only husband and wife do this and it is regarded as a sign of respect. After the birth of a child, teknonyms are used. If the name of the oldest child (male or female) is Alus, the wife calls the husband Pa Alus (*pa,* from *bapa*, father), and the husband calls the wife Nande' Alus (*nande',* mother).

Individual attraction or love is an important consideration in choosing a spouse (see Chapter 8), and during courtship affection is openly expressed. After marriage, however, feelings of affection are no longer referred to or publicly expressed. Indeed, to say of a man that he loves his wife is to imply that she is excessively jealous of him and is worried that he may be enticed by another woman. Only rarely and jokingly will a man sometimes express a liking for his wife. Pa Jabap, a small merchant inclined to humor, once said to his wife, "I like you very much. I have been travelling a lot but I never came across rice as good as you cook. You are very good at cooking rice." According to Pa Jabap, his neighbors in the adat house, and his wife too, laughed when they heard this.

"If eggs in a basket touch one another, why not also human beings who have ears and mouths?" This proverb expresses the Karo conviction that every intense social relationship will, in one way or another, give rise to interpersonal conflict. Thus, in the advice given to newlyweds concerning the sort of attitude to take if a quarrel arises between them, another proverb is frequently cited: "If one person comes from the western *ture',* the other goes from the eastern *ture'*; if one person comes from the eastern *ture'*, the other goes from the western *ture'*." (A *ture'* is an open platform on the adat house; there is one on the east end and one on the west end. See Chapter 4.) In this proverb "person" represents anger. The essence of the advice is this: Do not answer harsh words with harsh words. If your spouse is angry, do not contradict him or her; be silent or go away for the time being. Anger is said to be a condition of the soul, and an angry man cannot control himself, for "his heart is hot." In such a condition, a person should not be contradicted. If you want to contradict him, wait until "his heart is cool."

The major sources of conflict between husband and wife are jealousy, mismanagement of family monies, and disrespectful conduct toward the spouse's relatives.

A bit of conventional advice to a bride is "You are a married woman, do not let your eyes stray." A spouse possesses exclusive rights of sexual access to his or her partner and transgressions of this right readily give rise to quarrels. Since even a glance of the eyes may be interpreted as an expression of sexual desire, newlyweds may easily become involved in unexpected quarrels. Once, when Sura was going to town to visit his relatives and he and his wife were waiting for the bus, his wife said a few words to a young male acquaintance. Sura was not pleased by this and showed his displeasure by not speaking to his wife until they returned to the village. Most people would disapprove of the wife's conduct, but Sura's attitude was regarded as too severe. It would have been enough for him to admonish his wife so that she would not do the same thing again.

If a woman's jealousy is easily aroused, she may be counted as one "who loves her husband very much." The wife of Cari of Liren was such a woman. Once Cari went to town on business. He had made plans to stay away one night but his business took more time than expected and he stayed away two nights. When he returned to the village and gave his wife two fish he had bought for their meal, she threw them away. Cari could see no reason for this except jealousy, though he knew no girls in town.

Wives are usually more jealous than husbands, perhaps because married men lead less restricted lives than their wives and have more opportunities to meet and get acquainted with persons of the opposite sex. In some regards, a young married man may still behave as a youth; he may still participate in "youth dances" but a married woman may participate only in ceremonial dances.

Since married men lead less restricted lives than their wives, they also have more opportunities to spend money and they have different patterns of consumption. Men, but not women, visit the coffee shops and drink tea or coffee, and sometimes wine, smoke cigarettes, and eat biscuits or bread. Since any money earned by a family member is considered the money of the family, and since, especially in the rural areas, most family income derives from the sale of agricultural produce which is the joint product of husband and wife, women may resent excessive expenditures of this sort by their husbands.

Generally speaking, the husband manages the financial affairs of the family. He keeps the income from the sale of cash crops (tobacco and onions) and cattle; the wife, however, may keep the income from the sale of the chickens and pigs she looks after. If the husband mismanages the money he holds for the family and the needs of the wife cannot be met, a quarrel may arise. The most serious quarrels occur when the husband depletes the family money and goes into debt, often hiding this from his wife. One man I knew lost Rp. 2000 gambling in one week (the equivalent of about a month's pay and board for a rural laborer). To cover Rp. 500 of his debt, he took his wife's gold necklace and pawned it. His wife supposed that the necklace had been stolen, but when she discovered what had really happened, she demanded a divorce. At a family meeting the husband admitted his error and begged his wife's pardon. The necklace was redeemed by his father. Of course, this case involved more than just mismanagement of family funds; a man may not dispose of his wife's personal possessions without her permission.

In some families nowadays the wife holds all the family money and the husband receives a regular allowance from his wife. This is done in about 10 percent of the families in Liren and Kuta Gamber. But some people say of the men who permit this that they allow their wives to act as though they were their fathers, i.e., that they are men who follow their wives' orders.

Advice to the newly married couple usually includes "Be more respectful to the family of your partner than to your own family, when they come to visit." Respect to a guest is shown by the host's talkativeness, a clean face, and serving the best possible food. The epitome of tactless and rude conduct is to be cheerful, pleasant and generous when visited by one's own relatives but sullen, silent and stingy when visited by one's spouse's relatives.

Such behavior, the people say, is most common in the early stages of marriage. When Radu was visited by his second cousin, his wife did not exhibit the proper attitude. She did the cooking too slowly and told her husband to go out and buy some eggs at the coffee shop. Then she told him to boil the eggs. The guest, feeling unwelcome, excused himself by saying that he had already eaten and had to leave immediately because he had business elsewhere. When his cousin had gone, Radu took the eggs and threw them through the window, chased his wife out of the house and threatened to divorce her. Radu's neighbors, who heard him shouting at his wife, intervened and sent his wife to her mother's house. Everyone blamed her and the matter was patched up that very day. According to one informant, this tendency to discriminate between one's own and one's spouse's relatives may be found in older couples as well, but its expression is more subtle. He remarked "My wife is good and brings me good luck in financial matters, but she has one weakness; if we have a visitor from her side of the family she catches a fat hen to be killed, if we have a visitor from my side of the family she catches a thin hen."

Parent and Child

The strongest bonds of love are between parents and children, not husbands and wives. Love between husband and wife, the Karo often say, lasts only a year; after the first child is born the love of husband and wife turns to their child. The Karo say, however, that the mother loves the child much more than the father does. The Karo theory of procreation amounts to a horticultural analogy. The male semen is likened to the seed of a plant, and the female uterus is likened to a fertile field in which the seed is planted. The Karo say that many acts of sexual intercourse are essential for the creation of a child, since the foetus grows by accumulation of semen in the uterus. The Karo do not maintain, however, that the child is solely the physical creation of its genitor (*bapa*, father); offspring are said to share blood with their fathers and their mothers, and in ritual contexts Karo speak of the "white blood" of the father and the "red blood" of the mother. However, the concept of shared blood is most often mentioned when speaking of obligations between close agnatic kin. In speaking of obligations between close uterine kin, especially between a man and his mother's close agnatic kin (his *kalimbubu*), Karo say that these people (through one of their women) "gave birth" to that man. The question "Who gave birth to that boy (or man)?" is a conventional way of asking who his *kalimbubu* are. The Karo also attribute the "firmness of their heads and the fineness of their hair" to their mothers and say that they are obliged to their mothers, and therefore their *kalimbubu*, because of this.

Social and emotional relations between mother and young child are far more intense than those between father and child, for the mother suckles, nurses and pets the child. A Karo proverb likens the love of a mother for her child to the holding of sesame seed. Sesame seed, being very small, easily trickles out of the hand unless it is held very tightly. Since the term *nande'* (mother) has strong connotations of nurturance and succor, it is a conventional cry for help; and its connotations of love and affection account for its metaphorical use to mean "sweetheart" or "beloved". When a young man sings *"nande' Ginting,"* it is clear that his sweetheart, to whom the song is directed, is a woman of the Ginting clan.

In the customary division of labor, carrying and looking after children are woman's tasks. Nowadays this custom is becoming weaker and fathers too are often seen carrying their children to the rice fields or even in the village. Younger men even look after their children, and it is now quite common for a young man to bring his child to the coffee shop while his wife is busy. But even the young men go only so far in this respect. Although, while travelling from his own village to another, a man may carry his child for some distance, he will turn the child over to his wife before entering the other village so that its inhabitants will have no cause to think of him as a man who is at his wife's beck and call.

Although small children (nowadays anyway) may spend much of their time with their fathers and play with them, the father is the principal disciplinarian of the household. In lamentations at funeral ceremonies, the father is described as "one to whom questions go, one from whom advice is sought." This is not to say that the mother does not sometimes discipline the child, but if the child is particularly unruly or naughty she may well threaten the child with punishment by the father, thus appealing to his ultimate authority within the family.

In social relations between adult children and their parents, considerable reserve and respect is exhibited, especially between father and daughter and mother and son. There are no accounts of incestuous relationships between parents and children in stories and myths, and I heard of no actual instances of such relationships. It is said, however, that "other people" will regard it as unseemly if parents and children of the opposite sex exhibit much affection for and familiarity with one another. Young men past puberty do not hold conversations with their mothers, unless there is a real need, except in the presence of a third person. Because of this a widow who has only one child, who happens to be a son, finds it very awkward indeed. A widow aged about 40 had an only-child son who was about 21. She complained to me that her son had not yet married and she found the situation inconvenient and embarrassing. They were always having to avoid one another and if her son was alone in the rice field she could not go there. If he would get married, there would be a third person present and she could communicate with him.

While in certain circumstances a young man may be alone with his mother, in no circumstances may a man be alone with his adult daughter. A young man may go to eat at the house although his mother may be alone there. While they must sit well apart from one another, they may even discuss some essential business after the son has finished eating. In contrast, a man and his daughter must never put themselves in such a situation. One of them must leave the room if there is no third person present, and a man will not enter into a conversation with his adult daughter, unless there is a pressing need, even if there is another person present.

Social relations between men and their grown-up sons also are characterized by some restraint and, of course, by deference on the part of the son. For example, they may not bathe together and a son will give way to his father if by chance they meet at the bathing place. It is considered inappropriate for both of them to be present in a group holding a conversation touching on any sexual matter.

The Karo, like many other peoples, put a good deal of emphasis on the need to have a son to continue the family line, and they regard the birth of a son as essential for a happy and stable marriage. Unless a son is born to a couple, there is always the possibility that the husband will demand a divorce and then remarry. This places sonless women, especially young mothers, under considerable psychological stress. In 1961 a young woman who already had two daughters was about to give birth to a third child. Of course, she, her husband, and their relatives all hoped that the third child would be a boy, but it turned out to be a girl. As soon as this was apparent one of the female attendants shouted in disappointment, "A girl again!" The mother fainted, a priest was called because it was feared that she would die, but she regained consciousness after about half an hour. On another occasion when a sonless mother gave birth to a fourth daughter, the placenta was retained, perhaps because of her psychological distress, and it had to be removed under operation.

Siblings

Social relations between siblings are characterized, ideally, by strong mutual trust and solidarity. The Karo say that siblings should be almost as close as mother and child, and to express a very close friendship with someone Karo will say that he treats that person as he would a full sibling.

Important social distinctions among siblings are based on relative age and birth order. A person is obliged to respect and obey his older siblings, and as a sign of this respect, it is forbidden to mention the name of an older sibling. *Kaka* is the term of address for "elder sibling"; the eldest sibling in a set is *kaka tua* (*tua*, literally, old, senior); and the middle-elder siblings are *kaka tengah* (*tengah*, literally, middle). Younger siblings are addressed by name. The eldest son, in keeping with his status as the man who will "replace" the father, is entitled to the greatest respect and deference, and it often is said that he, like the father, is the *penggurun*, that is, the source of advice.

Brothers especially are obliged to trust and assist one another, and it is said that they should not allow themselves to be divided by their wives or other people, or allow their individual interests to come between them. The fact that they are *sembuyak*, that is, that they have their origin in one abdomen *(mbuyak)* or uterus, is appealed to as the basis of their mutual obligations. When two brothers are quarreling, it may be said that it is only a matter of time before harmony is restored between them, because they are *sembuyak*.

When a man has problems, he looks first and foremost to his brothers for help. "To whom else should one go for help if not to a brother?" explained Pa Tupa. Usually the expected assistance is a loan, in the form of rice or cash. Moreover, when a man quarrels with his wife, it is again his brothers to whom he makes his complaints. When Rasi fell out with his wife and decided to divorce her, he went to visit his elder brother in another village two kilometers away. His elder brother asked for the details of the quarrel and then set about persuading Rasi to abandon his intention. His advice: "Those of the same household have to advise each other when there is trouble. To divorce a wife is not an easy matter and it is even more difficult to find a replacement. Just think, you could get someone even worse. Wasn't your wife your own choice?" The next day the elder brother and his wife accompanied Rasi to his own home and helped him to make up with his wife.

Of course, social relations between brothers are not always harmonious. Their individual economic interests may conflict; since they have equal rights in respect of inheritance of their natal domestic family estate, quarrels may arise among them concerning its division. It is generally acknowledged that brothers may not be emotionally close despite their duty to support one another in time of need. In Nande Suruh's words, "quarrels and making up, such is the relationship between *sembuyak*."

Social relations between female siblings are somewhat different. Sisters, since they have no rightful interests in the economically most significant portions of their natal family estate, and since they are not obliged to assist one another financially, are not likely to become divided by conflicting economic interests. The strong bonds of friendship which develop among them as children are likely to continue in adult life. Moreover, the children of sisters classify one another as "siblings", though of a special kind (see Appendix II), and often social relations between maternal parallel cousins exhibit the same qualities as those between their mothers.

Among the most significant aspects of Karo social structure are social relations between opposite-sex siblings. In the first place, sexual intercourse between them is strictly forbidden, and this restriction is extended to all classificatory brothers and sisters, even to the clan level, so that a clan numbering tens of thousands of members constitutes one exogamous category. Although I heard of no cases of sibling incest, the theme is relatively prominent in Karo mythology. There are at least four myths whose principal theme is sibling incest; one is associated with the magical staff of priesthood and the other three with fertility cults. One of the latter is the myth of the creation of the rainbow. All have important ritual significance. The following is a summary of Si Aji Dunda Katekuten, the myth of the magical staff.[1]

It is said that the *gurus* Pakpak Pertandang (seven distinguished priests of Pakpak) made a trip from Pulo Cimcimen to Tuding si nu Purba. They were gossiping in the village about the king of the village who had no children. They knew this from their magical knowledge. A goatherd overheard the conversation and informed the queen who immediately gathered the seven *gurus* and invited them to eat at her house. She then asked for their help to obtain descendants.

The aid of the *gurus* brought results, for the king of Tuding si nu Purba had a son and a daughter. The *gurus* warned that they should be married off early.

When they were of marriageable age, they fell in love with each other. If the girl was pounding rice at the mortar or drawing water at the river, her brother would follow her. If the boy went hunting, his sister too would follow.

Their mother told them that such behavior was incestuous and would bring about a long dry season, the crops would die, the cattle would be struck down with thirst and mankind by thirst and hunger.

The children did not heed the advice. A dry season of seven years and seven months came. In consequence, there were terrible calamities: cows became deer, buffalo became elephants, domestic pigs became wild pigs and the people were struck down with thirst and hunger.

Once the siblings went to hunt a civet cat, using seven dogs and one snake. The civet cat climbed up a *tenggolan* tree followed by the dogs, the snake and the brother and sister.

At the top of the tree there was a female evil spirit (*jin*) who threatened to eat them. They prepared themselves to be eaten. The *jin* coaxed the boy so that he would stay with her and marry her. She said: marry me

[1] This myth has been published together with a Dutch translation in Joustra (1904).

without any marriage payment; it is sufficient to enjoy things here, food, drink and clothing in abundance.

The dogs, the snake and the sister returned to the village. After four days with the *jin* the food and drink was finished. Because of this the prince wanted to go. The *jin* asked him not to leave her but proposed that he should go to the king of the Pustima (west), called Datuk Rubia Gandé, to obtain food. He agreed

"Hai, I will eat you," said Datuk Rubia Gandé. The prince told how he had been commanded by his wife Tiang Manik, the *jin* who guarded the *tenggolan* tree. The prince was then given food, drink and clothing to take back.

On the way he met a girl who wished to go and meet Datuk Rubia Gandé to ask for medicine. Her mother was very sick. The prince offered her medicine. The girl took the medicine home and her mother was immediately cured. The girl was in fact his sister, but they failed to recognize one another.

"Find the medicine-man and marry him without a marriage payment," said the mother to her daughter. "But he was quite naked," said the girl. "Take clothing, a hat and a betel-holder for him," the mother advised.

The girl went to find the medicine-man and they were married.

Jin Tiang Manik was restless after waiting for four months for her husband to come back. Through her magic power she sent off a sparrow-hawk. The bird perched on the house of the husband.

The prince brought down the bird with a stone and it changed into a cat. When he fell asleep the cat came and annoyed him. He beat the cat which changed into a dog. Then he became angry with the dog because it kept licking the plate he ate from. He beat the dog which changed into a civet cat.

The civet cat ran off, chased by seven dogs, the snake and the husband and wife. The civet cat went straight to the jungle and climbed up the *tenggolan* tree of the *jin*. All of them finally climbed up the tree and changed into knots in the wood.

After they had been missing from the village for four days, the villagers went to look for them. The woman's parents and the other people heard a voice from the top of the tree: "It is a waste of time looking for us, we cannot come down; we have become knots in the wood; if you want to take us home call the *gurus* Pakpak Pertandang first."

They sent for the *gurus* Pakpak Pertandang from Pulo Cimcimen. One of the *gurus* said to the parents of the child: "I said before, marry your child off quickly; now your own child is also your son-in-law."

> The *gurus* cut down the tree and made a statue from it. They said to the queen that her son would be called Tuan Aji Dunda Katekuten and her daughter Beru Puang Tampė Raja Benawasen. "They will become the protectors of your family," concluded the *gurus*.

In another version of the myth the incestuous relationship is with a classificatory sister (first cousin) and the hunted animal is an ant-eater, not a civet cat. In this version, the tree turns into a magical staff from which the brother and sister, the ant-eater, the seven dogs and a snake are carved. Such staffs are possessed only by distinguished *guru* and no *guru* in Kuta Gamber or Liren has one.

In all the myths concerned with sibling incest, the act is magically punished. In the myth just cited the guilty parties turn into lumps of wood; in another they turn into a rainbow. This latter myth is well known to children, and when they see a rainbow they jump about and shout "Oh, Oh, he married his sister!" *(Eleė, Eleė, empoina turangna.)*

Social relations between grown-up siblings of opposite sex are characterized by some restraint and avoidance. They do not tell jokes to each other, and oral communication between them is minimal. In the absence of other members of the family, a girl will leave the apartment or the house when her brother comes home for lunch.

As already suggested, women are jurally inferior to their brothers; they have no right of inheritance in the family estate. Moreover, when a woman marries she is regarded as one of the *anakberu* of her brothers. Conversely, she regards them as her *kalimbubu*. The *anakberu* are jurally inferior to the *kalimbubu* in certain respects. When a man is performing a ritual or ceremony, his sister and her husband are obliged to assist; it is their duty to fetch the betel, catch and kill the pigs for the feast, do the cooking and serve the food.

There is, moreover, an asymmetrical metaphysical relationship between brother and sister. Harmonious social relationships between a married woman and her *kalimbubu* – her brothers in particular and her agnatic kin in general – are considered to bring happiness to her. If their social relations are poor and the brothers become extremely annoyed with their sister, she may be supernaturally punished. She will have bad luck in economic matters, become sick and perhaps even infertile. This condition, in which the brother's heart and soul becomes "hot" and therefore evil, may be ritually rectified. A woman who has wronged her brother may ritually present him with a drink of cold water, which has the effect of "cooling his heart" and rendering it good again.

One of the duties of a woman to her brother is to do her best to see to it that one of her sons marries one of his daughters. Thus, when one of her sons reaches marriageable age and begins to look about for a wife, she may encourage him to consider her brother's eldest eligible daughter. If she is successful in persuading her son to marry this girl, she may feel that one of her goals in life has been achieved (see also Chapter 8).

Chapter Four

The Adat House

One important characteristic of Karo social organization is the traditional house. "There are so many adat rules governing erecting and occupying the house," said Pa Sali, a prominent priest, "that is why it is called adat house." A number of complex rituals and ceremonies are performed at successive stages during the building of a house – choosing the site, selecting and felling the trees, erecting the piles, and establishing the hearths. In certain circumstances, the occupants of the house constitute a ritual group.

The majority of families – 87 out of 134, or about 64.8 percent – in Kuta Gamber and Liren live in adat houses. This ratio is more or less the same throughout the Karo highlands. In contrast, there are no adat houses in the lowlands where Karo live either in huts or modern houses. This may be ascribed to new cultural values resulting from Malay influence along the coast. Considering Karo as a whole, about 20 percent of the people still reside in traditional houses. The percentage was considerably higher in the past and has been falling steadily since Dutch annexation in 1906.

The adat house is a compact structure. Unlike a Dayak long house, which Geddes (1957: 29) describes as "a series of houses separately built but joined together," once an adat house has been built its internal and external structure remains unaltered until it is no longer used or is replaced by a new one, perhaps fifty to seventy years later. The Karo house is rectangular or square and is supported by strong wooden piles, about one-and-a-half meters high. It has low wooden walls slanting outward, and is topped by a gently curving saddle roof. The extremities of the roof gables at either end are adorned with buffalo horns. The roof is especially important, for the style of the house is described according to the shape of its roof. The roof is exceptionally high in comparison to the low and slanting walls. One house I measured had the proportions of pile to wall to roof of

1:1:9 respectively; the pile and wall each were one-and-one-half meters in height and the roof 14.5 meters high.

A house with the simplest hip and saddle roof is called *rumah beru-beru. Beru* signifies "woman" and the reduplicated form signifies "mean, average or normal." Thus, *rumah beru-beru* is an average or standard traditional house. This general type of house has been developed further by the Karo than by other Batak. On some houses of this type, called *rumah tersek*, the lower and sloping part of the roof is doubled. This produces a double-storied effect with the saddle roof above the lower part of the roof. This type is becoming increasingly popular because it makes possible a substantial improvement in the ventilation system and such a house is less smoky. A four-gabled house is called *rumah si empat ayo*, a house with four "faces" (gables). It is formed by crossing two saddle roofs at right angles. For purely decorative purposes a pole bearing a miniature adat house *(anjong-anjong)* is sometimes erected on the middle of the ridge-pole; a house with this feature is called *rumah anjong-anjong.*

The walls and the gables also are objects of artistic and symbolic expression. Each corner is adorned by a "lions head" *(takal singa)*, a wooden carving that looks more like a human head than a lion's.

Lizard-like figures (*pengeret-ret*), made from plaited cords of sugar palm fiber, decorate the external walls. These cords serve also to fasten the planks and the laths, the materials of which the walls are made. These figures, according to Neumann (1951: 45), represent *beraspati*, the grey lizard believed to be the incarnation of good spirits and the guardian spirit of the house. My informants were unaware of this symbolism. The triangular gable of the house, which resembles a buffalo head, is both decorative and ritually significant. After completion of the structure and before the inauguration ceremony is held, an outstanding priest (*guru mbelin*) performs a ritual called *mere' tandok*, feeding the horns, in which the priest feeds the figure *dalang-dalang*, a ritual food made specifically to placate dangerous spirits. This consists of raw offal, especially pieces of heart, liver, lung and the blood of a red rooster, mixed with salt and chili. The symbolic significance of this figure and of the ritual associated with it are no longer understood by Karo; but in Karoland, as in many other

Indonesian societies (Minangkabau, Dayak, and Toraja), the buffalo figures prominently in ceremony and ritual.

The adat house is divided into sections or apartments (*sence-pik*, a piece or portion), the number of which depends on the size of the house. There are three types of houses, small, medium and large; these contain four, eight and twelve apartments respectively. The majority of Karo traditional houses are of the eight-apartment type, and this type is regarded by Karo as the normal or standard type. *Rumah si waluh jabu* is the conventional expression for adat house; literally, it means a house with eight apartments (or domestic families). For this reason and also for the sake of simplicity, the following discussion concerns this type of house.

Each apartment consists of a kitchen, a living area and an enclosed sleeping place, and is, by Karo standards, a suitable dwelling place for one domestic family. Some families occupy two adjacent sections (a *seruang*) and for this reason the number of families residing in an eight-apartment adat house ranges from four to eight. However. the majority of families occupy only one section. Of the 97 domestic families living in adat houses in Kuta Gamber and Liren, 90 (92.8 percent) occupy one apartment and the remaining 7 (7.2 percent) each occupy two adjacent apartments.

Non-Karo visitors to an adat house are often surprised to discover that its roomy interior is not partitioned into compartments. Heine Geldern (1935: 321) remarked on this ascribed anomaly:

> Though the houses of the Toba and Karo are exceedingly attractive because of their phantastic roofs, beautiful proportions, and their lavish and tasteful ornamentation, no attempt whatever is made to dispose of their inward space. There are not even fixed walls separating the lodgings of the different families.

Despite the absence of interior walls, there is a distinctively Karo organization of this "inward space," and the organization is both physical and social. We may begin by considering the socially relevant aspects of the structure of the adat house.

Each adat house has two open bamboo platforms (*turé*), one on the east and one on the west end of the house (see Figure 1). Each platform is regarded as an integral part of the four adjacent divisions or apartments of the house. It serves as a verandah, a meeting place for youngsters, and as a lavatory in certain circumstances. To enter the house from ground level, one climbs a ladder that leans against the platform. From there the house is entered through a slanting door. In the late afternoon and evening the platform becomes a rendezvous for adolescents. Here a boy may meet his girl friend; it is contrary to adat to visit her inside the house. Small children use the platform as a lavatory, as do women at night. Pigs used to roam freely and scavenge under the house, but nowadays the people are obliged to keep their pigs in pens.

Figure 1. Plan of a Karo adat house.

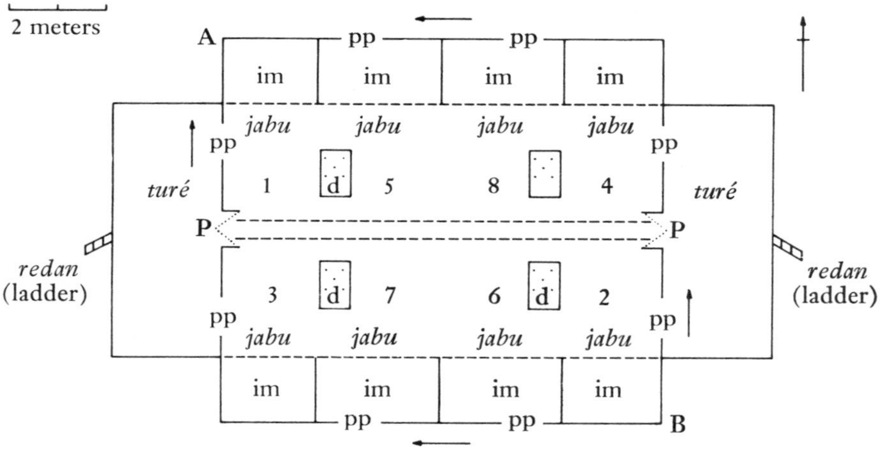

im = ingan medem (sleeping place)
d = dapor (kitchen)
p = pintun (door)
pp = pintun perik (window)
1 = benakayu ("the base of the tree")
2 = ujungkayu ("the top of the tree")

A central beam about ten meters long connects the east and west platforms, divides the house in half and serves as a corridor for its inhabitants. This beam has the shape of a long trough, the bottom of which is about twenty centimeters below floor level. It is called *dalan lau*, literally, the passage of water.

Each pair of adjacent apartments shares a kitchen area *(dapor)* which is in no sense a separate apartment. The hearth is sunk about twenty centimeters lower than the main floor. In the center of each kitchen, five stones are placed so as to form two fireplaces (A & B in Figure 2), one for each apartment. The middle stone, as the Karo call it, and the hanging racks (*para*) above the kitchen where various kitchen utensils and cooking ingredients are kept, are shared by the two adjacent apartments.

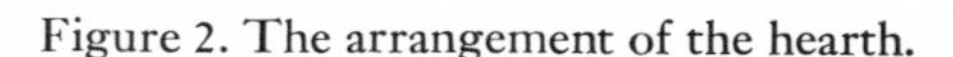

Figure 2. The arrangement of the hearth.

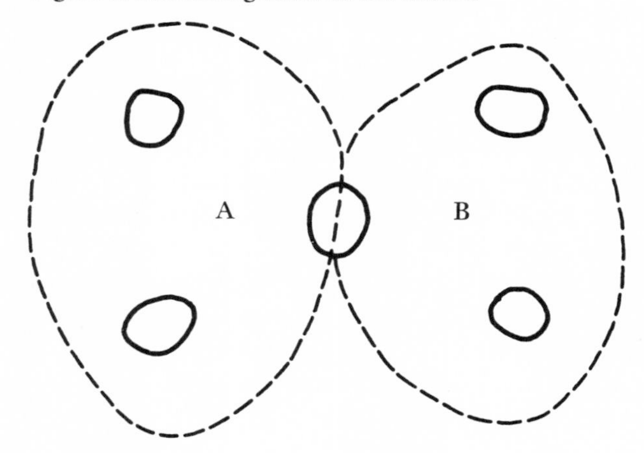

The *jabu* is the living room of the family where they take their meals, entertain guests and chat with neighbors. Family meetings, rituals and ceremonies are held there, children and girls sleep there, and women give birth there. When a member of the family dies, the corpse is laid out in the *jabu* where it is surrounded by wailing relatives.

The sleeping place (*ingan medem*) is the only part of the apartment that resembles a room; it is separated from the other sleeping places by a number of mats hung over a bamboo rod and from the living area by a curtain. The sleeping quarters usually are furnished with mats; nowadays, however, all but a small minority can afford mattresses, over which home-made mats are spread as sheets. As noted earlier, a well-to-do villager may own a bed (*peratas*) made by a local carpenter; this is a large rectangular wooden box about thirty centimeters high which also serves as a storage place for miscellaneous items such as pillows, small mats, pandanus baskets, traditional clothing and knives.

Because in Karo symbolism the floor is associated with dirt, inferiority and submission, and in contrast, the head connotes purity, supremacy and authority, it is regarded as improper, when lying down, for one man's feet to point to his neighbor's head; thus the rule "head meets head, foot meets foot." To manage this, those who sleep in the sleeping areas in apartments 1 and 8 (see Figure 1) must orient their heads to the east and those who sleep in apartments 4 and 5 orient their heads to the west; this arrangement applies also to the other parts of the house.

Above the sleeping place there is a two-story horizontal rack. The lower rack is used to store precious belongings such as traditional clothing, body ornaments, jewelry and other paraphernalia. The upper rack has an important religious function. Offerings are placed there for the family's *dibata*, a special category consisting of the spirits of ancestors who died unexpectedly or in an unnatural way, such as by drowning or suicide. They are also called *si mate' sada wari*, "who dies in one day," and they are the most important spirits in Karo religious life. They are believed to reside in the house; spirits of relatives who died in a "natural" way reside in various other places.

Each apartment has a generic name derived from the arrangement of the side beams of the house, and the system of names is related to the political organization of the house. Figure 1 shows how these horizontal beams are arranged: the point of the arrow indicates the "base" of each beam. The base of a beam is the lower part of the tree trunk from which the timber was hewn. The bases of the beams placed along the east and west sides of the house are oriented to the north, and the bases of the beams placed along the north and south sides are oriented to the west. Thus, all beams are oriented toward the northwest corner of the house.

The bases of the horizontal beams point to corner A and the upper ends of the beams point to corner B. On the basis of this arrangement, the apartments are designated as follows:

1. *benakayu,* base of the tree

2. *ujungkayu,* top of the tree

3. *lépar benakayu,* opposite the base of the tree

4. *lépar ujungkayu,* opposite the top of the tree

5. *sedapuren benakayu,* sharing a kitchen with the base of the tree

6. *sedapuren ujungkayu,* sharing a kitchen with the top of the tree

7. *sedapuren lèpar benakayu,* sharing a kitchen opposite the base of the tree

8. *sedapuren lèpar ujungkayu,* sharing a kitchen opposite the top of the tree

The points of reference are the two end sections, "the base of the tree" and "the top of the tree." The social organization of the house is related to this organization of its internal space because the apartment called "the base of the tree" is the place of the chief of the house (*pengulu rumah*), and opposite to him, occupying the apartment called "the top of the tree," is his deputy who is one of his jurally inferior *anakberu*.

The orientation of the house, which is always east and west, appears to be symbolically significant, though no priest in Kuta Gamber or Liren was able to explicate it. However, the Karo phrases *matawari pultak*, the rising sun, and *matawari sundut*, the setting sun, which refer to east and west respectively, may be a useful guide here. The eastern half of the house, represented by the apartment called "the top of the tree," faces the rising sun; the western half of the house, represented by the apartment called "the base of the tree," faces the setting sun. It seems probable that this orientation is related to the symbolic opposition between "cold" and "hot" which is widespread in Indonesia. In his book *The Achehnese,* Hurgronje gives an account of this opposition:

> In the native languages of the E. Archipelago all happiness, peace, rest and well-being are united under the concept of "coolness," while the words "hot" and "heat" typify all the powers of evil. Thus when a person has either just endured the attack of a "hot" influence, or has luckily contrived to escape it, the adat prescribes the method of "cooling" in order to confirm him in the well-being which he has recovered or escaped losing. The same methods are also adopted for charming away evil things and baneful influences, the removal of which is regarded as an imperative necessity. For instance, the completion of a house, and various domestic festivities, are made the occasion for a process of "cooling"; so also with a ship when newly built or after the holding of a kanduri on board; and before the padi is planted out the ground must be purified from "hot" or dangerous influences (Hurgronje 1906:305).

Among the Karo this twin dichotomy of "hot" and "cold" and "good" and "evil" is remarkably well developed. A "hot heart," "a hot liver," and "a hot mind" are expressions denoting anger, illness and a troubled mind caused partly by sickness but mainly by a disturbing supernatural power. Therefore, the "cooling" process is an important part of Karo ritual. Ritual "cooling" may be accomplished by drinking cold water, smearing the chest with cold water, smearing the forehead and cheeks with "neutralizing rice flour" (*tepong tawar*), or using "cold herbs" (*si-malem-malem*). Thus, I suggest, the Karo house has an east-west orientation and the apartment of the head of the house is located at the west end, facing the heat of the afternoon sun, because he is regarded as one who is able to confront "heat" or, in other words, evil.

Perhaps a more important symbolic dichotomy is that of "base" versus "top," the "base" being superior to the "top." The analogy is to a tree trunk, the base of which is larger, stronger and harder than the top.

The architecture of the adat house, its size and the absence of internal walls, has led some observers to describe it as a sort of lineage house. Wagner (1959:62), for example, describes Batak traditional houses as similar to the houses of the Toraja of the Celebes and the Minangkabau of central Sumatra, as the dwelling places of "large genealogical groups, or clans." This is incorrect, and the social organization of the Batak traditional house is quite different from that of the Minangkabau *rumah gadang* ("big house"). Cole describes the Minangkabau house in this way:

> The smallest unit is the *rumah* or house, the members of which trace their origin back to a single woman called *nini,* oldest woman, *ibu,* mother, or *inuk,* headwoman. Thus the family is made up of an original headwoman, her sons, her daughters, and their children and so to succeeding generations (Cole 1945:252).

A Minangkabau house "sometimes lodges seventy to eighty persons descended from the same ancestral mother" (Loeb 1935:99). In contrast, the Karo adat house is the dwelling place of several domestic families who are not necessarily related consanguineally, much less agnatically, to one another. It is true that the Karo house is inhabited by people who are related in one way or another, but, interestingly enough, affinal and non-agnatic cognatic relationships are just as important as agnatic relationships in the ideal composition of the larger household. Ideally, an adat house is occupied by the three major categories of relatives – agnates (*senina*), *anakberu* and *kalimbubu*. The focal individual here is the head of the house (*pengulu rumah*) who is, ideally, a member of the ruling lineage of the village, that is, an agnatic descendant of the founder of the village. For that reason his apartment is also called *jabu raja*, "the apartment of the king."

As already noted, the apartment at the southeast corner of the house is properly occupied by one of the *anakberu*, e.g., a sister's husband or daughter's husband, of the head of the house. In my experience, the ordinary Karo individual has little knowledge beyond this of who should occupy the other apartments, that is, of how the occupants of the other apartments should be related to the head of the house. In practice one finds a wide variety of arrangements, none of which are subject to general disapproval. Karo priests, however, are able to say how the occupants of the other apartments should be related to the head of the house. It should be noted that they do not attempt to coerce people to organize their larger households in this way and they refer to this arrangement most commonly in the context of ritual spells. So the arrangement is a ritual, not a normative concept.

In the esoteric knowledge of priests, then, occupants of an adat house should be related as shown in Table 6 (see also Tamboen 1952:90). In this model the particular types of *anakberu, anakberu menteri* and *kalimbubu* are not specified.

Figure 3. One possible arrangement based on the esoteric model of adat household composition.

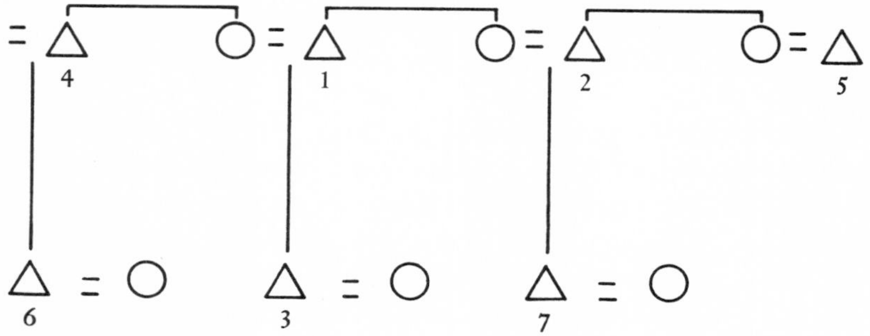

Table 6

Esoteric Model of the Social Organization of the Adat House

Apartment*	
1	*bangsa taneh* (member of the ruling lineage)
2	*anakberu* of 1
3	son of 1
4	*kalimbubu* of 1
5	*anakberu menteri* (the *anakberu* of *anakberu*) of 1
6	son of 4 (also *kalimbubu* of 1)
7	son of 2 (also *anakberu* of 1)
8	priest, non-kin

* These numbers correspond to those in Figure 1.

In my experience the composition of no adat household conforms in detail to this or any other possibility inherent in the esoteric model known to lineage priests. Since the model is unknown to most Karo and has no status in the adat, it is hardly to be expected that the composition of any household should conform to it. The composition of some houses does conform to the well-known expectation that the apartment at the "base" will be owned and occupied by a member of the ruling lineage and that the apartment at the "top" will be owned and occupied by one of his *anakberu*. But not all adat households are so organized.

Consider the following example of an actual house in Kuta Gamber. This house was built about forty years ago by four men, each of whom owned two adjacent apartments. These men were members of two lineages. A and B (see Figure 4), who occupied the "base" and the "top" apartments respectively, were agnatic first cousins and members of the ruling lineage. C and D were paternal half-brothers and the *anakberu* of A and B; C was married to a lineage "sister" of A and B (their FFBSD). Note that although the apartment at the "base" of the house was occupied by a member of the ruling lineage, so was the apartment at the "top" which ideally would have been occupied by one of the *anakberu*. Apartment no. 3 (again see Figure 1), instead of being occupied by a son of one of the members of the ruling lineage, was occupied by one of the *anakberu*, and apartment no. 4 was occupied by one of the *anakberu* rather than by a *kalimbubu*. To my knowledge this arrangement was subject to no disapproval, though it conformed to the esoteric model and to common expectation only in that the house was occupied by members of the ruling lineage and their *anakberu*.

Figure 4. The actual relations among the inhabitants of an adat house and their spatial distribution in the house.

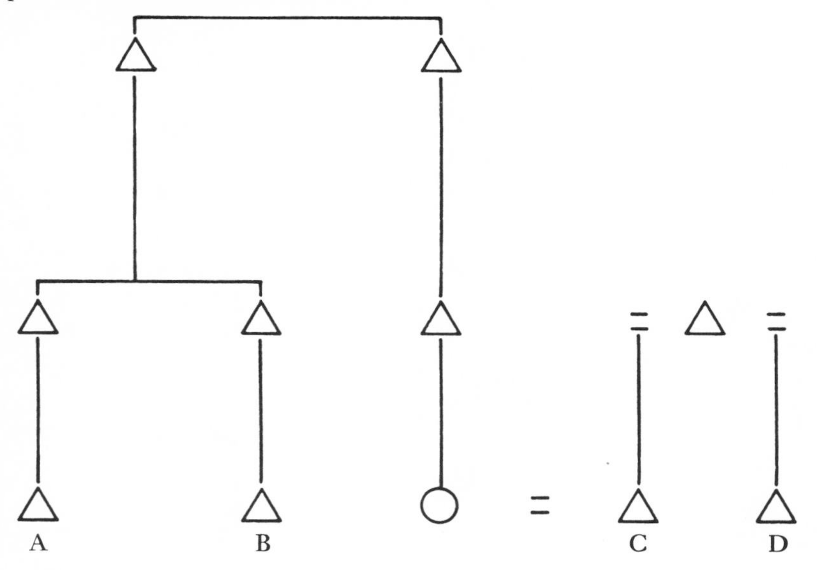

benakayu

A D

C B

ujungkayu

In 1960-1961 the four founders of the house were dead and it was occupied by persons as shown in Figure 5. The apartment at the "base" of the house (1) was occupied by the son (E) of its original occupant (B), and the apartment at the "top" (2) was

Figure 5. The subsequent composition of an adat household.

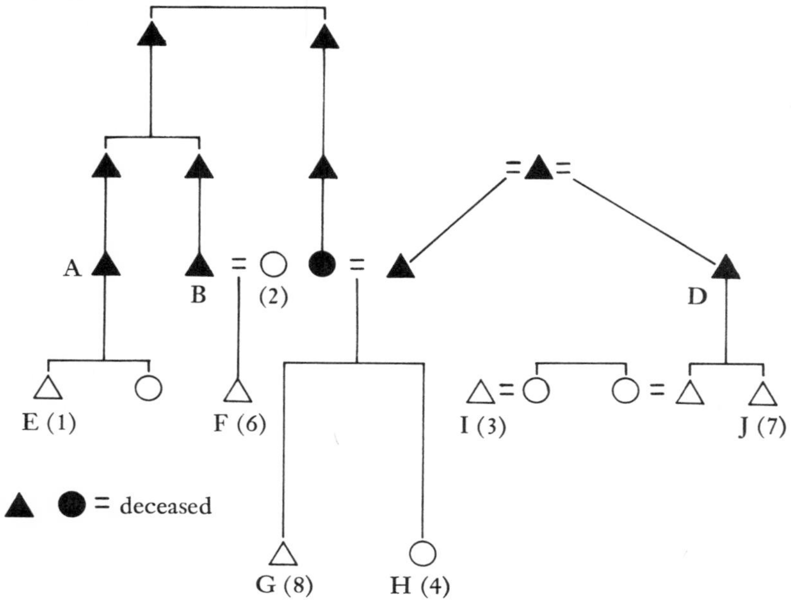

A B (2) D

E (1) F (6) I (3) J (7)

▲ ● = deceased

G (8) H (4)

benakayu E 1	A's clansman 5	G 8	H 4
I 3	J 7	F 6	B's wife *ujungkayu* 2

occupied by the widow of its original occupant (B). B's son (F) occupied the adjacent apartment (6). A grandson (G) of C, one of the original *anakberu* and himself *anakberu* of E and F, occupied one apartment (8). A son (J) of the other original *anakberu* occupant occupied one apartment (7). Another (5) was rented to a clansman of members of the ruling lineage. Yet another apartment (3) was occupied by (I) the WZH (a classificatory brother) of one of the sons of one of the original *anakberu* inhabitants (D). The one remaining apartment (4) was occupied by an *anakberu* (H, a ZD) of one of the sons of one of the original *anakberu* inhabitants.

As this example shows, there is a tendency for long-established houses to be occupied by descendants – though not necessarily agnatic descendants – of the house founders. This is in part a function of the fact that apartments are included in family estates. (The eldest son has no special rights to his father's apartment.) The house community, however, is an open group; families are entitled to leave and join at will and there are no genealogical or other restrictions concerning who may or may not reside together in a house. One of the principal determinants of the composition of the larger household is the simple non-jural constraint of the availability of space.

Although the larger household group is in no sense a corporate group, it is a small community. From the felling of the first tree until the house is abandoned, the occupants participate jointly in a number of rituals which center on the house.

The site of the house is chosen by divination. This rite is carried out not by a priest or elder but by a female *kalimbubu* (WM or MBW) of the head of the house (*pengulu rumah*) who will later occupy the "base" apartment. For this she takes a handful of rice from a container as a portent of whether or not the proposed place is favorable. An even number of grains is a good omen but if the number is odd – a bad sign in Karo augury – a new site, a few meters from the former place, is tried; the same rite is repeated until a favorable site is discovered. The pile at the "base" apartment corner (NW) is then erected at the very spot where the divination takes place.

The materials used to build the house should be gathered from many places. It is said that one should take into account the likelihood that some of this material may have come from places occupied by evil spirits. Consequently, it may be accompanied by harmful supernatural powers against which some routine precautions should be taken. The inauguration of the house has therefore a remarkable ritual significance besides being a great ceremonial occasion.

The inauguration ceremony and rites led by a priest (*guru*) commonly take place on *nggara sepuluh*, the tenth day of the Karo lunar calendar, which, according to traditional divination, possesses the most suitable mystical characteristics for such an occasion. It is said to be "the day of challenge on which those who are in a waiting position lose the fight." The allusion here is to pernicious spirits who are waiting in the house, and the inherent power of the day is supposed to assist the priest in chasing them away. Meanwhile an orchestra plays the well-known ritual song *gendang lima puluh kurang dua*, literally, the tune of fifty minus two, which contains forty-eight melodies. This again is an attempt to persuade the evil spirits to leave the house. They are invited to dance and a spirit can hardly resist this strong temptation. After dancing the spirits leave the village.

The occupants then enter the house in a ritual procession, accompanied by their agnates, *kalimbubu*, and *anakberu*. Dressed in ceremonial attire they enter the house solemnly via the western ladder, porch, and door. The occupants of the apartment at the "base of the tree" lead the procession, followed by the occupants of the apartment at "the top of the tree;" the occupants of each section enter the house in a fixed sequence corresponding to the apartment numbers in Figure 1. The priest awaits their arrival on the *ture'*, close to the ladder with his ritual device, *tepong tawar*, neutralizing rice flour. This is made of rice flour mixed with water and is put in a white porcelain cup. With a stick the *guru* puts some *tepong tewar* on the forehead and cheeks of everyone who enters the house to "cool" him or her from any "hot" effect of the newly built house.

Other minor rites are conducted when a new family moves to the house and when a resident dies, but there is no joint rite when a baby is born within the house. The new residents perform a small ceremony by serving food to all residents of the house. This rite is called *persadan tendi*, uniting the soul. According to Karo belief, it is the means whereby a new resident is spiritually incorporated into the household community. When a resident dies, a farewell rite is performed by his housemates. Each scrapes his or her nails and the surface of the tongue; the scrapings are put on a betel-leaf which is placed beside the corpse in the coffin. The housemates, according to adat, must provide a carrying pole and a binding rope for the coffin. In return each family in the house receives a slice of meat from the funeral feast and is entitled to dance at the funeral ceremony.

The head of the house is the focus of the house community. He is "the man who knows the adat of the house." His authority is restricted, however, and he is not entitled to interfere in the internal problems of the resident families. As a rule, he makes no decisions relevant to life within the house without consulting all other residents. For example, if a man wants to move into an adat house after finding an empty apartment there, he must first seek the permission of the head of the house, who makes a decision only after consulting with the other residents of the house.

Social life in the adat house is characterized by intense daily contact and lack of privacy. Residents of the house meet at the door, on the porch or at the ladder and see each other within the house. Vegetables, chilis, onions and other everyday cooking ingredients are exchanged between women in the house. A part of the meat obtained by hunting and trapping should be distributed to the residents of other apartments, and so too homemade cakes and bananas grown in one's own garden. A professional sugarmaker should also follow this custom. Brown sugar is made from tapped palm sap and the product of the first day's work is distributed to fellow residents of an adat house. Purchased food is not distributed in this way.

The advantages of living in such a house were repeatedly stressed by my informants. A gravely ill resident of an adat house never feels isolated; he is surrounded by neighbors who consider themselves responsible for giving help whenever the need arises. They are a great help in collecting herbs, fetching a medicine man from a neighboring village, and in conveying an invitation to a close relative. When a man dies, the whole house is used to entertain visitors, as though the whole house belonged to the dead man. All the occupants customarily participate in the mortuary ceremony; their apartments are fully occupied by guests or used for the dancing floor. For two or three days they do not cook for themselves in the usual way but have their meals at the mortuary ceremonies. When the ceremonies are over, the housemates are expected to console the family of the deceased. During the first two or three months following the death the bereaved relatives, especially the women, may cry, and their housemates will hasten to console them.

Chapter Five

Descent Groups

According to a Toba Batak myth (see Ypes 1932:24-6; Vergouwen [1933] 1964:6), all Batak are descendants of a single divine ancestor. In this myth a high god called Mulajadi na Bolon sent away his daughter Si Boru Deak Parujar. After a violent but victorious battle with a huge serpent (Naga Padoha) and after chaining this disturbing creature, she created the world out of a lump of earth that she had brought from the heavens. Then her father sent a man named Raja Odap-odap to become her husband. Their union resulted in the founding of the first Batak village Sianjur Mulamula, which is situated on a slope of the sacred mountain Pusuk Buhit on the western side of Lake Toba. Twins – a son Raja Ihatmanisa and a daughter Boru Ihatmanisa – were born of this union; they married and bore a son, Si Raja Batak, the progenitor of all Batak. Here, one of the many great-grandsons of Si Raja Batak is regarded by the Toba as the founding ancestor of the Batak Karo.

This myth is unknown to most Karo however; the few who have heard it suppose it is an invention of the Toba designed to assert their cultural and political superiority among the Batak generally. Tamboen (1952:64), himself a Karo, presents a somewhat different account of Karo origins. In Tamboen's account the ancestor of all Batak was named Batak. He had five sons, Toba, Angkola, Mandailing, Karo and Pakpak. (The Simelungun are not included by Tamboen, probably through an oversight.) These five sons then became the ancestors of the several Batak peoples. Thus, according to Tamboen, the Karo did not originate from Tobaland. This theory, too, is not widely known among Karo – it may be Tamboen's own invention. The Karo do not possess any myth of the origin of their own society.

CLANS

There are five dispersed patriclans (*merga*) among the Karo and the whole population is divided, so to speak, into these five categories. Every Karo is a member of one or another clan and no person can be a member of more than one clan concurrently. The Karo are aware that this division into five clans distinguishes them from other Batak (the Toba, for example, see Vergouwen 1964:5-44). Thus they sometimes speak of themselves as *merga si lima*, the five clans, or the people of five clans. This designation is used on many occasions, especially in adat negotiations. Interestingly enough, the bookshop recently established in Kabanjahe bears the name Merga Si Lima. It was chosen also as the name of a Karo association founded by urban Karo at Padang Bulan, a suburb of Medan.

The Karo have no clear idea how the five clans came into existence. They possess no story or myth to account for the fact that there are five clans. Neumann (1926:2) recounts a story according to which the five clans – Ginting, Karo-karo, Perangin-angin, Sembiring and Tarigan – are each named after their founding ancestors. They are said to have been full siblings, the sons of Nini Karo (Grandparent Karo), though their birth order is not mentioned. Neumann suggests that this story is a recent invention. Tamboen (1952:64) repeats this story, and provides an explanation of the term *merga*. He asserts that the father of the five apical clan ancestors was Me(he)rga (expensive, outstanding), the only son of Karo, one of the five sons of Batak. Again this story is unknown to or not taken seriously by most Karo villagers. Still, it is interesting to note that the Karo term *merga*, Toba *marga*, and Pakpak *mego*, all of which refer to patrilineal groups, probably are derived from the Sanskrit *mrga*, which means track, way or custom.

The Karo clan names Ginting and Tarigan are just that and nothing more. That is to say, no one can explain their significance or offer an etymology for them. While the other names can be explicated, the explications are of no social significance. Karo-karo is simply a reduplication of Karo and the expression may be taken in other contexts to mean "resembling a Karo" or "like a Karo." Perangin-angin is composed of a reduplication of *angin*, wind, and a prefix *per*. Joustra (1907:11) translates

Perangin-angin as *windhoekers*, "those who stay in the windy section." The clan name with the most straightforward interpretation is Sembiring, from *mbiring*, black, thus "the black ones." These apparent etymologies have led to some scholarly speculation on Karo clan origins (see, e.g., Neumann 1926, 1927), but these speculations need not detain us here.

The clan name or a derivative term is not normally used in everyday speech but serves as a form of dramatic or poetic address. For instance, *mama biring* (*mama*, MB) and *nandé biring* (*nandé*, mother) refer to male and female members respectively of the Sembiring clan; these terms are employed particularly in romantic songs or when making love. Members of the Perangin-angin clan are referred to as *mama tambarmalem* (males) and *nandé ribu* (females). *Tambarmalem*, literally, a cooling medicine, is undoubtedly associated with the clan name in which the root *angin*, wind, is reduplicated, but there is no known explanation for the word *ribu*. Elder female and married members of the clan are referred to, by their grandchildren and others, by abbreviated clan names, e.g., *karo* for Karo-karo, *iting* for Ginting, *tigan* for Tarigan, *biring* for Sembiring, but for members of Perangin-angin the term *ribu* is employed.

The Karo clan is not a corporate group. Its members are dispersed throughout Karoland, own no property in common, have no chief, possess no common emblem or ritual center, and on no occasion do they assemble as a group. There are no reasons to believe that Karo clans ever possessed any of these features. The total number of members of each clan is not known, but if we estimate the total number of Karo (in 1962) at about 300,000, the total membership of each clan may range from 40,000 to 70,000.

Strictly speaking, Karo clans are not descent groups; they are mere aggregates of named groups, here termed subclans, which have no history of common origin and which do not regard themselves as agnatically related to one another (see also p. 76). Clan mates call one another brother or sister (*senina*, same-sex sibling, *turang*, opposite-sex sibling) and treat one another socially as distant classificatory siblings. This is not because they suppose that, since they belong to the same clan they must be agnatic kin of one another, but as a matter of courtesy. Their "siblingship" is entirely a polite social fiction.[1]

Even so, and despite their great size, the clans are exogamous. The people say that those of one clan, subclan, or lineage, should not marry one another. However, only three of the five clans are strictly exogamous. Marriage is permitted between certain subclans of the Perangin-angin and Sembiring clans, though this arrangement is regarded as anomalous.

In the case of Perangin-angin clan the explanation given for the anomaly is as follows. The two Perangin-angin subclans Sebayang and Pinem are descended from two (mythical) siblings, Raja Lambing and Raja Enggang. (Thus they form a subclan cluster; see below p. 78.) In the distant past the Sebayang took over as the ruling lineage of the village of Perbesi after driving out the members of the Pincawan subclan, also of Perangin-angin clan, who had been the ruling lineage. After that, according to legend.

> One day the village chief invited a silversmith to make *padong-padong*, heavy silver earrings, for his beautiful daughter. When the smith had all but completed working the earrings on his anvil, they suddenly sprang up into the sky and disappeared. The chief was filled with despair, fearing he might not retrieve the lost earrings. He issued a proclamation that whoever found and returned them could marry his daughter without paying brideprice. The earrings happened to fall into the lap of the son of the village chief of Kuta Buluh, about ten miles away. He then married the beautiful daughter of the Sebayang chief even though they were of the same clan, Perangin-angin.

Since then, the story continues, members of the Sebayank subclan may intermarry with members of any other Perangin-angin subclan except Pinem, the one subclan to which Sebayang is supposed to bear an agnatic relationship.

There is no similar explanation for the case of the Sembiring exception to the rule of clan exogamy. In this clan members of the Milala subclan are permitted to intermarry with some of the other subclans (those in category A, Table 7). Some informants speculated that this was allowed because the Milala belong to

[1] If it were not that the term clan is well established in the ethnographic literature on Karo, I would prefer to describe these groups as phratries.

Table 7

List of Karo Clans and Subclans

Ginting	Karo-karo	Perangin-angin
1. Ajartambun	1. Barus	1. Pinem
2. Babo	2. Bukit	2. Sebayang
3. Beras	3. Jung	3. Bangun
4. Jadibata	4. Gurusinga	4. Benjerang
5. Bukit	5. Kaban	5. Kacinambun
6. Garamata	6. Kaciribu	6. Keliat
7. Gurupatih	7. Kemit	7. Laksa
8. Sugihen	8. Ketaren	8. Mano
9. Suka	9. Purba	9. Namohaji
	10. Samura	10. Penggarun
10. Manik	11. Sekali	11. Pincawan
11. Munte	12. Sinubulan	12. Perbesi
12. Tumangger	13. Sinuhaji	13. Singarimbun
	14. Sinukaban	14. Sinurat
13. Jawak	15. Sinulingga	15. Sukatendel
14. Seragih	16. Sinuraya	16. Tanjung
15. Sinusinga	17. Sitepu	17. Ulunjandi
16. Capah	18. Surbakti	18. Uwir

Sembiring	Tarigan
A. Those who do not eat dog meat	1. Bondong
	2. Jampang
1. Muham	3. Ganagana
2. Pandia	4. Gereng
3. Colia	5. Gersang
4. Gurukinayan	6. Pekan
5. Berahmana	7. Purba
	8. Selangit
6. Bunuhaji	9. Sibero
7. Busuk	10. Tambak
8. Depari	11. Tambun
9. Pelawi	12. Tegur
	13. Tua
10. Keling	
11. Milala	
12. Pandebayang	
13. Sinukapur	
14. Tekang	
B. Those who eat dog meat	
15. Keloko	
16. Kembaren	
17. Sinulaki	
18. Sinupayung	

that group of Sembiring subclans (see below p. 79) who used to practice the custom called *pekualuh.* These subclans used to "drown" the ashes of their cremated dead in Lau Biang, the largest river in Karoland. This was done in the course of a large-scale communal ritual held approximately every twelve years. The ritual was the occasion for a mortuary feast, *Pekualuh,* whose lavishness and high cost have become proverbial. Since the husbands of women of these subclans were obliged to contribute substantially to the cost of the feast, it was suggested to me, these subclans may have found it difficult to get men from other clans to marry their women. It was pointed out to me that the requirement to perform this ritual (the last one was held in 1902) was a stigma. The myth of the origin of the ritual tells how a Sembiring man once deceived the King of Acheh, and to appease the King of Acheh the Batak King punished the Sembiring by forcing them to "drown" the bones and ashes of their deceased agnates so that they would not remain in Batak soil. All of this is interesting enough, but it hardly explains the fact that not all of the Sembiring subclans who performed this ritual may intermarry with one another. The exception to clan exogamy here is that Milala may intermarry with members of certain other Sembiring subclans, but those other subclans are not free to intermarry among themselves.

The fact that there are some exceptions to the rule of clan exogamy does not prevent the Karo from regarding the clans as exogamous in principle. In general terms Karo consider both the Perangin-angin and Sembiring clans to be exogamous, though a limited amount of marriage within the two clans is permitted. Members of those subclans that may intermarry still regard one another as classificatory siblings. However, when members of two subclans within the same clan become more closely related because of a marriage between their subclans, this closer relationship takes precedence, for purposes of kin classification and the regulation of social relations between them, over their clan siblinghood.

The clan then is principally an exogamous group. The fact that clans are exogamous, even though they are not regarded as patrilineal descent groups and have no corporate features, may be related to the fact that they serve to extend relations of agnatic kinship – and by implication other kinds of kinship relations as well – throughout the whole of the society. The system of five clans provides a means whereby virtually any Karo may establish some kind of kin-like social relationship with virtually any other Karo, if they so choose. In the final analysis, however, social relations based on nothing more than common clan affiliation, or on extensions of *anakberu-kalimbubu* relationships to distantly related or unrelated members of other clans, are highly attenuated versions of social relationships based on close genealogical or marital connections, and are not subject to strong moral or jural sanctions.

SUBCLANS

The subclan is the highest-order patrilineal descent group in Karo society. The members of each subclan are said to descend from a common ancestor; each subclan has a specific name, a history of origin, and certain taboos are common to all its members. Subclans, like clans, are called *merga*, but no confusion arises (on the part of Karo) because of this. If a man is asked the name of his *merga* he replies with the name of a specific group, e.g., Perangin-angin. Since every Karo knows that this is the name of one of the five Karo clans, they know that the man is referring to his clan affiliation. To find out his subclan affiliation, the inquirer will then ask "Which Perangin-angin?" (P. *apai*?). If the initial response is more specific, say Mano, the inquirer will know that the man is giving the name of his subclan. If the inquirer does not know to which clan this subclan belongs, he will ask to which *merga* the Mano *merga* belongs.

Most subclan names are said to derive from the name of the founding ancestor of the group or from the name of the village founded by this man. Sometimes the name of the alleged apical ancestor, the name of the village allegedly founded by him, and the name of the subclan are all much the same. For example, Gurukinayan, a subclan of the Sembiring clan, is said to originate from Nayan who was a well-known priest and who was therefore referred to as Guru Nayan. The village he founded (Gurukinayan) was named after him, and similarly the subclan comprising his agnatic descendants. In some cases, such as Ulunjandi and

Sebayang, subclan names are associated with historical events experienced by the subclan ancestors. Ulunjandi means "the source of agreement." This refers to a peace agreement that concluded an ancient war. The term Sebayang is associated with an imprisoned (*terbayang*) ancestor. However, there are some interpretable subclan names whose significance is now unknown to the people because their history has been forgotten; and there are some subclan names that have no literal meaning.

The fact that a number of Karo subclan names resemble the clan or subclan names of neighboring peoples deserves special attention. Karo subclan names like Pinem, Seragih, Munte', Manik, Maha, Sibero, Purba, Sinulingga and others, are also the names of patrilineal groups outside Karoland. Pinem is found among the Alas, Seragih and Munte' among the Simelungun and the Toba, Manik and Maha among the Pakpak, and Sibero among the Pakpak (Cebero) and the Gayo (Cebero). Though in some instances the historical connection is scarcely known, the similarity is nevertheless attributed to common descent. This attribution is confirmed in many cases by legends and myths. It might be supposed that, in view of the geographical separation of these groups and their identification with different ethnic groups, their alleged common descent is of minor social significance, particularly when compared with common clan affiliation within the *merga si lima*. On the contrary, however, it is an effective means of relating people belonging to these different ethnic groups. By these means, where circumstances require, a Simelungun, Toba, Alas or Gayo may identify himself as a Karo and similarly for a Karo who wishes to identify himself as one of those peoples. Thus, a member of Pinem subclan in Alas may claim to be a member of the Pinem subclan in Karo and therefore a member of the Perangin-angin clan. According to a Pinem myth, both the Pinem in Karo and Alas originated from a common ancestor, Raja Enggang who came from Jambu village in Pakpakland and who is therefore believed to have been a member of the Jambu subclan in Pakpak. Among the Pakpak, members of the Jambu, Solin and Padang subclans considered themselves agnatically related and so, by implication, they may identify themselves as members of Pinem subclan and Perangin-angin clan in general.

It was noted above that members of the same clan classify and treat one another as classificatory siblings even though they do not consider themselves as necessarily agnatically related. Of course, it follows that members of the same subclan do the same, though at this level there is a supposition of common agnatic descent. Thus, members of the same subclan are described as *sembuyak*, of one abdomen. Persons related only as clan mates are not so regarded. Some subclans, however, are regarded as agnatically related.

My informants (see also Tamboen 1952) were able to name 83 Karo subclans (see Table 7). If this list is exhaustive – I think it is – the range is 13 to 18 subclans per clan, an arithmetical mean of 16.6. The brackets in the list presented in Table 7 enclose sets of subclans that may be described as subclan clusters. These are sets of subclans claiming common agnatic descent. Their members count one another as *sembuyak*. There is no special generic term for such clusters; they are not regarded as *merga*.

In general, it is said that the founding ancestors of the subclans constituting a subclan cluster were siblings, and there are no stories relating how one or the other subclan was founded by someone who belonged originally to one of the others. There is one exception. The founding ancestors of the three subclans Muham, Pandia and Colia are said to have been brothers (see Figure 6). Gurukinayan, a priest and a wanderer, was originally

Figure 6. Relations between the subclans of one cluster.

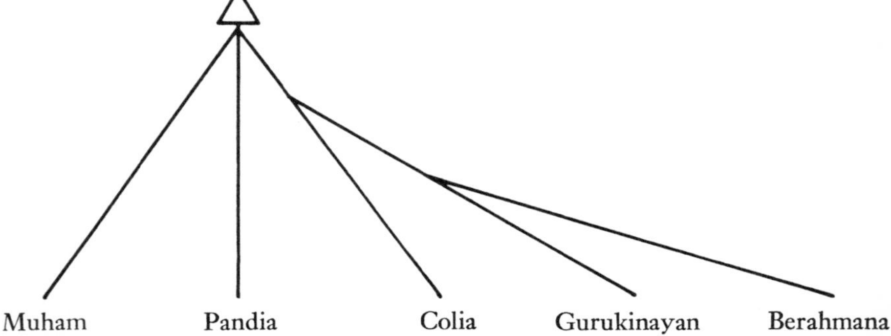

a member of the Colia subclan. Berahmana subclan was founded by a member of Gurukinayan subclan who, according to this story, left his village of birth in search of a lost herd of buffalo. There had been a prolonged drought and the herd had wandered off in search of food and water. The owner found his herd in a remote place but had difficulty recovering the animals, so he built a hut at the place and settled down there. Later that place became the village of a subclan founded by this man.

The largest cluster of subclans (nine) is in the Ginting clan. This subclan cluster is identified by the expression *siwah sada ginting*, nine (subclans) in one *ginting*. This cluster has an elaborate and popular myth which makes it the most renowned subclan cluster among the Karo. The myth is still generally known both by members of the cluster and other Karo, and it is preserved in the traditional *pustaka* (book of bark) called Pustaka Ginting, written in Batak script. This myth has been transliterated and translated into Dutch by Neumann (1930). (See Appendix I.)

There are no subclan clusters in the Tarigan and Karo-karo clans. There are two such clusters in the Sembiring clan. The subclans of this clan are divided also into two categories, those who eat dog meat and those who do not. These two categories do not constitute subclan clusters. "Those who do not eat dog meat" are so called because they observe a ritual prohibition on dog meat; these are the same subclans as observe the mortuary ritual mentioned above (p. 75), and so they may be described also as Sembiring *si ngombak,* who drown. The Karo have no explanation for this dual division of the Sembiring subclans. It may be, however, that the subclans who abstain from eating dog meat and who "drown" the ashes of their dead were founded by Indian immigrants, while the other four subclans are of genuine Batak origin. This is a popular theory among Dutch scholars of the Batak (see Joustra 1902, 1903, 1918; Ronkel 1918; Tideman 1936). According to Ronkel (1918) the custom of *pekualuh* originated in south Dekan where it is observed as the *tabut* feast, a mourning feast held in commemoration of two martyrs, Hasan and Husain. The clan name and several subclan names might be taken as evidence in support of this theory. As already noted, Sembiring (or Simbiring) means "the black" and this may indicate that the Sembiring ancestors were dark-skinned immigrants to Karoland. The subclan names Milala, Pandia, Colia, Pelawi and Berahmana are similar to the Dravidian dynastic names Malayalam, Pandya, S'oliyan, Pahlava and the Indian caste name Brahmana.

Although the lineages of a subclan are said to have common agnatic ancestors, little or nothing is known about these ancestors, except for the apical ancestor, the alleged founder of the subclan. Some subclans have elaborate myths concerning this man and his activities. All but two subclans (see below) have a traditional village-of-origin allegedly founded by the apical subclan ancestor.

As noted above, the members of a subclan observe certain food taboos. Thus, the members of one subclan may not eat a specific variety of mushroom, those of another may not eat certain varieties of banana, others may not eat dog, deer, white buffalo, or turtle dove, and so on. The Karo do not regard these as sacred objects. In most instances there is a sort of mythological charter for the prohibition. The members of one subclan tell the story that one of their ancestors, when a child, was saved from starvation when he was suckled by a white buffalo. They and others say that in abstaining from the prohibited foods they recognize the assistance given by the plant, animal or whatever to one of the subclan ancestors. They say also that failure to observe the taboo causes a skin disease which primarily affects the lips and mouth.

Each subclan possesses a pair of nicknames which may be applied to children of the group. The most common explanation is that the nicknames originated from the names of mentally retarded members of the subclan and were jocularly extended to all juvenile members of the subclan until, in the course of time, they became common nicknames for all the young people of those subclans. Thus, male children of the Sebayang subclan may be called Balandua and female children may be called Jengok. For the Sibero subclan the names are Batu (male) and Pagit (female). So a Karo child may be addressed by one of two names, either his personal name or his subclan nickname. The personal name of a boy is chosen for him by his mother's brother, and that of a girl by her father's sister. Just as the personal name forms the basis of the teknonym, so does the subclan nickname. Thus Amat, a man of the Sebayang subclan, has as his first-born child a son whose personal name is Sali; Amat may be referred to as Pa Sali or Pa Balandua. The former designation of course is more specific and gradually displaces the latter, which is commonly used only in a child's earliest years.

Subclans and subclan clusters, like clans, are not corporate groups. In no economic, religious or political activities do they act as wholes, nor are their members jurally or morally liable for one another's actions. Although members of these groups classify and treat one another as siblings, social relations based on common subclan affiliation, or on genealogical or marital relations between members of different subclans, are regarded as only slightly more binding than similar social relations based on clan affiliation. Common subclan affiliation becomes the basis for effective social relationships only when individuals so related live together in the same or adjacent villages over a long period of time.

LINEAGES

Each Karo lineage acknowledges its ultimate descent from a particular subclan founder and is identified partly by reference to the name of that subclan. As already noted, Karo in general have little knowledge of the exact nature of the genealogical relationship between subclan and lineage founders. For the most part it is merely asserted that the lineage founder is an agnatic descendant of the subclan founder, that the lineage founder left the village-of-origin of the subclan (or in some cases the village of another lineage of the subclan) and established his own village (or village ward). The village established by the lineage founder is the village in relation to which his agnatic descendants have the status of *bangsa taneh*, people of the land, or ruling lineage. The lineage, then, is terminologically identified by reference to the name of its subclan plus the name of its village; the ruling lineages of Liren and Kuta Gamber both belong to the Pinem subclan; they are identified as Pinem Liren and Pinem Kuta Gamber. The various lineages of a subclan are not politically ranked in relation to one another; each lineage is a politically autonomous group and has no specific rights or duties in respect to any other lineage of the same subclan. Thus, for example, although the ruling lineages of Liren and Kuta Gamber allegedly were founded by two paternal half-siblings, they have no specific rights and duties in respect to one another because of this relationship.

The depth of known lineage genealogies is correlated to some extent with the putative relative ages of the villages allegedly founded by their apical ancestors. The older the village, the greater the number of generations represented in the lineage genealogy. Most lineage genealogies, however, are only six to eight generations deep, though many villages surely are much older than that. Doubtlessly, the lineage genealogies recited by their older members are not accurate historical records, especially at their upper levels. We may assume that "telescoping" regularly takes place at these levels (cf. Peters 1960), though I have little data on this process at work.

It is important to distinguish between the lineage itself and the group constituted by its members who happen to reside in its village of origin. To say of a man (or woman) that he is, for example, a (member of) Perangin-angin (clan) Pinem (subclan) Kuta Gamber (lineage), is not necessarily to imply that he lives in Kuta Gamber village. Many people (men as well as married women) reside in villages other than the villages-of-origin of their lineages, but they do not become identified as members of the founding lineages of those villages, no matter how many generations they and their ancestors may have lived there. Thus Dolu, a Pinem Liren man, was born and still lives in Kuta Gamber; he says that he is *anak* (an inhabitant of, one of the people of) Kuta Gamber, but not that he is Pinem Kuta Gamber, or that his *merga* is Pinem Kuta Gamber.

The lineage, then, is not a local group. It is a unilineal descent group many of whose members reside in its traditional village-of-origin. There is no rule that all the men of a lineage must reside in this village, nor would Karo regard this as an appropriate arrangement. Villages, like adat houses, are ideally (and in fact) heterogeneous in terms of the lineage (and subclan and clan) affiliations of their inhabitants. Even the *bangsa taneh*, people of the land or ruling lineage, is not a local group. The *bangsa taneh* of a village is its alleged founding lineage, and anyone identified as a member of that lineage enjoys the status of *bangsa taneh* in relation to that village, whether or not he or she lives there.[2] The same principles apply to the *kesain* or village ward.

For one reason or another, not all Karo are able to claim the status of *bangsa taneh* in relation to some village or village ward, though theoretically nearly all Karo should be able to do so. As noted above, there are two subclans that have no traditional villages-of-origin. These are Busuk of Sembiring and Keliat of Perangin-angin. The various lineages of these subclans have no villages-of-origin either. The explanation given for this anomaly is that none of the ancestors founded a village or ward. The ancestors of the Busuk subclan are alleged to have been four full brothers who were great warriors and who were not interested in founding villages of their own. According to Pa Radu, a member of the Busuk subclan, this was because the brothers were honored and respected wherever they went. There is no known reason why the Keliat subclan has no traditional village-of-origin. Members of both subclans expressed some regret about this negligence on the part of their ancestors, who in their view should have founded at least one village.

The members of some lineages of other subclans are unable to specify the villages-of-origin of their lineages, though they assume that their ancestors must have founded villages. In addition, some individuals are unable to specify their lineage affiliations. Various explanations are offered for these conditions. In some instances, it is said, the known apical ancestor of the lineage had a serious quarrel with other inhabitants of his village-of-origin, left the village and, being determined to sever all social relations with his natal lineage, did not tell his descendants where he came from. In some instances, it is said that some agnatic ancestor had been exiled from his natal village because of his repeated, intolerable misbehavior. In other instances, some ancestor is alleged to have been a wanderer (a gambler or a petty trader, for example) who finally settled down in a village far distant from his natal lineage village, so that he and his descendants no longer had any social relations with that village and eventually lost track of it.

[2] To my knowledge this arrangement is characteristic of Batak village communities in general. Thus, ter Haar's (1948:65) description of the Batak "community" as a localized, exogamous, patrilocal clan or subclan inhabiting its own territory is seriously misleading. See also Tugby (1958).

In the traditional village community the perogatives of the ruling lineage include the right to hold the village or ward chieftainship (*pengulu*). The chief is the principal administrator of village affairs; he is the leader of its council of elders and is responsible for maintaining the social and moral order of the community. He enjoys some economic privileges such as unpaid labor to prepare his fields, and he has a right to part of the foreleg of any wild animal caught in his area. In addition, he enjoys some ceremonial privileges such as the exclusive right to dance at a certain stage in village ceremonies and to receive special meat and other foods at these ceremonies. Only after he has commenced cultivation of his own fields may other people in the village sow paddy in their fields.

This traditional political institution has been officially abolished by the Indonesian national government and replaced by the status of village headman (I, *kepala kampung*). The village headman is elected by popular suffrage and has lost most of the minor ritual and economic perogatives of the traditional office. Even so, the old political and ritual values survive and find expression in various ways. The ruling lineage is still regarded as a politically privileged group, and in adat matters the voices of its elder members carry considerable weight. The religious status of the ruling lineage is unaltered; only an elder male of the ruling lineage (or his wife) can communicate with the guardian spirits of the village. Finally, in Liren and Kuta Gamber the elected village chiefs have always been members of the ruling lineage.

It is important to note that the chief of a village or ward is not the head of the lineage that enjoys the status of *bangsa taneh* in relation to the village. The chief's authority is restricted to the village (or ward) and its land. Since this area is occupied necessarily by members of a number of different lineages, the chief's authority is not confined to members of his own lineage. Also, he has no authority in relation to members of his own lineage who happen to reside elsewhere.

Ordinary members of the ruling lineage of a village have few perogatives as such (see also Chapter 2), though the older men of this lineage are accorded some deference in the village council. Only members of the ruling lineage have the right to be head of an adat house in the village, but this status is not highly valued and a man's influence in village affairs is not dependent on his being head of an adat house.

Finally, it should be emphasized that members of a lineage are not jurally responsible for one another. Responsibility for revenge in the case of a homicide, for example, rests with the brother of the man who has been killed. His sister's husband (his closest *anakberu*) is obliged to assist him, and they may be assisted by other close kin of the victim. They take their revenge on the culprit himself, not on his brothers, lineage mates, or other close kin. Of course, in paying compensation for an offense a man may call upon his brothers and close *anakberu* (again, his sister's husband, or his sister's son) to assist him, and in some instances these kin may be held liable for his debts (see p. 118). In any event, his lineage mates in general are not liable for his actions or his debts.

Lineage Segments

The lineage is internally differentiated in a number of respects. The Karo often compare the internal structure of the lineage to the fingers of the human hand: "They are fingers of a single hand; one finger is close to some but not so close to others, even though one finger can touch any other finger." Every Karo knows his genealogical position in the lineage. He knows that he is genealogically closer to some of his agnates than he is to others, and he knows that this affects his social relations with them. He knows also that it is considered improper and impolite to mention or to discuss such matters in public. Privately, however, one may observe to another that he treats the other as though he were a close relative when he is in fact a distant relative, with the implication that this is something extraordinary. Karo often speak of the solidarity of lineage mates without qualification with regard to genealogical distance, as though all were equally obligated to one another, but they neither expect nor demand equivalent services from their close and distant lineage mates (or kin of any kind, for that matter). They know full well that distant lineage kin do not feel as strongly obliged to assist with their time and resources as do close kin, and they refrain from making unreasonable demands of them. The weight of rights and duties among agnatic kin falls on close agnatic kin, especially those who share the same father or father's father.

Aside from the domestic family, then, the socially most significant lineage segment consists of the domestic families of married brothers. This is the *sada bapa* segment (sometimes referred to as *jabu sada bapa*), the "one father" group (or family). During his lifetime the father himself is the head of this segment and its members (his children, his sons' wives, and his sons' children) usually ask for his advice in matters of importance. As he grows old, however, his authority and influence gradually pass to his eldest son, but in matters of importance to the segment as a whole his decision is final. The solidarity of this segment is especially great as long as the parental family estate remains undivided (until the deaths of both parents, see above p. 41), for until then the constituent families of this segment have a common economic interest. The *sada bapa* segment also is a religious group, for the constituent domestic families share the same guardian spirits, those of the deceased parents of the brothers who are the heads of those families. The several families of the brothers may make communal offerings. Misfortune within one of the domestic families often is attributed to one of these guardian spirits, but the guardian spirits are not said to punish one member of a family (domestic or "one father") for the misdeeds of another member.

The members of a "one father" segment share the same *anakberu jabu* and *kalimbubu jabu*. Their *anakberu jabu* is the domestic family of their married sister(s) and, conversely, their *kalimbubu jabu* is the domestic family of their mother's brother. That is to say, they have the same political, economic and ritual rights and duties in respect to these families. The social significance of this is discussed more fully in the following chapters.

The next highest lineage segment is the *sada nini* segment (sometimes *jabu sada nini*), the "one grandfather" segment (or family). This segment consists of the families of married agnatic parallel cousins. The organization of this segment is less clearly defined than the organization of the "one father" segment. Authority and influence within it are more diffuse and its members usually no longer have a common interest in an undivided family estate. Members of the same "one grandfather" segment co-operate in everyday activities and commonly render economic assistance to one another, but they do not act together as a group. Beyond this range ties of lineage kinship become considerably less important as the basis for mutual aid and assistance. Members of the same "one grandfather" segment have one set of *anakberu* in common, i.e., the families of their father's sisters and father's sisters' husbands. But these latter families have closer *kalimbubu* to whom they are more strongly obligated, and so interfamily alliances at the level of "one grandfather" relations are not as significant as those at the level of "one father" relations.

In theory, Karo may distinguish still higher-level segments within the lineage. They may speak, for example, of those who are related as *sada empong*, i.e., those who have one great-grandfather, or of *sembuyak empong*, those who have one great-great-grandfather. But these are purely genealogical distinctions and pertain only to interindividual relationships. The various domestic families of individuals so related are never described as constituting a *jabu* (family, of one order or another) or a *merga* (clan, subclan, lineage).

Lineage and Locality

The nature of the normative relationship between lineages and villages was discussed above. We may now consider the village of Kuta Gamber as an example of how this works out in practice.

All five clans are represented in Kuta Gamber, and each is represented by members of several (three to six) of its subclans (see Table 2). Thus, 21 of the 83 Karo subclans are represented in this village. Perangin-angin, the clan to which the ruling lineage (Pinem Kuta Gamber) belongs, is represented by more inhabitants (112) than is any other clan, and so is Pinem subclan (97), but a much smaller number of inhabitants (64) belong to the ruling lineage itself. Members of this clan constitute only 30 percent, and members of the ruling lineage only 17 percent, of the village population. It seems safe to suppose that, in order to maintain a dominant influence in village affairs, the ruling lineage must be represented by a fair number of its members; but of course the jural status of the lineage is not dependent on its having any particular number, or proportion, of its members resident in the village.

Pinem subclan contains eighteen lineages whose thirteen villages and five wards of origin are distributed in three adjacent subdistricts (see Table 8). One of the wards is one of the seven wards of Kidupen village. The four wards are parts of Juhar village, the largest village in Karoland. Juhar village has about 4,000 inhabitants and is divided into twelve wards.

Table 8

The Distribution of Perangin-angin
Pinem Lineages in Three Subdistricts

Kecamatan	Village	Ward
I. Taneh Pinem	1. Pinem	
	2. Kuta Gamber	
	3. Liren	
	4. Kempawa	
	5. Kuta Buluh	
	6. Butar	
	7. Balandua	
	8. Pamah	
	9. Lau Gunung	
	10. Taneh Pinem	
	11. Sembetek	
II. Tiga Lingga	12. Rantebesi	
III. Juhar	13. Jandi	1. Ulunjandi (in Kidupen village)
		2. Jambor Gerga
		3. Jambor Pengambaten
		4. Ulunjandi (2-5 in Juhar village)

According to a myth, the various lineages of Pinem subclan derive not only from Pinem village in Karoland but ultimately from a mythical ancestor, Raja Enggang, who was born in Jambu village in Pakpakland. He was a renowned traveller whose exploits included founding Pinem village. After that he travelled to Keluat and to Alas in Southern Acheh, where he died. Lineage elders in Kuta Gamber claim that his descendants in Keluat and Alas constitute descent groups which also go by the name

Pinem. Karo Pinem refer to these groups as Pinem Alas and Pinem Keluat and say that these groups refer to the Pinem of Karoland as Pinem Karo. Although all Pinem lineages are alleged to derive from Pinem village, there is no unitary myth or legend to account for the origins of the eighteen lineages.

Kuta Gamber lineage elders tell the following story about how their village came to be established. Long ago a man from Pinem village founded a village called Mbacang, about four miles north of Kuta Gamber. The village has long been abandoned but the villagers know the site well because there are still a few remaining coconut palms. It is said that the reason for the desertion of the village was a serious quarrel between two siblings over a pig. Both felt a strong desire to eat pork and decided to slaughter their mother's pig. As they did not have sufficient salt, the elder brother went to purchase some at the coast. The younger brother, hungry and unable to resist temptation, killed the pig before his brother returned. The elder brother was furious about this and decided to leave the village. He went away and founded another village, Balandua, about four miles from Mbacang. In due course, the younger brother, Raja Katana, also left and founded Liren village. One day Raja Katana went hunting near Lau Rimbon river and heard a strange voice that aroused his suspicion. He approached the place with his dogs and to his astonishment saw four men suddenly run away leaving behind a girl whom they had stolen from her natal village, Gurubenua, about twenty miles away. She was a member of Tarigan (clan) Sibero (subclan) Gurubenua (lineage) and a member of the ruling lineage of that village. The four men had bound her hands tightly with a length of rattan. Raja Katana took her to his home and she became his second wife. His first wife, a member of Karo-karo (clan) Sitepu (subclan) Kutambaru (lineage), totally disagreed with this and prohibited the second wife from staying in the same village. The second wife then lived in a hut in her field near Liren. The first wife protested again that this was too close to her own dwelling place. She could not bear to hear the other woman's cock crowing. The second wife was removed to a new place which later became Kuta Gamber village. She bore two sons. The elder son was named Gombang, literally, abuse, which suggested his mother's maltreatment by his father's first wife. Gombang became the founding ancestor of the ruling lineage in Kuta

Gamber. His younger brother, Sukuten, founded a new village, Kuta Buluh, about five miles away from Kuta Gamber, where his descendants are now the ruling lineage.

Taking Gombang as the apical ancestor of Kuta Gamber lineage, its genealogical depth is six or seven generations (see Figure 7). It is six generations from Gombang to the youngest

Figure 7. Skeletal genealogy of Kuta Gamber lineage, Pinem subclan.*

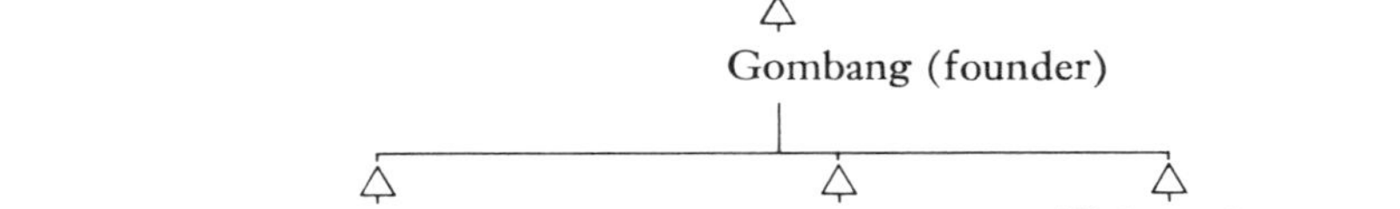

* All of Gombang's sons and grandsons are included.
For the subsequent generations I have included only one son of each son.

married male members of the lineage; their unmarried children add one more generation. The living members of the Kuta Gamber lineage total 130, 72 males and 58 females. Sixty-four members (49.2 percent) live in Kuta Gamber and the other 66 (50.8 percent) live in various other places. So slightly more than one-half reside outside the lineage village-of-origin, but only 17.2 percent (64 our of 372) of the residents of Kuta Gamber belong to this lineage.

Members of Kuta Gamber lineage who live outside Kuta Gamber village are residents of sixteen different villages and towns at varying distances (1 to 130 kilometers) from Kuta Gamber (Table 9). It appears, however, that there is a strong tendency

Table 9

The Distribution of the Dispersed Members of Pinem Kuta Gamber Lineage

Name of place	Distance from K.G. in km.	Male	Female[a]	Male and Female
I. Liren Kempawa Kuta Buluh Butar	1-8	21	16	37
II. Lau Petundal Lau Peranggunen Kuta Bangun Lau Gunung Taneh Pinem	8-12	4	7	11
III. Tiga Lingga Kede Berek	12-20	-	3	3
IV. Kabanjahe[b] Berastagi[b]	40-50	4	4	8
V. Simpang Selayang Medan[b] Lubuk Pakam[b]	100-130	4	3	7
		33	33	66

[a] Membership by birth.
[b] town.

to stay fairly close to the lineage village-of-origin. The spatial distribution reveals an approximate inverse proportion between the number of Kuta Gamber lineage members resident in these villages and towns and their distance from Kuta Gamber. Most of them (37 out of 66) live in villages not more than eight kilometers from Kuta Gamber. (This is not topographical distance but the approximate length of the path connecting the villages.) This means that they can reach Kuta Gamber within two hours by foot. Such a distance is generally regarded as "not far away," the criterion being that one can make a visit and return within a day. A lineage member who lives within that range can attend a ceremony in Kuta Gamber and return to his own village before nightfall. In contrast, lineage members who live in town are "far away" and their visits to the village-of-origin, it is said, require at least two days' travel. They have to walk four hours before reaching the main road in Tiga Binanga and then travel by bus about one-and-a-half hours to Kabanjahe and five hours to Medan. The villagers' calculation is not an exaggeration, since it is not uncommon to spend many hours waiting before one is able to catch a bus.

The figures presented in Table 9 show that there is a slight tendency for female married members of the lineage to reside elsewhere than in the lineage village-of-origin less frequently than male married members (see Table 10). About 50 percent of male

Table 10

Residence of Kuta Gamber Lineage Members

	Married	Not married	Total	
Resident				
male	13	26	39	64
female	11	14	25	
Non-resident				
male	13	20	33	66
female	16	17	33	
Total	53	77		130

married members of Pinem Kuta Gamber lineage reside in Kuta Gamber village but only about 41 percent of the female married members do so. The ratio is more or less the same in other Karo villages I visited. As noted in Chapter 3, there is no rule of patrivirilocal post-marital residence, such that a newly-married couple is obliged to live with or near the father of the husband. Also, villages, like adat houses, are ideally heterogeneous in terms of the lineage affiliations of their inhabitants. Thus, quite properly, many people reside with close maternal relatives and relatives by marriage. Nevertheless, there is a tendency for men to bring their wives to live with their fathers' domestic families for the first year or so of marriage, but this is not necessarily in the husband's lineage village-of-origin. This tendency is attributable to the duty of a father to provide food and lodging for his son and son's wife until the newly-married couple can harvest food from their own garden. If similar support is offered by the wife's family, the couple may reside with them. But this is not the only constraint that operates to make it slightly more likely that a couple will continue to reside patrivirilocally if theirs is an intervillage marriage. For one thing, it is considered proper for at least one son to stay with his father and support him in his old age. Also, it is often said that it is good and desirable, all other things being equal, to stay with one's "own people" rather than "other people" and to reside in one's own lineage's village-of-origin. While "own people" includes all close relatives, close agnatic kin especially are obliged to support one another. There is, thus, a sense of security associated with residence with close agnatic kin. Of course, most of these considerations do not necessarily entail residence in one's own lineage's village-of-origin, and in certain circumstances they may favor residence in another village – if, for example, a man is the only son of a man who does not live in his lineage's village-of-origin. Also, there is the proviso "all other things being equal." Thus, if a man is likely to be economically better off living in some other village, he is not usually under great pressure even to remain in his own lineage's village-of-origin.

THE STATUS OF WOMEN

The situation of women with respect to descent group affiliation is somewhat different from that of men. Both sons and daughters are regarded as members of their father's *merga* (lineage, subclan, or clan), but their affiliations are expressed in different ways. A man says, e.g., *Mergangku Tarigan*, My clan is Tarigan; but his sister or daughter says, *Aku beru Tarigan*, I am a Tarigan woman. Similarly, other people say of the man that his *merga* is Tarigan, but of his daughter or sister that she is a woman of Tarigan. The difference may reflect the jural dominance of men in descent group affairs.

For both men and women it is important to know also the natal lineage, subclan and clan affiliations of their mothers. A person's mother's natal lineage, subclan and clan are his or her *bere'-bere'* (see also p. 104). A married woman, however, has yet another set of identities. For many purposes a married woman is identified by reference to the lineage, subclan and clan affiliations of her husband. These are her *je'*. For several reasons it may appear that she is regarded as a member of these groups in much the same way as her husband's unmarried sisters and daughters are. For example, she and others refer to her natal family and lineage as her *kalimbubu*, and they are the *kalimbubu* of her husband and his lineage mates. Conversely, she is counted as one of the *anakberu* of her natal family and lineage, and so are her husband and his lineage mates. Also, when a woman marries, she comes under the protection of the guardian spirits of her husband's family and lineage segment; when she dies, her ghost is reckoned as one of the guardian spirits of her sons' families and their lineage segment. When ancestral spirits are called on in rituals held by families and lineage segments, the names of mothers and fathers' mothers are mentioned, but not those of FZs and FFZs who married and went to "other people."

Nevertheless, when Karo say of a married woman, "She has been sold by her people and purchased by her husband's people, she belongs to other people," they are talking about families and, at most, small-scale lineage segments which, as we have seen, are little more than extended families. They are emphasizing that certain rights and duties in respect to the woman, but by no means all such rights and duties, have been transferred from some persons to others; other rights and duties in respect to her are retained by her parents and brothers, and of course by the various other categories of kin. Certain rights in respect to her are transferred from her father and mother to her husband (e.g., the right to her domestic services), and her husband acquires certain rights in respect to her which no one had before she married (e.g., the right of exclusive sexual access and the right to engender children by her). Her husband and his father and brothers also take on the responsibility to look after her welfare; should her husband die and should she choose to remarry elsewhere, they have the right to custody of her children. On the other hand, should she divorce her husband she returns, jurally if not always physically, to the custody and authority of her father or her brothers if her father is dead. Also, her father and brothers retain the right and the responsibility to look after her if her husband and his people do not treat her well, and it is their responsibility to discipline her if she causes trouble for her husband and his people (see also Vergouwen 1964:156-157).

Marriage does not entirely dissociate a woman from her natal family or agnatic kin. Rather, the family formed by her and her husband constitutes a bridge between two sets of kin, the families and agnatic kin of her father and brothers, and those of her husband and his father and brothers. This is clearly demonstrated by the fact that any family may be counted, in different contexts of course, as a family of the husband's or of the wife's natal lineage. A man who belongs to Pinem Kuta Gamber lineage may say that the lineage consists of twenty-six *jabu*, each constituted by a married male member of the lineage and his wife and children, *and* of twenty-seven *jabu* (of) *anakberu*, each constituted by a married female member of the lineage and her husband and children. Many of these women and their families reside elsewhere than in Kuta Gamber, and so the families of female lineage members are counted as families of the lineage even if they do not reside in the village where that lineage is the ruling lineage. (Of course, the families of procreation of male members of the lineage are counted as families of the lineage regardless of where these men reside.) These same families of procreation of female lineage members are counted, of course, as the families of the lineages of their husbands.

In short, in some contexts Karo count the families of their daughters and sisters as families of their lineages, thus again showing that a married woman is not entirely dissociated from her natal family or agnatic kin.

The fact that a woman comes under the protection of the guardian spirits of her husband's family, and is no longer under the protection of the guardian spirits of her father's family, does not imply that she is dissociated from her natal lineage and is assimilated to her husband's. The guardian spirits are family, not lineage, guardians (see also pp. 138-139). The interests of guardian spirits may span lineage segments, but seldom beyond "one father" range, because the spirits are concerned only with the welfare of their children and sons' children (the latter because their sons, but not their daughters, perpetuate their families).

What then of the fact that a married woman describes her natal family and lineage as her *kalimbubu* and, conversely, members of those groups describe her as their *anakberu*? One way to interpret this is suggested by the theory of so-called asymmetric prescriptive alliance systems (see Needham 1962; Lévi Strauss 1969). We might suppose, in accord with this theory, that the two lineages were related prior to the marriage as *kalimbubu-anakberu*, that is, as wife-giver and wife-taker, that the marriage was an expression of this relationship, and that on marriage, the woman joined the wife-taking group in this dyad. For a number of reasons, however, this interpretation would be quite mistaken. The main difficulty is that, for this interpretation to be valid, the *kalimbubu-anakberu* relationship would have to be primarily a relationship between descent groups, whereas for Karo it is primarily an interfamilial relationship which is extended to all of the agnatic kin (and their spouses) of the principals. It is shown in the next chapter that the central or primary *kalimbubu-anakberu* relationship is between a woman's family of orientation and her family of procreation. So any previous *kalimbubu-anakberu* relationship has no bearing on the point to be made here, which is that a married woman stands as the *anakberu* of her natal family, lineage segment, etc., not because she joins or is assimilated to a lineage segment which was already the *anakberu* of her natal lineage segment, but because this is par excellence the relationship of her natal family to her family of procreation. It is only by extension that she regards the rest of her father's lineage, etc., as her *kalimbubu* and that they regard her (and her husband and children) as their *anakberu*.

Chapter Six

Anakberu-Kalimbubu Relations, I

CATEGORIES

All persons to whom any Karo is related by genealogical connection or by marriage are his *kade'kade'*, relatives. His agnatic relatives are his *sembuyak* (see p. 78). The opposed category of non-agnatic relatives (including non-agnatic cognates and relatives by marriage) has no single-word designation in the Karo language. This category is divided into two reciprocal categories, *anakberu* and *kalimbubu* (cf. Toba Batak *anakberu* and *hulahula,* Vergouwen 1964:45), each of which is further subdivided according to whether the relationship is by birth or by marriage. The structure of the category *kade'kade'* is diagramed in Figure 8. The three overlapping categories, *sembuyak, anakberu* and *kalimbubu,* together comprise all of anyone's relatives by birty or by marriage; thus the Karo speak of them as *sangkep si telu,* the three complete.

Figure 8. The structure of the *kadékadé* categories.

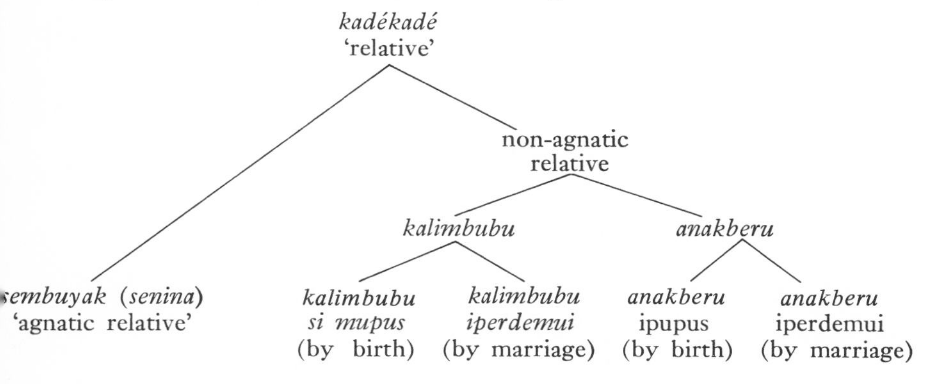

Primary Kalimbubu-Anakberu

In addition to distinguishing between *kalimbubu* and *anakberu* by birth and by marriage, Karo distinguish among *kalimbubu* and *anakberu* according to their genealogical distance from the focal individuals. The principal or structurally primary *kalimbubu-anakberu* relationship is between a woman's family of orientation and her family of procreation. Thus, a married woman's parents and siblings are among her *kalimbubu* (as well as being, some of them, her agnates) and, conversely, she is their *anakberu*. A person's principal *kalimbubu* by birth (*kalimbubu si mupus*) are his or her MF, MM, MB, MZ (unmarried); conversely, the principal *anakberu* by birth (*anakberu ipupus*) are DC and ZC. The principal *kalimbubu* by marriage (*kalimbubu iperdemui*) are a man's WF, WM, WB and WZ (unmarried); conversely, the principal *anakberu* by marriage (*anakberu iperdemui*) are one's DH and ZH. The families of origin of one's mother and a man's wife are *kalimbubu jabu*; conversely, the families of procreation of a man's sisters and daughters are his *anakberu jabu*. (The families of procreation of a woman's sisters and daughters are, ideally, families that are agnatically related to her own family of procreation, thus neither *anakberu* or *kalimbubu jabu*.)

Of course, the practice of matrilateral cross-cousin (MBD-FZS) marriage makes it possible for a man's MB's and WF's families to be one and the same, that is, for some of his *kalimbubu* by birth to be also his *kalimbubu* by marriage. Conversely, a man's ZS's and DH's families may be one and the same, so that some of his *anakberu* by birth may be also his *anakberu* by marriage. Such marriages, however, are relatively infrequent; one's *kalimbubu* by birth usually are distinct from one's *kalimbubu* by marriage, and so too for the reciprocal *anakberu* relationships.

Immediate Kalimbubu-Anakberu

In addition, a person counts as his (or her) *kalimbubu* by birth all members of the domestic families of his mother's "one father" lineage segment, i.e., the families of his mother's married brothers. Thus, in addition to his MB who is one of the primary *kalimbubu*, a person counts his MBW and MBC as *kalimbubu* also. Although the Karo language has no simple modifying expression by which to distinguish *kalimbubu* within this range from more distant *kalimbubu*, we may describe them as immediate *kalimbubu*. It is important to make this distinction analytically, even if Karo do not make it lexically, because Karo do make important jural distinctions between these and more distant *kalimbubu*. The reciprocal immediate *anakberu* by birth are one's father's sisters' families of procreation, i.e., FZ, FZH, FZC.

Similarly, the domestic families of a man's wife's "one father" lineage segment, i.e., the families of her married brothers, are counted as his *kalimbubu* by marriage. We may describe them as his immediate *kalimbubu* by marriage. The relationships included within this range, in addition to WF, WM and WB, are WBW and WBC. The reciprocal *anakberu* by marriage are the families of one's ZH's "one father" lineage segment.

Close Kalimbubu-Anakberu

Another socially significant category of *kalimbubu* by birth, though again without a distinctive designation in the Karo language, consists of the domestic families of one's mother's "one grandfather" lineage segment, i.e., MFB's and MFBS's families. The reciprocal category of *anakberu* by birth consists of the families of procreation of women of one's own "one grandfather" lineage segment, for instance, the families of FFBDs and those of more closely related female agnates. The corresponding category of *kalimbubu* by marriage consists of the domestic families of one's wife's "one grandfather" lineage segment, i.e., WFB's and WFBS's families. The reciprocal *anakberu* by marriage are the families of one's ZH's "one grandfather" lineage segment. We may call these close *kalimbubu* and *anakberu* by birth or by marriage.

Distant Kalimbubu-Anakbubu

Beyond this, the families of all the men of one's mother's lineage, subclan, and clan are counted as *kalimbubu* by birth; conversely, the families of procreation of women of one's own lineage, subclan and clan are counted as *anakberu* by birth. Similarly, the families of one's wife's lineage, subclan, and clan are counted as *kalimbubu* by marriage, and the families of one's ZH's lineage, subclan and clan are counted as *anakberu* by marriage. (It is important to note that this applies to ZH's ascendant and collateral agnates; a man's ZH's descendant agnates are his sister's children and his *anakberu* by birth. Thus, ZH's lineage, subclan and clan mates are divided between the *anakberu* by marriage and *anakberu* by birth categories.)

The *kalimbubu* who belong to one's mother's or one's wife's subclan and clan, but not to her lineage, may be called *kalimbubu ndaohndaoh*, distant *kalimbubu.* Conversely, the families of procreation of women of one's own subclan and clan, but not one's own lineage, and the families of one's ZH's subclan and clan, but not his lineage, may be called *anakberu ndaohndaoh*, distant *anakberu.* The lineage mates of the principal *kalimbubu* and *anakberu* are not called distant *kalimbubu* or *anakberu,* but neither are they regarded as particularly close relatives. In some ways, the lineage mates of the principal *kalimbubu* and *anakberu* are treated like close *kalimbubu* and *anakberu,* but in other ways they are treated like distant *kalimbubu* and *anakberu.*

Extensions

Because of the mistaken anthropological theory that categories of relationship of the sort described here are primarily or fundamentally intergroup relations (see Lévi-Strauss 1969; Needham 1962; Dumont 1968), it should be emphasized that the primary *kalimbubu-anakberu* relations are the consanguineal and affinal (marital) relations between the members of a woman's family of origin and her family of procreation. *By extension* the agnatic kin of persons so related stand also in *kalimbubu-anakberu* relationships. Because *kalimbubu-anakberu* relations are extended along lineage, subclan and even clan lines, it follows that agnatic groups as well as individuals may be regarded as *kalimbubu* and *anakberu* of one another. It is important to realize, however, that the agnatic relatives of two men related as, for example, WB and ZH are not *kalimbubu-anakberu* in their own right but as the agnatic relatives of those two men. Just as their category relationship is indirect and mediated by their agnatic relationships to the principal parties, so too are their social relationships. The rights and duties of *kalimbubu* and *anakberu* are essentially those prescribed between the members of a woman's families of orientation and procreation. The agnatic relatives of men so related, especially their brothers and first parallel cousins, are implicated in their social relations only as *their* close agnatic kin, not as *kalimbubu* and *anakberu* in their own right.

The non-Karo observer could easily be misled on this matter, for in some aspects of their manner of speaking about *kalimbubu-anakberu* relations, the Karo may appear to stress intergroup rather than interpersonal relationships. Thus, for example, a man may speak of his own brother's WB as "our *kalimbubu*" or as the *kalimbubu* of his lineage (and similarly of his FFBWB, etc.). He avoids speaking of such a man or of his lineage as "my brother's *kalimbubu*" (or "my grandfather's *kalimbubu*," etc.). This is not because his brother's WB is just as much his *kalimbubu* as is his own WB – far from it! It is sensible to say that BWB is "not my *kalimbubu* but my brother's *kalimbubu*," but it is not polite or tactful. The Karo avoid making such distinctions because they imply invidious comparisons and are regarded as discourteous. In this example, it might be to suggest that the speaker's brother, rather than the speaker himself, has certain duties toward the man and that the speaker's principal obligation is to help his own brother meet those duties, not to meet them himself, unless his brother is unable to do so. The speaker's obligation is principally to his brother, not to his brother's *kalimbubu*. This is true enough and is understood by all Karo, but it would be tactless and discourteous to make a point of it without good reason.

Conversely, the brothers of a man's ZH are regarded as his *anakberu*, but it is recognized that they have obligations elsewhere – most particularly to the brothers of their own wives – and so he cannot make demands on them at will in the way that he can reasonably make demands on his own ZH. Again, a man's brothers and classificatory lineage brothers are obliged to assist him in meeting his obligations to his own WB, but they themselves are not directly obligated to assist his WB. Similarly, more distant agnatic relatives may assist one another to meet their individual obligations to their individual *anakberu* and *kalimbubu;* and where the principal *anakberu* or *kalimbubu* of someone is not available to perform a ritual or ceremonial duty or to act as a go-between (as required by custom), a more or less distant agnatic relative of the principal *anakberu* or *kalimbubu* may take his place. Closeness of agnatic relationship to the principal *anakberu* or *kalimbubu* usually determines priority in choice of a substitute, if such a choice is possible under the circumstances.

Thus, when the Karo speak of two agnatic groups as the *anakberu* and *kalimbubu* of one another, they do not imply that the groups as wholes stand in a unitary jural relationship. They usually refer, though not necessarily directly, to some particular pair of individuals and to their close agnatic kin who are implicated by extension in their *anakberu-kalimbubu* relationship. The single and only partial exception to this generalization is the *anakberu tua-kalimbubu tua* relationship between two lineages.

As previously noted (p. 23), a village is properly founded by a man and one or more of his *anakberu* and *kalimbubu.* The lineages of these *anakberu* and *kalimbubu* them stand in a special relationship to the founding lineage, and representatives of these groups are required to participate in certain of its ritual and ceremonial activities (see p. 26). The *kalimbubu tua* and *anakberu tua* (*tua* = senior) also are called the *kalimbubu* and *anakberu taneh,* i.e., the *kalimbubu* and *anakberu* of the land. The *kalimbubu tua* is described also as the *kalimbubu si majekken lulang,* the *kalimbubu* who planted the *lulang,* the plant that serves as a hedge around the village. Usually the *anakberu tua* is the lineage of the ZH of the lineage founder, and the *kalimbubu tua* is the natal lineage of the founder's wife' The *kalimbubu tua* of the ruling lineage in Kuta Gamber is Jambor Lateng lineage of Tarigan clan, Munte subclan. The *anakberu tua* of Kuta Gamber lineage is Rumah Padang lineage of Ginting clan, Munte subclan. Some members of both lineages reside permanently in Kuta Gamber village and they usually represent their lineages on the appropriate occasions.

THE DEVELOPMENT CYCLE OF *ANAKBERU-KALIMBUBU* RELATIONSHIPS

Since the Karo distinguish between *anakberu* and *kalimbubu* by birth and by marriage, any individual's field of *anakberu-kalimbubu* relationships must undergo changes in structure and composition as he (or she) progresses from childhood to adulthood and acquires a spouse. An extended example, focusing on a man I call Sudip, will serve to illustrate the process and to introduce some further categories of *anakberu-kalimbubu* relationships.

Sudip belongs to Kuta Gamber lineage, Pinem subclan, Perangin-angin clan; these are his *merga.* His mother belongs to Rumah Tengah lineage, Gurukinayan subclan, Sembiring clan; these are Sudip's *berébere*, his maternal lineage, subclan and clan affiliations. Members of these agnatic groups are regarded as his *kalimbubu*; they are his father's *kalimbubu (kalimbubu bapa)* also, but while they are Sudip's father's *kalimbubu* by marriage, they are Sudip's *kalimbubu* by birth. Conversely, Sudip's father is an *anakberu* by marriage of Rumah Tengah lineage, Gurukinayan subclan, Sembiring clan, and Sudip is an *anakberu* by birth of members of these groups. The creation of the *anakberu-kalimbubu* relationship between Sudip and his mother's brother, etc., depended, of course, on the marriage of Sudip's father to his mother, which marriage established an *anakberu-kalimbubu* relationship between Sudip's father and his mother's brother, etc. To that extent the *anakberu-kalimbubu* relationship between Sudip and his mother's brother, etc., may be said to derive from his father's *anakberu-kalimbubu* relationship with the same man. It must be emphasized, however, that Sudip is the *anakberu* of his mother's brother in his own right, not merely as his father's son. If Sudip's father were to divorce his wife, Sudip's mother, his father's *anakberu-kalimbubu* relationship with Rumah Tengah Gurukinayan would be jurally annulled, but this could have no effect on Sudip's status as the *anakberu* of Rumah Tengah Gurukinayan, for this *anakberu-kalimbubu* relationship is by birth and is regarded as indisolvable. Thus, Sudip's status as the *anakberu* of Rumah Tengah Gurukinayan is not dependent on or mediated by his father's status as the *anakberu* of the same people, certainly not in the same way as his status as, say, the *anakberu* of his brother's WB.

The Karo regard the *anakberu-kalimbubu* by birth relationship as inalienable; they say that the relationship commences prenatally, "before the child sees the light of day, before his head is hard and his naval cord falls off." It commences when the fetus is about one month old and is recognized as a human being (*jelma*). At that time the fetus acquires a soul (*tendi*), a paternal agnatic affiliation (*merga*), and a maternal agnatic affiliation (*berébere*), and thus becomes an *anakberu* of its mother's natal family and, by extension, her agnatic groups. Once acquired, these identities are integral and inalienable aspects of a person's social identity. Should a person die "before seeing the light of the day" (through abortion or the death of his mother during pregnancy), his kinship status is not affected. He may choose his own name and proclaim it to his relatives through a spirit medium. Such a soul-spirit (*butara guru*) usually chooses an unusual name, such as Raja Kumilap, King of the Lightning, and is regarded as one of the guardian spirits of its family and lineage segment. The principal *kalimbubu*, represented by one of their wives (usually a MBW), are obliged to make presentations of food to such a soul-spirit on the occasion of certain family rituals.

Sudip's *merga* and *berébere* affiliations provide him a ready-made field of social relations and the normative means for ordering his social relations with virtually anyone he may meet. They do this by enabling him to fit any Karo into one of the three major categories of relationship, *senina* or *turang*, and *anakberu* and *kalimbubu*. Thus, if Sudip should encounter a stranger whose *merga* is Pinem or one of the other subclans of Perangin-angin clan, they may regard one another as agnates; they may also classify one another under one of the appropriate kinship terms (see Appendix II), depending on their ages relative to one another. (They do this not because they suppose that, as members of the same clan, they must be agnatically related, but because of the polite social fiction that they are.) Similarly, if Sudip meets a man whose *merga* is Gurukinayan or some other subclan of Sembiring clan (Sudip's mother's clan), he may regard this man as his *kalimbubu*. Conversely, if Sudip meets a man whose *berébere* is Pinem or some other subclan of Perangin-angin clan, he may be regarded as Sudip's *anakberu* because his mother may be regarded as Sudip's agnate. The final possibility is that Sudip may meet a man who belongs to a different clan but who has the same *berébere* as Sudip himself – their mothers belong to the same clan. Since women who belong to the same clan are regarded as "like sisters," Sudip and this man may regard one another as "like the children of two sisters" (*senina sepemerén*), that is, as classificatory siblings. From this it should be clear that one of the functions of the wide extension of *kalimbubu-anakberu* relationships is provision of an egocentric genealogical framework into which any Karo may fit any other Karo (and many non-Karo too), for purposes of ordering their interpersonal social relations. By this means, the moral order associated with relations of close genealogical connection is widely extended and is used to order social relations between persons whose genealogical relationships are greatly attenuated, if they exist at all.

When the time comes for Sudip to marry, he is confronted with two alternatives. One of these is that he may choose to marry a matrilateral cross cousin (MBD) or the close classificatory lineage sister (second parallel cousin) of such a relative. If he does this, he will strengthen his social relations with his immediate *kalimbubu* by birth by making them also his immediate *kalimbubu* by marriage. Alternatively, as most commonly happens, he may choose to marry some other woman, perhaps a woman who does not belong to his mother's lineage, subclan, or even her clan. Of course, if Sudip marries a woman (not a MBD or close classificatory MBD) of his mother's lineage, subclan, his wife's relatives who were his distant *kalimbubu* by birth become also his principal *kalimbubu* by marriage, and his own *kalimbubu* by birth become also his distant *kalimbubu* by marriage. Finally, if he marries a woman not even of his mother's clan, Sudip's *kalimbubu* by birth and his *kalimbubu* by marriage do not overlap at all.

Anthropologists familiar with the theoretical literature on asymmetric prescriptive alliance systems, so-called, may think it strange that the alternatives are classified in this way – especially that the case of marriage with a woman of one's mother's lineage who is not a MBD or close classificatory MBD is grouped with the case of marriage to a non-kinswoman. This, however, is the Karo view. The Karo say that marriage between distant *impal* (cross cousins) is not a proper *impal* marriage; the consequences of such a marriage are not the same as the consequences of a marriage between MBD-FZS or between a man and a woman who belongs to the same "one grandfather" lineage segment as his own MBD. The consequences are not the same for the simple reason that, beyond the range of the "one grandfather" segment, agnatic kin are not greatly implicated in one another's affairs. Thus, if a man marries a woman not of the same "one grandfather" segment as his own MBD, those people who become his *kalimbubu* by marriage are not likely to be the people with whom he and his parents already have close and active social relationships as *kalimbubu* and *anakberu.* The obligations arising from such a marriage are bound to compromise a man's ability to continue to treat his *kalimbubu* by birth just as he had before the marriage. The compromise is not likely to be any less if a man marries a distant *kalimbubu* by birth or a woman who is not even a member of his mother's natal clan.

In short, as the Karo see it, unless a man marries a MBD or one of her second agnatic parallel cousins (a MFBSD), there is an unavoidable conflict of interests between the two *kalimbubu,* the "old" and the "new," the *kalimbubu* by birth and the *kalimbubu* by marriage, even if these should overlap to one degree or another. The *kalimbubu* by marriage always "win" in this conflict, and it is the common expectation that they will. The conflict can be prevented only by resorting to cross-cousin marriage, by which a man's principal *kalimbubu* by birth become also his principal *kalimbubu* by marriage. Of course, such conflicts of interest would not exist if it were not that the *kalimbubu-anakberu* relationship is primarily one between individuals as particular kinds of kin, rather than between agnatic groups.

The shift of focus in *kalimbubu-anakberu* relations that is bound to result from marriage to a woman other than a MBD or her close classificatory sister is reflected in the way in which Karo understand the question "Who is Sudip's *kalimbubu*?" This depends on whether or not Sudip is married. Prior to his marriage, Sudip and others answer with the name of his mother's brother or his lineage or subclan. After Sudip's marriage, the expected answer is the name of his wife's father or brother or that of their lineage or subclan.

This shift in focus in *kalimbubu-anakberu* relations is evident also in certain aspects of divination procedure. The asymmetry between *anakberu* and *kalimbubu* pervades almost every aspect of their social relations and is deeply rooted in Karo religion. The Karo say that harmonious relations with one's *kalimbubu* bring happiness and prosperity, but if the *kalimbubu* feels neglected or injured by his *anakberu,* this may bring mystically-inflicted misfortune to the *anakberu.* The source of the misfortune is *menek-menek kalimbubu,* the frustration of the *kalimbubu.* This diagnosis of a misfortune, or of one that is about to occur, may be made by a male priest or a female spirit medium who purports to discover it in an augural object such as an egg, a chicken head, or an areca blossom. Thus, healing a disturbed social relationship between *kalimbubu* and *anakberu* may have a curative or a preventative potency. The priest or spirit medium does not specify a particular *kalimbubu* as the frustrated one. Identification of the particular *kalimbubu* who is frustrated is accomplished through a process of elimination. For a married man, the starting point in the inquiry is always some possible misconduct toward his wife's parents or her brothers. His *kalimbubu* by birth are considered only after it is clear that the frustrated *kalimbubu* is not a member of his wife's natal family or her brother's family. Since a man's *kalimbubu* must participate in a divination rite for which he is the patient, for a married man the representative is usually his WF, WM, WB or WBW.

The birth of Sudip's first child strengthens his ties with his *kalimbubu* by marriage. In theory, once a marriage is consummated, an enduring *anakberu-kalimbubu* relationship is established, but in practice it is only after the birth of a child from that union that the relationship becomes relatively permanent. This is because it is then that the marriage itself becomes more likely to endure. Obviously, since Sudip's status as the *anakberu* of his WF and WB is defined as "by marriage," it is terminated if the marriage itself is dissolved.

Let us assume that a son, Teras, is born to Sudip from his marriage to a woman of Ginting Munte subclan. These Munte who are Sudip's *kalimbubu* by marriage are Teras' *kalimbubu* by birth. Moreover, since the *kalimbubu* of one's *kalimbubu* are regarded as *kalimbubu* too, Teras' mother's mother's brother and his lineage, etc., are Teras' *kalimbubu,* specifically his *puang kalimbubu.* He is their *anakberu menteri,* the *anakberu* of *anakberu.* As with the closer *kalimbubu* and *anakberu,* there are two kinds of *puang kalimbubu* and *anakberu menteri,* those by birth and those by marriage. As just noted, the first kind of *puang kalimbubu* are a man's MMB and his lineage, etc. The terms *soler* and *kempu* designate the senior and junior parties, respectively, to a *puang kalimbubu-anakberu menteri* relationship by birth. Thus, Teras may say of his mother's mother's natal subclan, Gersang let us say, "My *soler* is Gersang" or "I am the *kempu* of Gersang." Today, the *puang kalimbubu-anakberu menteri* relationship by birth has only a relatively minor ceremonial significance. That its social significance may be decreasing seems indicated by the fact that only older people (generally those over fifty) understand the terms *soler* and *kempu.* They say that in the past the identity of one's *soler* was one of the four inquiries made in the identification procedure called *ertutur.* In *erutur* two persons take turns asking about each other's identities in order to establish their *senina-senina* or *anakberu-kalimbubu* relation. First the *merga* (*beru* for a woman), is asked, second the *berébere*, third the *binuang* (one's father's mother's agnates), and fourth the *soler.* Today, the identity of the *binuang* and *soler* are no longer asked, but inquiries are still made as to the identities of one's *merga* and *berébere.* Nevertheless, the mother's mother's agnates are still invited to attend the ceremonies at which such inquiries are made (see p. 140).

A man's WMB and his lineage, etc., are regarded as *puang kalimbubu* by marriage – they are the *kalimbubu* by marriage (WF, etc.) of his own *kalimbubu* by marriage. The social significance of this relationship is stronger, perhaps better preserved, than the *puang kalimbubu* relation by birth. The bride's mother's agnates still receive the portion of the marriage payment called *berébere* (which term also signifies one's mother's – in this case the bride's mother's – agnatic group). In return, they are obliged to participate in the rite performed on the occasion of the bride's first pregnancy (see p. 140).

Beyond this, there are a man's *kalimbubu si ngaloken perkempun,* the *kalimbubu* who receive the *perkempun.* This, too, is a portion of the marriage payment, and it is presented to the agnatic kin of the bride's mother's mother, who are the *kalimbubu* by birth of his *puang kalimbubu* by marriage. As a rule, the *perkempun* is half the size of the *berébere.* In 1962 the main part or trunk of the bride price (*unjuken*) was commonly Rp. 2000, the *berébere* Rp. 600, and the *perkempun* Rp. 300. Those who receive the *perkempun* also are obliged to participate in the pregnancy rite mentioned above. Little else is normatively entailed by either of these fairly distant *kalimbubu-anakberu* relationships.

Figure 9. The various kinds of *kalimbubu*.

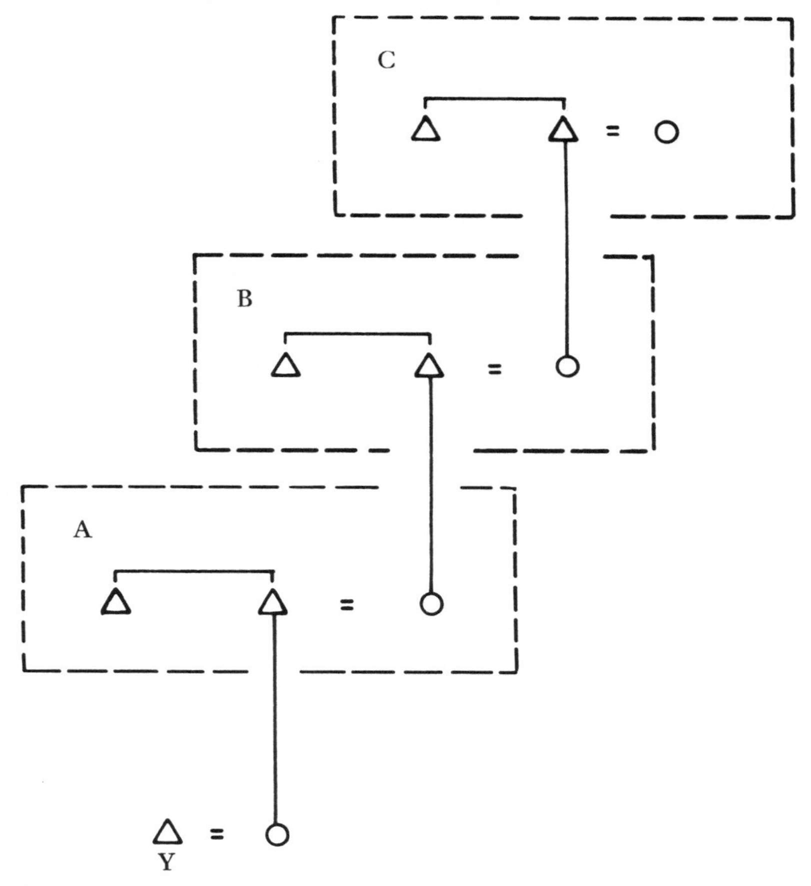

From Y's point of view:

A = *kalimbubu* by marriage or the *kalimbubu* who receive the *tukor*.
B = *kalimbubu* who receive the *berébere*, the *puang kalimbubu*.
C = the *kalimbubu* who receive the *perkempun*, the *kalimbubu* of the *puang kalimbubu*.

The proliferation of formal *kalimbubu-anakberu* relationships ends with the *kalimbubu* who receive the *perkempun*.

Of course, it is not only a man's own marriage that may add to his *kalimbubu-anakberu* relations. The extension of *kalimbubu-anakberu* relations to the agnatic kin of the principals implies that any marriage contracted by an agnatic relative may add to the range of one's *kalimbubu-anakberu* relationships. Moreover, in principle, any *kalimbubu* of a *kalimbubu* is one's *kalimbubu* and, conversely, any *anakberu* of an *anakberu* is one's *anakberu,* too. However, as previously noted, every Karo distinguishes among his many *kalimbubu* and *anakberu* by degrees of importance to him, and these degrees are directly correlated with the genealogical distance of the relationships. For any individual, there are only a few primary and immediate *kalimbubu* by birth or by marriage. These are the *kalimbubu* who matter most to him. His social relationships with other persons whom he may classify as *kalimbubu* are only indirect and mediated, either by his status and obligations as an agnatic relative of some man who is the immediate *anakberu* of those people, or by his status and obligations as the *anakberu* of their agnatic kinsman. Conversely, the most important *anakberu* are the families created by the marriages of one's own sisters and daughters.

Finally, brief mention should be made of the expressions *kalimbubu si empat* and *anakberu si empat,* the four *kalimbubu* and *anakberu.* These expressions, often used on ceremonial occasions when large crowds of people gather to participate, refer to the four clans other than the one to which the host lineage belongs. There are no traditions or rules of unidirectional wife-giving – wife-taking relations between the five clans; the men of any one clan are free to take their wives from among the women of any other clan, and to give their sisters and daughters as wives to the men of any other clan, subject of course to the rules prohibiting marriage between certain kinds of kin. Thus, the logical extension of *kalimbubu-anakberu* relations to the clan level implies that all of the clans are related to one another both as *kalimbubu* and *anakberu.* The apparent logical contradiction and the mixing of directly opposed categories does not trouble the Karo, for it matters little in terms of its social implications that a particular man or set of men may be both *kalimbubu* and *anakberu* to another man or set of men, if that relationship is only at the clan level. Furthermore, it may be a matter for small concern that such a dual relationship may exist at the subclan level. It can usually be decided which is the closer relationship and therefore the one that should be given priority, or neither relationship may be close enough to matter very much.

WIFE-GIVERS AND WIFE-TAKERS

Some comment should be made on the argument advanced by certain anthropologists that terms like Karo *kalimbubu* and *anakberu* are best translated as "wife-giver" and "wife-taker" respectively (cf. Needham 1962; Maybury-Lewis 1965; Dumont 1968). The argument assumes that societies like Karo are best described as "asymmetric prescriptive alliance systems," where this expression refers to a social order based on a division of the society into three kinds of lineal descent groups which are engaged, prescriptively, in the unidirectional exchange of women in marriage. It is an essential part of the argument that the systems of classification usually described by ethnographers as systems of kin classification are in reality something quite different, i.e., "systems of social classification" whose categories are not genealogically defined; they are defined, as Needham (1962) puts it, by relations of descent and alliance, not by relations of individual genealogical connection and individual marriage.

In almost every particular, this would be a misleading characterization of Karo society. It is not that Karo do not speak of *kalimbubu-anakberu* relations between descent groups, or of descent groups as giving and taking women (as wives) from other such groups. They certainly do! It is rather than, in Karo society, such relationships are structurally derivative. All *kalimbubu-anakberu* relationships between sets or groups of individuals originate in particular individual marriages between particular members of those groups, and the groups stand in *kalimbubu-anakberu* relationships only by virtue of the extension of these inter-individual relationships to the agnatic kin of the principals. Of course, any two groups may already stand in a *kalimbubu-anakberu* relationship prior to some marriage between two of their members, and such a marriage may (it does not necessarily) reinforce the established *kalimbubu-anakberu* relationship between members of those groups. But it should not be lost sight of that the temporally prior intergroup relationship, though formally viable as long as descendants of the original marriage exist to remember it, becomes socially insignificant if it is not reinforced – perhaps it would be better to say recreated – by further marriages between members of the groups.

So when Karo speak of intergroup *kalimbubu-anakberu* relations, this is merely an abbreviated and convenient way of expressing the extension along agnatic lines of relationships created by individual marriages, ultimately to the whole lineages, subclans and clans of the principals to the marriage. Karo know perfectly well that to say, for example, "Munte is Sudip's *kalimbubu*," is only to say that Sudip is married to a Munte woman, and therefore her agnatic kin, principally her father and her brothers, are his *kalimbubu* and he is their *anakberu*. It is not to imply that Sudip regards all members of Munte, or even just the members of his wife's lineage within Munte subclan, as equally his *kalimbubu*. They know, furthermore, that Sudip's wife was given to him by her father's lineage or clan only in the sense that she was given to him by her father, who happened to be a member of Munte subclan.

A further difficulty with the glosses "wife-giver" and "wife-taker" is that, while they describe a very important aspect of the social relations between *kalimbubu* and *anakberu*, they do not specify what it is that makes people the *kalimbubu* and *anakberu* of one another (see also Lévi-Strauss 1966:17). This is most clear in the case of one's *kalimbubu* and *anakberu* by birth. A man's father and his father's collateral agnates are his mother's brother's *anakberu* by marriage. Thus, two quite different sets of relatives are implicated in these two *kalimbubu-anakberu* relationships, though there is some overlap in the composition of the two sets.

On the other hand, neither can the *kalimbubu-anakberu* relationship by marriage be reduced to the *kalimbubu-anakberu* relationship by birth. As already noted, the primary *kalimbubu-anakberu* relationship is that of a woman's family of orientation to her family of procreation, and so a number of consanguineal and affinal relationships are equally focal to it. The consanguineal relationship is no more reducible to the marital relationship than is the marital to the consanguineal. (It is important to note, however, that this has no necessary implications for the structure of Karo kin classification; see Appendix II.)

Although it is clear that the glosses "wife-giver" and "wife-taker," much less "wife-giving group" and "wife-taking group," are not particularly appropriate, it is difficult to find simple English glosses for the terms *kalimbubu* and *anakberu*. This is only to be expected since similar categories are not part of the culture of English-speaking peoples. It is possible to guess at the etymology of the terms, but this is not necessarily a valid guide to their present signification. The *-mbubu* in *kalimbubu* probably derives from a common Indonesian root meaning skull (cf. Nias *kamu'u* and Angkola Mandailing *ambubu*), and Neumann (1951:134) suggests that *kalimbubu* refers primarily to the crown or rearmost part of the human head. This accords well with its connotations of great respect and entitlement to jural and ritual superiority. *Anakberu* is more transparent. It appears to be a compound of the two roots *anak,* child or person, and *beru,* woman or female. In the ethnographic literature, preference is usually given to the meaning "child" and the expression is glossed as "the children of the woman" (cf. Tugby 1958:347). However, since *anak* is often used in expressions to indicate "the people of" (e.g., *anak gugung,* upstream or highland people; *anak jahějahě,* downstream or lowland people), the expression *anakberu* might better be glossed as "people of the woman" or "the woman's people," or simply "one's daughter's (or sister's) family." This takes us back to the notion (see pp. 95-96) of women as the links between families and ultimately the several descent groups to which these families belong.

Whatever their etymology, nowadays the terms *kalimbubu* and *anakberu* have a number of meanings. They refer first and foremost to the relationship between a woman's family of origin and her family of procreation and to those relatives who are parties to this relationship. The woman herself is the link between the families and belongs, in a sense, to both, certainly as long as her father is alive; but as a member of the domestic group headed by her husband, she is one of the *anakberu* of her natal family and of her brothers' families of procreation. Of course, her husband is implicated in this interfamily relationship, but since he is (or may be) related to his wife's familial kin only by marriage, they are his *kalimbubu* by marriage rather than by birth. Beyond this, the terms are extended, as previously noted, to all agnatic kin of the principal parties, and various ranges of *kalimbubu* and *anakberu* may be distinguished by the use of specific lineage, subclan, and clan names. Since certain social relationships are prescribed between the various members of the families concerned, depending on the specific nature of their respective genealogical or marital relationships, the terms *kalimbubu* and *anakberu* also connote these jural, affective, and ritual relationships. As the terms are extended to progressively broader categories of relatives by birth and by marriage, so are the social relationships they connote. But while the categories may be extended almost indefinitely, the social relationships are another matter. The organization of social relations between *kalimbubu* and *anakberu,* close and distant, is the topic of the next chapter.

Chapter Seven

Anakberu-Kalimbubu Relations, II

Social relations between *anakberu* and *kalimbubu* are asymmetrical. The *anakberu* is the junior party and must defer to the *kalimbubu* and render him a variety of services. So diverse and pervasive are these services that Karo say "You cannot do anything without *anakberu*."

THE *ANAKBERU* IN EVERYDAY AFFAIRS

Some indication of the role of *anakberu* in the everyday life of the people may be given by reporting some incidents in the life of the family of Pa Randal, with whom my wife and I shared a house during our stay in Kuta Gamber.

Pa Randal has six children. The two eldest, a daughter and a son, are married and live in Kuta Gamber (but not in the same house as Pa Randal). His third child, a boy named Ngapin, is a high school student in Kabanjahe. The family ambition is for Ngapin to acquire the academic title *sarjana hukum* or *doktorandus* (both equivalent to an M.A. degree), for this would enhance the family's social status. (Karo villagers are strongly aware of the importance of education in social and economic mobility. Material and political success, once the predominant criteria of social differentiation, are now being replaced by education.) Thus, the family has great hopes for Ngapin and they treat him with honor when he returns home once a term during the vacation period. On the evening of his arrival home there is a big dinner attended by his sister's and brother's families. Another joint meal is served on the evening of his return to school, and there is a further meal the next morning. On each occasion a chicken is killed and eaten, and this marks the occasion as a more or less formal one.

Although the joint meal is a simple family affair, the *anakberu*, Ngapin's sister and her husband Tambat, have a definite, prescribed role to play. The meals are served at the house of Ngapin's father and he provides the food, but it is prepared and served by Ngapin's sister and her husband. Ngapin's sister sits near the fire, cooks the rice and prepares the ingredients for the curry; her husband sits beside her and plucks and cleans the chicken. He then asks if there is anything else he can do to assist his wife, like picking some unripe tangerines for vinegar or fetching down a cooking pot from the rack. In the meantime, Pa Randal and his sons are at their leisure in the coffee shop. When the food is cooked and ready to serve, Tambat goes to the shop to inform his *kalimbubu* that everything is ready.

The relative statuses of the participants are reflected in the seating arrangements. First, there is a distinction according to sex; the women sit nearest the kitchen, a low prestige position. Pa Randal, as head of the family, sits in the most honored place, the *bataruang,* close to the sleeping area. His eldest son sits closest to him. His daughter's husband Tambat sits near the door, the least honored place in the house. Tambat hands out the plates in a sequence also based on relative status. Pa Randal is given his first, then his eldest son, and Tambat serves himself last. The participants fill their dishes with food in the same order.

On these occasions and others, Tambat's conduct toward his wife's father and her brothers is restrained and reserved and they do not talk much to one another. Tambat behaves as though he were the servant of the family. Indeed, if Pa Randal needs something from the shop, such as matches or pandanus leaf for smoking, and Tambat is around, he will ask Tambat rather than one of his own sons to go for him. The same thing may happen when one of Pa Randal's sons want something. Moreover, Tambat usually refuses to accept the money required for the purchase: "No, no, I have some," he says.

Tambat is expected to be even more restrained and reserved in his conduct toward certain of his female *kalimbubu*, particularly his WM (*mami*) and his WBW (*turangku*). Such relatives may not speak to each other's faces. They are not supposed to stay in the same house without the attendance of a third person. I was told that in the past it was forbidden even to sit on the same floor board with one's WM or WBW. Thus, when Tambat is in the kitchen helping his wife with the cooking, his WM and

WBW must withdraw. Only when he goes to sit near the door and they are sure that he has nothing more to do in the kitchen may they return there. Because of the stronger restrictions on their interaction with Tambat, these female *kalimbubu* do not demand services of him in the same way as his male *kalimbubu* do. Nevertheless, they sometimes issue orders in a doubly oblique manner. For example, Tambat's WM may say to her daughter in Tambat's presence, "We are very short of areca, do you think *kèla* (DH) can fetch some?" Tambat does not wait for his wife to speak but immediately says to her, "Please say to *mami* that I certainly can." The Karo say that, if a man's *mami* expresses a desire or need, he must take this as his command and let no obstacle deter him. They say also that the purpose of the avoidances observed between a man and his female *kalimbubu* is to make them respect one another, and especially to ensure that the *anakberu* respects the *kalimbubu*. One man expressed the opinion that if the custom of avoidances were to lapse, men would not respect their mothers-in-law as they do now. They would say "I will do it tomorrow" or "I will do it when I have time."

Tambat's relations with his other close *kalimbubu* are quite different. He may talk freely and joke with his WZ, who may be a prospective (second) wife, and may interact freely with his WBC. Although he is their *anakberu* and in principle subservient to them, he is also considerably older than they are and therefore is entitled to some respect from them. The respect to which he is entitled, however, is familiar rather than formal. He is expected to be kind and gentle with them. Tambat may mildly discipline his WBC but he does not get angry with them or order them about the way their father does. He might say, "If you are naughty I will not cook food for you. I will refuse to arrange your wedding," but the child may only laugh and reply, "Well, then, I will never get married." Such jocularity is more pronounced with the WBD than with the WBS. More often than not the joke is about marriage. A man may joke with his WBD by telling her that he would like her to marry his son (her FZS). Other people may tease a little girl to tears by suggesting to her that her *impal* (FZS) wants to marry someone else, but her FZH would not be so unkind.

When the time comes for Ngapin to return to school, he leaves the village in the morning. This is considered the most appropriate time for departure – Karo say that the rising sun represents rising fortune and happiness. Some final inquiries are made before he goes. Is the usual amount of money enough? Does he require new books or clothing? Is he content with his accommodation? His father usually gives him Rp. 300 for his board and lodging. His older brother gives him Rp. 50, and his *anakberu* Tambat gives him another Rp. 50.

On some occasions it is necessary for a representative of the family to visit Ngapin in town. News may reach them that he is ill, and the first thing they ask is "How seriously ill is he?" On hearing such news Tambat is expected to visit Pa Randal, his WF, to show his concern and say "I hear *silih* (WB) is not well. Don't you think I had better go to town to see him? Who knows, it may be serious." On one occasion, after consulting his parents, Ngapin moved to the house of a friend with whom he used to study. A few days later Tambat went to town to see Ngapin's new host. This visit by Ngapin's *anakberu* was essential to let the host know that Ngapin had relatives, especially an *anakberu* who was concerned for him. Ngapin was thereby made known as a man of specific origin and of good social background, a person who may be trusted. The host then knew to whom he might refer in case of trouble, for one's *anakberu* is also his guarantor.

THE *ANAKBERU* AS GUARANTOR

A man is expected to give a guarantee for his *kalimbubu* on many occasions. On major economic and political occasions, both one's *anakberu* and *senina* (sibling) may act as guarantors, but there is no occasion on which a *senina* alone does so.

Oath-taking

In the traditional political system, taking an oath was one of the essential procedures to test the innocence of an accused person. This ancient procedure is still practiced occasionally and belief in its effectiveness is still an important element in social control. Even an innocent man is reluctant to take a formal oath if he can avoid doing so, for to take a false oath, even unwittingly, is to invite death. The act of taking a formal oath is called *erduhum.*

Erduhum is a formal occasion on which a definite ritual procedure must be observed. *Duhum* means pouring food, particularly rice, into the mouth, with the hand holding the food well above the mouth. As the term suggests, something must be consumed by the person who takes the oath. The ritual objects used for this are small quantities of rice, turmeric, pepper, garlic and salt. These are mixed with water in a white porcelain bowl (*mangkok meciho*). The ingredients represent the basic needs in human life. Rice is the staple food and it is thought that man cannot survive without it; at any rate, life would be miserable without rice. Water is essential, because without it the rice cannot be cooked. The failure of a love affair or of a marriage that ends in divorce is usually expressed in the euphemism "rice is separating from water." Turmeric, pepper and garlic are components of a traditional herbal salve (*kuning*) that is regarded as essential to human welfare, particularly in the early stages of life. The salve is supposed to prevent several diseases and is smeared on an infant twice a day after its bath. Salt also is an essential item in the daily diet. "We are weak and feel cold without salt."

The Karo explain that these ritual objects, "the sustainers of our life," turn into harmful objects and kill the person who takes the oath if he tells a lie. This idea is expressed in the formula uttered by the oath-taker while he holds the ritual bowl before drinking the potion. The formula, in the case of an accused who is alleged to have attempted to kill someone by poisoning, is: "Please hear me rice, water, turmeric, pepper, garlic and salt. If I do or did keep poison by which I ever attempted to kill anyone in this village, I will die, killed by this rice, water, turmeric, pepper, garlic and salt."

For the oath to be valid, the accused must be accompanied by an *anakberu* who also drinks the potion. Thus, no one can take an oath if he has no *anakberu* or if there is no one among his *anakberu* who is prepared to take an oath on his behalf. In taking an oath with his *kalimbubu,* a man must be prepared of course to risk his own life. It is important to note that a sibling of the accused cannot substitute for an *anakberu,* nor can a man be obliged to take an oath on behalf of an agnate. So after the accused takes an oath it is repeated, but with a slightly different formula, by one of his *anakberu.* The *anakberu* comes forward, holds the same bowl, drinks the same ritual water, and says, "Please hear me rice, water, turmeric, pepper, garlic and salt. If my *kalimbubu* does or did keep poison by which he has attempted to poison someone in this village, I will die, killed by this rice, water, turmeric, pepper, garlic and salt."

This form of oath-taking is primarily associated with two types of criminal behavior, theft and sorcery or poisoning. In both cases the accuser is usually a group of people and the accused an individual. The accusers may be co-members of an adat house or co-villagers. In the last twenty years there have been only two cases of oath-taking in Kuta Gamber and Liren and two others in adjacent villages (Kempawa and Lau Perimbon); three of the four cases were related to sorcery accusations, the other to theft. In addition, I heard of one case in a distant village where the accused was alleged to have caused *batang karé,* a chronic disease of the skin around the neck, to inflict three persons.

Unfortunately, I was unable to gather detailed information concerning most of these cases. For three, however, I did ascertain the relationship between the accused and his *anakberu* who joined him in the oath. These were in one case a ZS, in another a ZH, both primary *anakberu,* and in the third a BDH, an immediate *anakberu.* The details of this third case were still fresh in the minds of my informants because the incident had occurred only two years before. According to my informants, Pa Sate was arrogant and used to pretend to be a *guru* who knew many things about medicine, divination and magic. He suffered from a chronic skin disease and a Pakpak *guru* treated him and stayed with him. The villagers did not like this priest and regarded him as potentially harmful. At that time Sura, Pa Sate's BS, proposed to marry a classificatory cross cousin (third cousin) but the girl refused his proposal. Sura's parents were very disappointed by this. Some people suspected that Pa Sate would attempt to take revenge through a form of sorcery called *tahan* which would result in the girl remaining a spinster all her life.

One evening a distant agnate of the girl saw someone standing near the ladder of her house. He thought the man was Pa Sate and suspected that he was preparing black magic. He immediately went to see the FB of the girl (who was also his agnate) and told him what he had seen. They set off to search the place but the man had gone. However, they did find a fresh betel leaf under the ladder and the leaf had a red substance on it which they supposed was blood. (A betel leaf and the blood of a chicken are the two most important ingredients in this kind of sorcery. The relevant spell is: "This leaf must become green, and the chicken to which this blood belongs must live again, before So-and-so may get married.") They convinced themselves that Pa Sate had placed this object of sorcery there, and this was confirmed by someone who said he had seen Pa Sate around the place a short while before. Both of them conveyed the news to other agnates.

In panic they went angrily to Pa Sate's house with the intention of attacking him. Someone hurriedly warned Pa Sate of his danger and he immediately locked his house. Two other families shared the house, Pa Sate's son and his brother. The girl's relatives surrounded the house and beat on the door. They demanded that Pa Sate open the door and kept beating on the door, windows and walls of his house. This continued through the night; most villagers joined in the attack because they hated the accused man. In the morning two policemen came from Kuta Buluh, invited by an *anakberu* of the accusers. Discussions were held between both parties and it was decided that a reconciliatory ceremony would be held, accompanied by an oath-taking ritual, and attended by the subdistrict officer. The *anakberu* who took part in the oath-taking was the DH of Pa Sate's brother. He was Pa Sate's closest *anakberu* because Pa Sate had no sister and his own daughter had not yet married. Even though this man was Pa Sate's closest *anakberu*, Pa Sate had no right to expect him to take the oath voluntarily. As the Karo see it, a man may reasonably expect his DH or ZH to take an oath with him, because these *anakberu* can be fairly certain that the accused would not take the risk of making his daughter or sister a widow if he were not sure of his innocence. In this instance, the accused and his *anakberu* survived the ordeal and Pa Sate was declared innocent.

Nehken tangko acem cina

The role of the *anakberu* as guarantor is manifest also in a rite called *nehken tangko acem cina,* literally, reporting the theft of vinegar and chili, which is performed when a family moves into an adat house. As noted in Chapter 4, the residents of an adat house share common ladders and doors and the apartments are not separated by walls. There is no physical barrier to prevent anyone from going into another apartment. Thus, any apartment is open to theft, and in the interests of the inhabitants of the house, adat prescribes that every newcomer should have a guarantor. The guarantor is an *anakberu* who, on the day his *kalimbubu* moves into the house, proclaims to all residents of the house that he is the person to whom complaints should be addressed. He does this in the evening at about eight o'clock when all the residents are present. The *anakberu* stands on the *jabu* of his *kalimbubu* says loudly in a formal manner, "Dear residents of the house, I am the *anakberu* of this newcomer who has moved into your house this morning. I hope that in this house you will all help each other. In case my *kalimbubu* steals vinegar or chilies, please report to me."

Anakberu and Senina as Witnesses and Guarantors

As previously noted, both *anakberu* and *senina* may serve as guarantors. This traditional arrangement was described by Joustra as follows.

> No case can be treated as a court session without the presence of the *anakberu* and *senina* of each party. Every adult should always be able to indicate his *anakberu* and *senina.* If he fails to do so, he is liable for punishment, and if he is unable to provide them immediately he is regarded as *anak lajang,* a wanderer. These *anakberu* and *senina* are natural guarantors, the *adat* guarantors (Joustra 1926:232).

Under the old political and administrative system, this requirement was expressed at the village level in the form of an executive body consisting of three persons. These were the chief of the village, a member of the *anakberu tua* lineage, and one of the chief's distant classificatory siblings (*senina*). This *senina* was chosen from another subclan of the chief's clan. In both Kuta Gamber and Liren these *senina* were always of the Bangun subclan.

Nowadays the use of *anakberu* and *senina* as legal guarantors not only has no status in national law, it is expressly forbidden in statutes prohibiting the use of close relatives as witnesses. Nevertheless, there has been no systematic attempt to suppress the practice at the village level, and so it is sometimes observed even today.

In the past, almost every contract made by an individual had to be witnessed by both an *anakberu* and a *senina*. Should a man sell his house or pawn his tangerine grove, the attendance of the two witnesses was essential. In their absence the transaction was impossible. (The presence of the buyer's *anakberu* and *senina* was not required.) Similarly, when a man built a house, the contract with the carpenter would be binding only if witnessed by an *anakberu* and a *senina* of the man who proposed to build the house. (The carpenter's *anakberu* and *senina* were not needed to witness the transaction.) It is difficult to obtain reliable information concerning what happened in the event of a breach of contract in the past, but according to my informants the injured party could confiscate some of the belongings of the immediate *anakberu* and *senina* (in this case *sembuyak*) of the defaulting party.

Under traditional adat, the responsibility of *anakberu* and *senina* extended well beyond legally contracted obligations to which they were guarantors. According to Tamboen (1952:165), a man who failed to pay a gambling debt could be punished by putting him in stocks until he was redeemed by his *anakberu* and *senina*. A captive in war might be treated the same way, and a murderer might be punished by imposition of a heavy fine for which his *anakberu* and *senina* were held liable if he could not pay. According to Tamboen, their refusal to pay could result in their being attacked by the kin of the victim.

The procedure of identifying the *anakberu* and *senina* of the principals to any agreement is called *sijalapen*. The root word here is *jalap*. According to Neumann (1951:78), *jalap* means potency (of medicine), trust and sincerity (of mind); and *njalapi* means "to make a note, as happens now and then in the village, in order to know the *anakberu* and *senina* of the inhabitants; to send for someone's *anakberu* or *senina* (thus looking for reliable information in a lawsuit)." The expression *sijalapen* signifies a reciprocal action between two parties to a discussion, each making a formal enquiry as to the identities of the *anakberu* and *senina* of the other. This formality must be carried out even though both parties may know each other well and may know the answers to their questions before they ask them.

To illustrate how the *sijalapen* operates, I will describe the formal meeting at which the brideprice is handed over to the bride's relatives. The other formal meetings and discussions that take place between the principals before this stage is reached are discussed in Chapter 8.

As a rule the wedding takes place at the bride's village, and the brideprice is handed over before noon, that is, while the sun is still rising. A group of thirty or more people may gather to witness this event, which takes place publicly, in the midst of all the wedding guests. This inner group is composed of two parties, the fathers of the bride and groom and their respective agnates and *anakberu*. They sit facing each other. The *anakberu* of each party sit in front so that the givers of the feast are separated by their *anakberu*. Everyone sits on mats with their legs crossed, the proper and formal way of sitting. The "talking *anakberu*" of each father is one of his *anakberu tua*, and they lead the procedure. First they check informally to see whether everyone concerned is present. This is followed by a formal check. Either of the talking *anakberu* may initiate the parley.

X You, the party of the bridegroom, are you complete already?

Y Yes, we are, and you, the party of the bride, are you complete already?

X Yes, we are complete already.

Y So, may se start *sijalapen?*

X Yes, we certainly may.

Y Who is the *anakberu* of the person who will give the bride away?

X I am.

Y What is your name please?

X Sinek, my clan name is Tarigan.

Y (to his party)
Have we all heard that? The *anakberu* of the bride-giver (*si nereh*) is Sinek Tarigan.

Y's party:
Yes, we have.

X Who is the *bapa* (classificatory father) of the bride? (The question is implicitly directed to Y).

Y (to his *kalimbubu*)
My *kalimbubu*, the *anakberu* of the groom has asked: "Who is the father of the bride?"

A classificatory father of the bride, to Y:
Please tell the *anakberu* of the groom that I, Rikat Ginting, am the *bapa* of the bride.

Y The father is Rikat Ginting.

X (to his party)
The father of the bride is Rikat Ginting. Have we heard that, all of us?

X's party:
Yes, we have.

Y It is now my turn to question you. Who is the *anakberu* of the bridegroom?

X I am; (jocularly) the man to whom you have been talking. My name is Simpar, my clan is Karo-karo.

Y (to his party)
The *anakberu* of the bridegroom is Simpar Karo-karo. Have we all heard that?

Y's party:
Yes, we have

Y Who is the *bapa* of the bridegroom?

X (to his *kalimbubu*)
You may have heard the voice of the *anakberu* of the bride. He asked: "Who is the *bapa* of the bridegroom?"

A classificatory father to X:
Please tell him that I, Mbalo Sembiring, am the *bapa* of the bridegroom.

X The *bapa* is Mbalo Sembiring. Do you hear me?

Y Yes I do.

Y (to his party)
The *bapa* of the bridegroom is Mbalo Sembiring: is it clear already?

Y's party:
Yes, it is.

X Now as we have finished *sijalapen,* do you think we can proceed to transfer of the brideprice?

Y No, I am sorry. I think we have first to ask the approval of both the bride and the bridegroom, that is, whether they approve the proposed contract for their marriage.

X I am sorry, you are right.

Although the inquiry about the identity of the *anakberu* precedes the inquiry about the identity of the *senina* (the bride's or groom's father's classificatory brother), this does not mean that the *anakberu* is more important than his *kalimbubu* (the principal's *senina*) in the discussion. This order depends on the *anakberu's* role as formal mediator and on the rule that the agnates of the principals cannot directly communicate with one another. The speaker must be an *anakberu* of the party he represents, and he must identify himself first of all so that the other party will know with whom they are dealing.

THE *ANAKBERU* AS MEDIATOR

Anakberu serve not only as guarantors but also as mediators (*kelang*). On important public occasions, such as the transfer of brideprice, when larger groups of people are involved in a transaction, they are represented by one of their *anakberu tua.* In everyday life a close personal *anakberu* acts as an individual's mediator. For example, should a dispute arise about the boundaries of a field or the terms of an economic contract, the dispute will be mediated by the ZHs, ZSs or DHs of the disputants. They will meet to discuss it and try to arrange an amicable settlement. Also, if a man is uncooperative with his relatives, they may turn to his *anakberu* for help, as in the following example.

The people of Kuta Gamber have organized a sort of mutual aid society. They call it *persatun piring,* literally, the dish association. Every family is expected to join the association because it is "for the benefit of all." Its main purpose is to help a feast-giver to borrow kitchen utensils, dishes, mats and other things needed for the feast. Any ceremony, whether it is "for joy" or "for tears," must be accompanied by a meal, and it is common for the participants to number between 200 and 300; large ceremonies may attract a thousand or more participants. The utensils of the Kuta Gamber dish association can cater for 200 people. Each member contributes Rp. 50 and pays Rp. 50 each time he borrows utensils but non-members must pay Rp. 100. Only two people in the village did not join the association. The chairman of the association reminded both of them once but they did not respond. He then conveyed his complaint to their respective *anakberu,* in both cases, their ZHs. Because it is "for the benefit of all," this association is not regarded as a voluntary organization. One man did not join because he was considering moving to another village and eventually he did. The other man joined immediately after his *anakberu* did nothing more than say to him, "I am told by the chairman that you have not joined the dish association and this I think is embarrassing; Rp. 50 is not much and it is for the benefit of all."

The *anakberu* also are called in to mediate in disputes between agnates. The *anakberu* must always "stand in the middle" and not take sides with one of the disputants. Since partition of family estate is often a source of conflict, partition usually takes place in the presence of *anakberu.* I have heard of cases where the *anakberu* went to a field in dispute and divided it according to their judgment.

THE *ANAKBERU'S* SERVICE IN ARRANGING FEASTS

The Karo regard feasts as very important. Giving a feast is a significant event in the life of an individual and one's social status is closely related to the number, size and quality of the feasts he gives. A family, a segment of a lineage or even a lineage is sometimes judged according to the feasts they have given. Some families used to give large and successful feasts; others were only moderate (*bujur-bujur*) feast-givers; still others gave no memorable feasts; finally, some families had bad reputations because they gave no feasts at all.

There are two types of feast, *kerja mehuli* and *kerja raté céda,* joyful and sorrowful festivities. The first includes weddings, inaugurations of new houses and *erpangir kulau,* feasts for the guardian spirits which are sometimes given to fulfill a promise. For example, a man may promise his guardian spirits a feast if they bring him a good harvest or if they cure him of a grave illness. Sorrowful feasts are confined to mortuary festivities. However, the death of a person whose children have all married is not recognized as a sad occasion, because he has passed an ideal life. He has fulfilled his responsibilities in life; "he has paid his debt." Thus, there is no reason to shed tears. His mortuary feast is called *kerja meriah,* a glad feast, though not quite as joyful as those mentioned above.

Feasts (*kerja-kerja*) are distinguished according to their size as small, medium and large. The main criterion for distinguishing the size of the feast is the animal or animals killed for the occasion. For a small feast the standard is four chickens, but the others require animals with four legs. For a medium feast one or two pigs are killed. A large feast requires at least one cow or buffalo. Small feasts are quite rare. They are held only by poor people who have few or no relatives. No such feasts were held during my stay in Kuta Gamber and Liren. In general, then, when people talk about feasts, they refer to medium or large ones.

The type of feast given obviously reflects the economic status of the feast-giver. Only well-to-do families hold big feasts of which they can be proud. For them, killing a pig is a trivial matter and they sometimes do it even without holding a feast. This is particularly common in urban areas today.

Wealth, however, is not enough. For a feast to be successful, many people must attend it; there must be many guests. The Karo say, "You need people to eat your food, your pig or your cow." Otherwise the food will be wasted, "eaten by dogs," and this is embarassing. Only those who are sociable and have many relatives can expect that there will be enough guests to consume all the food prepared for a large feast, because one cannot "pay to come." Attending a feast is an expression of solidarity with the host. Apart from kinship obligations, attendance is based on the principle of reciprocity and only those who are willing to respond to the invitations of others can expect other people to respond to theirs. Those who try to disregard this basic principle are said to have two *tumba* (a bamboo measure of volume, about two liters), that is different *tumba* for buying and selling, a large one for buying and a small one for selling. He does not like to respond to others' invitations but he would like many people to respond to his. The Karo say that a feast given by such a person will be "eaten by dogs."

Another criterion in the evaluation of a feast is implied by the question, "Is it well organized?" A large well-attended feast will not bring its giver a good reputation if it is poorly organized. A well-organized feast of medium size will bring a better reputation than a large but disorganized one. People praise a medium size, well-organized feast by saying, "It was not a big one but it was excellent. The sunshades were well arranged. The guests were well cared for and they knew where to sit (there was someone to usher them). The food was tasty and well distributed. The feast-giver was well-mannered; he moved around and had a word for every guest. It is worth spending money for such an excellent feast." In contrast, a poorly-organized feast is the butt of jokes and gossip. I heard this comment about one such feast: "Although it was a big feast, it was horrible. I have never seen such a feast. The food was tasteless. The distribution was so poor that some did not get any meat at all. What a waste of money."

The organization of a feast is exclusively the responsibility of the *anakberu* of the host. So whether a feast is successful or not largely depends on the attitude and the capability of the *anakberu* concerned. Indeed, a feast is the occasion on which the ability of the *anakberu* to serve their *kalimbubu* and their guests is put to the test. In this context the role of the *anakberu* as the servants of their *kalimbubu* finds its fullest expression. A man can work for himself in his field, in his house, or anywhere else but he cannot work for himself on the occasion of his own feast. On this occasion his close *anakberu* act as a group and take the responsibility for organizing the affair. There is a division of labor in the *anakberu* group; there are usually two leaders, an *anakberu tua* and an immediate *anakberu,* usually a FZH or a ZH. The *anakberu* have a number of jobs to do – erect the sunscreens, prepare the food, serve the guests, guide them to their seats, distribute tobacco and palm-leaf wrappers for cigarettes, betel and other ingredients for chewing betel, clean up after the meal, collect gifts and make a note of them, lead the formal adat discussion, and so on. In short, they do everything. The *sukut,* the giver of the feast, and his *senina,* do nothing. The Karo say of the *sukut,* "They wait." If one of them should notice, for example, that the distribution of the food is not going well, he may not get up and go to help the *anakberu.* The most he can do is approach one of them without attracting attention and casually say a few words about it.

THE ROLE OF *ANAKBERU* IN TIME OF CRISIS

In certain circumstances, assistance may be expected from any and all categories of relatives, though the kind and degree of assistance given by a particular person and expected of him depends in part on the kind of relative he is and on how close a relative he is. Thus, on some occasions one's *anakberu* cooperate with other relatives in meeting their duties. If a person becomes seriously ill or suffers from a prolonged illness, his family will need help in various ways. They may need help to collect herbs from the fields or from a distant forest, or to summon the medicine man from a neighboring village, or to consult a spirit medium, and so on. If the patient's life is thought to be in danger, messages must quickly be sent to close relatives who live elsewhere. In such a situation, there are many relatives whose assistance may be expected and requested. Besides relatives, co-residents of the adat house and co-villagers are a great help. Sometimes the patient's condition is such that the family decide to take him to the hospital in town, usually to Kabanjahe, and this presents an immediate problem of transport. Three sets of four people each are required to carry the litter. Even so, it is seldom difficult to find the required number of people, for carrying the patient is, according to adat, the responsibility of his co-villagers.

The group must be organized, however, by the *anakberu* of the patient. Thus, an *anakberu* should go to the young people of the village and tell them that their help is required. When a patient is carried to town, there is always a long procession of some thirty to thirty-five people, so that it looks like a small ceremony. In addition to the bearers, many people join the procession to express their sympathy for the patient. This may present a problem for the family of the patient, for they are obliged to feed all those who join the procession. By the time they reach the main road it is usually high noon; they have their lunch there and most of the carriers return to the village.

With that, the duties of the co-villagers as such have been met; they are not responsible for conveying or accompanying the patient all the way to the hospital. This is the duty of close relatives, particularly *anakberu* and *senina*. One day's *sabat*, i.e., a man's absence from his own work, is the maximum one may expect from a co-villager who must be reimbursed for any additional expense he may incur. Once at the hospital, the head of the family takes care of the patient, and the other relatives return to the village. If the patient recovers speedily and the head of the family is able to pay the medical costs himself, then his *senina* and *anakberu* will not be called on again. They accompany him to the hospital, spend one night there and return the next morning, revisit the patient once or twice, and accompany him when he returns to the village.

The degree of involvement of the relatives depends on many factors such as the nature of the disease, the economic condition of the head of the family, and the social status of the patient. It is a grave situation if the disease is serious or chronic, and if the patient's economic situation is difficult, either because the head of the family cannot afford the costs or because the patient is himself the head of the family. How the Karo handle such a situation is illustrated by the following case.

Pa Tolong of Kuta Gamber, aged 37, is the head of a family consisting of his wife and three children whose ages range from 9 to 15 years; he has tuberculosis. To be polite, the villagers call it a chest or cough disease (besides coughing, the principal known symptom is "vomiting blood"), but whisperingly they call it *tébésé* (from T.B.C.) or refer to it as the disease of the rich, because its treatment consumes much money and only the rich can afford to pay the costs. Pa Tolong has suffered from this illness since 1958 when he was treated in the hospital in Kabanjahe for about three months. He was told he had recovered and he returned to Kuta Gamber, but he had to see his doctor periodically in Kabanjahe and to go to Medan for periodic X-ray examinations. This treatment cost him a great deal of money and he had little earning power because he was advised not to do any hard work. By the end of 1959 he was reluctant to see his doctor and had abandoned the idea of having a further check-up because of his financial difficulties. He had been about to build a house in 1958 and had purchased a sufficient quantity of timber and corrugated iron for that purpose when he had had his first attack of this so-called disease of the rich. He had to sell all the materials to pay the medical costs and was left without anything else that could be sold. He told his wife that he would never again go to town for treatment.

Pa Tolong's wife spoke to her husband's eldest brother who then conferred with Simak, the son of another brother, and with his own *anakberu* Ndati who is both his son-in-law and his classificatory sister's son (FBDS). A family meeting was held at the house of the eldest brother and nine families were represented: four *senina* (1 - 4) and five *anakberu* (5 - 9) of the patient (see Figure 10). The former were two brothers (1 and 3) and two brothers' sons (2 and 4); the latter were a sister's husband (6), his son (7) and his two brothers (8 and 9), and Ndati, the patient's FBDS who is also the DH of the patient's

Figure 10. The kinship relation between the patient and the nine families.

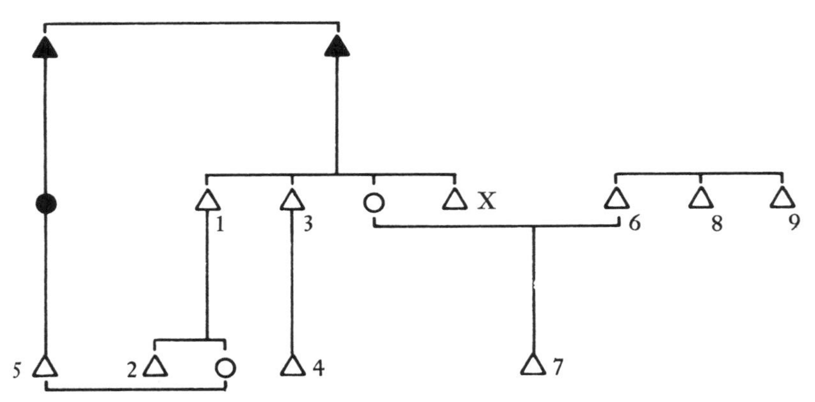

brother. The decision was reached that the nine families should each contribute Rp. 150 so that Rp. 1350 were handed to the patient for the cost of his treatment.

When Pa Tolong returned from town, he had Rp. 300 left. The amount was not sufficient for the cost of another consultation strongly advised by his doctor who urged him to have a further X-ray in Medan within a few weeks. Ndati (5) took the initiative in collecting more money for this consultation, for which another Rp. 1,000 was necessary. For this a family meeting was held in his house. Seven of the nine families represented at the first meeting were represented at this meeting. The two brothers (8, 9) of Pa Tolong's ZH were not invited because they are not primary *anakberu*. Everyone recognized that it was too much to ask them to contribute again. This time the *senina* each contributed Rp. 100 and the three primary *anakberu* contributed Rp. 100 (7). Rp. 200 (5) and Rp. 300 (6) respectively. Thus, the *senina* contributed Rp. 400 and the *anakberu* Rp. 600.

Two years later, in November 1961, Pa Tolong's condition deteriorated suddenly and he urgently needed treatment in the hospital. There was widespread gossip in the village that he had "vomited blood" again and that his illness had taken a turn for the worse. In despair Pa Tolong came close to committing suicide by throwing himself into a deep and stony ravine near the village. His wife suspected the attempt and ran to the ravine where she found her husband rolling a cigarette intended to be his last.

Pa Tolong's physical and economic condition was critical. Moreover, the interests of the co-residents of the adat house in which he lived had to be taken into account. As far as the villagers know, there are two communicable diseases, tuberculosis and leprosy. A person who suffers from either is a potential source of infection, not only to his family but also to co-residents of the adat house. The adat provides a preventive measure by prescribing that a person who suffers from a communicable disease must leave the house. Thus, Pa Tolong had another serious problem – the residents of his adat house had the right to ask him to leave his apartment. If circumstances prevented him from going to town for further treatment, he would still have to build a hut away from the village in his field. It was already rumored that his *senina* and *anakberu* were considering building a hut for him. Their plan was set aside, however, because his *kalimbubu* volunteered to collect some money to help Pa Tolong solve his financial problem. This was initiated by Pa Tagar, the patient's *kalimbubu* by birth, his MFBSS (second cousin), who also lived in Kuta Gamber. Pa Tagar and his wife invited people to a meeting held at the patient's house. About twenty people came and the three categories of relatives, the *senina, anakberu* and *kalimbubu,* were represented. It was a successful meeting because it resulted in the collection of Rp. 2,225, sufficient for Pa Tolong's further treatment. Five *senina*, five *kalimbubu,* and eight *anakberu* each contributed Rp. 100; of the five *anakberu menteri* present, three contributed Rp. 100 each and the other two contributed Rp. 50 each; Rp. 25 came from Nande Tampil, an old widow and a co-resident of Pa Tolong's house. Further details about the relation of the patient to the contributors is given in Table 11.

Preparations for the patient's departure from the village were well in hand. However, after spending two weeks in Seribudolok, Pa Tolong did not feel any better; the earlier plan to build a hut for him was then renewed. A small *lalang* (I) hut was eventually erected for him near the main road in Kutabuluh. The labor was provided by six relatives of the patient, three *senina,* two *anakberu* and one *anakberu menteri.* He moved into the hut a few weeks before I left Kuta Gamber and I was told whisperingly that he was likely to spend the rest of his life there.

As should be evident from this case, close *anakberu* and *senina* are the most important sources of economic assistance; the *kalimbubu* come to the fore only in special circumstances. Further, the amount of aid rendered by each category of relative strongly suggests that in practice the *anakberu* are of primary importance (see Table 12). There are contingencies, however, so that it occasionally happens that the *senina* or even the *kalimbubu* are of greater assistance. This is particularly so because, besides kinship norms and values, there are other considerations to be taken into account, such as the geographical proximity and the economic condition of the relatives themselves.

Nevertheless, Pa Tolong's case is fairly representative of the way in which the various categories of relatives are called upon and fulfill their duties as such. There are many instances in

Table 11

The Relationship of the Patient to the Contributors

Kinship category	Number of families represented	No.	Contributor's relationship	Residence
Senina	5	2	brothers	co-resident[a]
		2	brothers' sons	
		1	classificatory brother	
Anakberu	8	1	brother-in-law (Y)	"
		1	Y's son	"
		2	Y's brothers	"
		1	BDH (also ego's FBDS)	"
		2	FFZSS	
		1	immigrant whose wife belongs to the subclan of the patient	"
Anakberu Menteri	5	1	ZDH	
		1	father of above	
		1	ZHZH	"
		2	brothers-in-law of the above, FFZSS	one co-resident, one not
Kalimbubu	5	1	WB	resides elsewhere
		4	members of his mother's lineage, i.e. MFBSS (2) and MFBSSS (2)	two co-resident and two not

[a] Co-resident in the village.

Table 12

The Contributions of the Relatives
Toward the Three Treatments

		A	S	K
1st treatment	Rp	750	600	-
2nd treatment	Rp	600	400	-
3rd treatment	Rp	1200	500	500
		2550	1500	500

Legend: A = anakberu

S = senina

K = kalimbubu

which it would appear to be appropriate to call on agnates but in which assistance is sought from among *anakberu*. For example, when Sapa Pinem of Kuta Gamber was due to get married about two months before the harvest, there was a shortage of food for the wedding feast. It was estimated that another fifteen *pelgan* of paddy was necessary, and this was borrowed from relatives on the condition it would be repaid after the harvest. Since his father lived in his natal village and was a member of the ruling lineage, there should have been no difficulty for him to get this amount of paddy from his close agnates. Even so, the major part of the borrowed paddy came from his (Sapa Pinem's father's) *anakberu*: three *pelgan* from *anakberu tua,* three *pelgan* from his son-in-law, five *pelgan* from two of his brothers' sons-in-law, and only three *pelgan* from his brother's son. Thus, of the fourteen *pelgan* he obtained from kinsmen, eleven were from *anakberu* and three from *senina* (*pelgan* = 40 liters).

"REQUESTING FOOD"

The preceding account should make it clear that Karo regard it as natural to seek the assistance of *anakberu* in time of need and that *anakberu* often volunteer this assistance without being asked. For the most part, substantial sacrifice is expected only of close *anakberu,* but even very distant – one might say fictitious – *anakberu* may be called on to render fairly minor services, as in the custom of *erkata nakan,* literally, requesting food.

If a stranger spends the night in a village where he has no relatives, he sleeps in a rice barn and takes his meals with one of the village families. He first inquires whether the village chief is in the village, because travelers have the right to take their meals with the chief's family. Under the traditional political system, a chief is obliged to offer physical protection and food to strangers passing peaceably through his territory. If the chief is away, the stranger attempts to determine if there is someone in the village to whom he may claim to be related. He inquires first whether he has a fellow clansman (*senina*) among the inhabitants of the village; if so, he may ask to take his meals with that man's family. If the stranger has no fellow clansman in the village, his next inquiry is whether there is someone who stands as *anakberu* to him. For example, if his clan is Ginting, he inquires where there is someone whose *berèberè* (mother's clan) is Ginting. If he has no *anakberu* in the village, he tries to locate a *kalimbubu.* If his own *berèberè* is Tarigan, he asks for someone who belongs to that clan. Since there are only five clans, and since most villages include members of most if not all of the clans, strangers normally have no difficulty finding a family with whom to take their meals.

"THE VISIBLE GOD"

Every Karo child is taught from infancy to regard his *kalimbubu* as a "visible god," *dibata niidah.* The expression *dibata* has a number of meanings. According to Neumann (1951:75), "*dibata* is god, gods, the world of gods; the pregnant womb; *i dibatana* (in its *dibata*) being still unborn; *dibata niidah* the way of naming the *kalimbubu; dibata si nangkih nusur* (the up and down *dibata*) the sun . . . ." The first meaning noted by Neumann may be, like the word itself, ultimately of Hindu origin (compare Sanskrit *devata*), and Karo and other Batak also recognize the trinity of god. This, however, is esoteric knowledge and these gods are mentioned only in the spells uttered by *guru*, some of which begin with the phrase, "Please come down Upper Dibata, please sit down Middle Dibata, and please come up Lower Dibata." There are no cults associated with these gods and no offerings are made to them.

It is curious that Neumann does not mention the most common use of the term *dibata*, to refer to a special class of guardian spirits. (Neither does he mention its use euphemistically to refer to the penis, as in the expression "he feels itchy on his *dibata*"; further, I have not heard it used to refer to the pregnant womb.) The souls of all human beings become *bégu*, ghosts, at death. The ghosts are said to remain sentimentally attached to the surviving members of their families, and they look after the welfare of their relatives by intervening between them and evil spirits of non-human origin that bring illness and misfortune. The ghosts of persons "who die naturally" (*maté gerpagerpa*) are called *jinujung* or simply *bégu*. They are propitiated in family ceremonies called *perumah bégu* and they are said to reside in and around cemeteries. These ghosts are interested only in their own offspring and are of no significance to other persons. They are soon forgotten. In contrast, the *dibata* of a family (*dibata jabu*) are the ghosts of family members "who die in one day," i.e., of persons who die unnaturally or unexpectedly. These *dibata* include the ghosts of persons who die accidental deaths, or who commit suicide, of miscarried or aborted fetuses and small infants who die before their teeth appear, and of women who die in childbirth. In addition, the ghosts of persons with exceptional talents, such as carpenters, players in the traditional orchestra, and *gurus,* also become *dibata.* As previously noted, these spirits are said to reside in the houses of their families; they are propitiated in ceremonies called *perumah dibata.*

The ancestral ghosts of greatest importance to any individual are the ghosts of his parents, but he may be influenced by the ghosts of more remote ancestors, especially those of former members of his "one father" or "one grandfather" *jabu,* i.e., of his lineage segments. Of course, such spirits are likely to be male agnatic ancestors such as father's fathers, but they are not necessarily so. Since the focus here is on one's family, the guardian spirits of importance to an individual may include the ghosts of his mother or his father's mother, the latter especially if his father is still alive or if he is one of several married brothers. A person's *anakberu* or *kalimbubu,* should they become *dibata,* are concerned only with the welfare of the families of their own children and son's children; they have no influence on him or his family.

It is important to note that although lineage segments have guardian spirits, lineages as wholes do not. The guardian spirits of a village are Pa Megoh and Nandě Megoh who are not genealogically related to the ruling lineage. Members of the ruling lineage who live in the village have the same guardian spirits as other villagers, but the former enjoy a privileged ritual status with regard to these spirits. As previously noted, these spirits are propitiated for the good of the village as a whole (not just its ruling lineage) by a priest who belongs to the ruling lineage of the village.

As noted above, a person's *kalimbubu* may be referred to as *dibata niidah,* the visible god. The expression does not imply that the *kalimbubu* is deceased and has a mystical influence on the life of the *anakberu,* but rather that in life the *kalimbubu* has such an influence. This influence is confined to close *kalimbubu* by birth. This does not imply that a man does not have to respect and obey members of his wife's family, his *kalimbubu* by marriage; rather, it sanctions that respect and obedience. Thus, one of the reasons why a man must maintain good social relations with his *kalimbubu* by marriage – aside from the fact that "they gave him a wife" and he is therefore indebted to them for one of the most precious things in life, a woman to bear his children – is that if his conduct "frustrates" them (see p. 106), their condition will have an adverse effect on the welfare of his children.

Everything good in life is ascribed to these two powers, the mediating influence of the familial guardian spirits in the spirtual world, and the metaphysical influence (*tuah*) of the *kalimbubu* on the *anakberu* among the living. Any particular event or condition may be ascribed to either of these. Thus, a man may say that his family enjoys good health and prosperity because of the protection of his guardian spirits, or he may say, especially when speaking to one of his *kalimbubu,* that this is because of the good influence of his *kalimbubu.* No particular kind of misfortune is associated with one or the other of these influences. The cause must be determined in each case by consulting a *guru*, a spirit medium, or some other expert in such matters.

The influence of the *kalimbubu* on the *anakberu* begins early in life. As noted earlier (p. 103), an individual becomes the *anakberu* of his mother's family of origin (including her brothers) when he becomes a human being, that is, only one month after conception. The first ritual recognition of this relationship, and of the potential influence of the *kalimbubu* for good or for evil, does not occur, however, until the seventh month of pregnancy (reckoned by the lunar calendar from the last menstruation).

"THE *KALIMBUBU* GIVE FOOD"

This ritual is called *kalimbubu mesuri man,* literally, the *kalimbubu* make it satisfied with food, but more simply, the *kalimbubu* give food. Another name for the rite is *kalimbubu nungkir jabu,* the *kalimbubu* call the *jabu.* In the past, large feasts were sometimes held on this occasion and they were called *kalimbubu ngembahken naroh mbentar,* the *kalimbubu* deliver white egg. The ritual procedure was the same whether or not a large feast was held.

As the name suggests, this rite is performed by the *kalimbubu* for the benefit of the *anakberu* still to be born. It cannot be performed by members of the child's family on behalf of the child's *kalimbubu.* Also, the rite is performed only for the first-born child of a couple.

Three sets of *kalimbubu* (of the unborn child) take part in the ritual. These are: (1) members of the mother's natal family (the child's MF, MM, MB), (2) members of the natal family of the mother's mother (the child's MMF, MMB, MMBW, or if they are dead, their closest living agnatic descendants), and (3) members of the mother's mother's mother's natal family (the child's MMMF, MMMB, or since they are likely to be dead, their closest living agnatic descendants). From the perspective of the husband of the pregnant woman, these are his several *kalimbubu* by marriage, and in the context of the ritual, they are identified according to that portion of the brideprice that they received (see pp. 174-176). All of the child's relatives who fall into these three categories of *kalimbubu* normally are invited to attend, especially if they live within ten miles or so (a day's journey) of the village where the rite is to be performed. The closest relatives of these categories are obliged to attend the ceremony, or to arrange for "substitute *kalimbubu*" to attend in their stead.

It is said that the purpose of the rite is to give the child its first meal. The child is fed by its principal *kalimbubu* and they are assisted by the other sets of more distant *kalimbubu*. It is said also that if the rite is not performed, the child will suffer throughout life from *teratera mulana*, literally, the first frustration; he would not enjoy good health and he would experience difficulty in getting married, and if he managed to do so he might not have any children.

Since, for the welfare of the child, his parents should be on good terms with both the visible and the invisible "gods" when he is born, one part of the rite consists in determining whether there are any disturbances in the social relations between the parents and either the *kalimbubu* or the spirit world or both. This is done by a spirit medium through two divinations, one before the meal and one after. The ritual object used in the first is a boiled egg; that used in the second is a chicken head. By "reading" the objects the medium may reveal that a *kalimbubu* is frustrated or that a guardian spirit is claiming a promised feast or feeling neglected, or perhaps that the soul of one of the parents is "away" (perhaps detained by a sacred spirit in whose place the parent experienced "shock" sometime ago), and so on. If some such disturbance is revealed, it must be rectified as soon as possible.

The following is a description of one such rite that I witnessed in Kuta Gamber in December 1961.

The pregnant woman was the wife of Malem. He had married uxorilocally, as had his WF, so he was living in the village of his *puang kalimbubu* by marriage (his WMF's village). Malem belongs to Sembiring Milala subclan; his wife belongs to Ginting Munte (the *kalimbubu*); his wife's mother is Perangin-angin Pinem (the *puang kalimbubu*, or the *kalimbubu* who receive the *berébere*); and his wife's mother's mother is Tarigan Gersang (the *kalimbubu* who receive the *perkempun*). The ceremony was attended by sixty-one adults, twenty-seven males and thirty-four females. (It is common for small feasts or rites to have more female than male participants.) Among these sixty-one people were four *anakberu* of Malem, ten *senina,* eighteen *kalimbubu* who receive the *tukor,* seventeen *kalimbubu* who receive the *berébere,* and twelve *kalimbubu* who receive the *perkempun.* Almost all the participants were residents of the village. Only four were outsiders: Malem's father, mother, brother, and sister. Because the rite took place in the village of the *puang kalimbubu,* they, of course, could participate in person. However, the other *kalimbubu* lived some considerable distance away and could not directly participate in the rite. As is usual in such cases, knowing in advance that they would not be able to meet their ritual obligations in person, they had attended the wedding feast, received the portion of the marriage payment to which they were entitled, and distributed a substantial part of it to their closest agnatic kin who resided in the village and whom they had chosen to represent them on future occasions when their attendance would be required. They also left some money to purchase the chicken, the egg and the two liters of rice that they were obliged to donate to the rite.

The rite and feast took place at Malem's house. His *kalimbubu* by marriage (the primary *kalimbubu* by birth of his unborn child) donated four chickens, one egg, and twenty liters of rice to the occasion. The second and third sets of *kalimbubu* each gave one chicken, one egg and two liters of rice. Malem himself, his agnates and his *anakberu* gave nothing. One chicken, the one egg and the two liters of rice donated by the first and principal *kalimbubu* were used for the ritual meal. The food was put in a large sacred Chinese porcelain dish, and Malem and his wife were joined by three other people, two *senina*, and one *kalimbubu,* so that there were five (*lima*) to eat the ritual meal. (This is regarded as a good ritual number because it rhymes with *ertima,* to wait, and is said to imply that the *tendi,* the souls of the living, are waiting at home; they are not "away.") The rice was placed in a heap with the egg on top and the cooked chicken to one side.

The spirit medium took the egg, opened it and "read" it. She found nothing wrong with it and so the ritual meal started. As the five people ate the meal, the participating *kalimbubu* addressed the unborn child: "Here we, your *kalimbubu,* are bringing food, chicken, egg, and rice, to you. Be satisfied with it. We bring this to prevent you from suffering from *teratera mulana* in the future. May we have good health. May your father and mother achieve their aspirations. Please eat the food. Do not hesitate."

The meal was followed by the "reading" of the head of the chicken. According to the medium, the head revealed the existence of a frustrated *kalimbubu*. She addressed an inquiry about this to each group of *kalimbubu* and eventually Malem's WM admitted that she had had a grievance. The spirit medium urged her to tell the whole story because it had to be made public.

Malem's WM explained that one day she found her daughter at home and asked her why she had not gone to the fields with her husband. The daughter explained that she felt very tired and wanted to rest; her husband had asked her to go with him because there was much work to be done. He wanted to cut tobacco and needed her to pluck the leaves. When she refused, they quarrelled. Malem was furious and said, among other things, "Is this what you learned from Minter (her F) and Simpan (her M)?" Malem's WM was deeply injured when her daughter told her this. (It is taboo to mention a senior person's name, especially the name of a parent or parent-in-law or MB. Moreover, it is regarded as gravely insulting to mention a person's parent's name to him or her.) Eventually Malem's wife set off for the tobacco field. Her mother went along and helped her work and then stayed to have a meal with the couple. After the meal she asked her daughter, in Malem's presence, whether she was on good terms with her husband. She pretended not to know what had happened earlier in the day. Her daughter then repeated the story. Malem's WM then commented angrily, "That is a grave insult! That is a shame! Everyone knows that at one time or another husband and wife must quarrel. It is unavoidable. But why must our names be brought into it? I think you should divorce your husband!" Malem then apologized to his wife and her mother. A few days later he and his wife took a chicken to her parents and made a formal apology. So, apparently, the matter had been settled.

The Karo believe, however, that a person's soul may harbor an unconscious grudge. Even though he may consciously "forgive and forget," his soul may remain frustrated. And it is this kind of frustration that divination often reveals, for relatives who have quarrelled usually try to compose their differences and to re-establish amiable relations as soon as possible. Thus, when the divination revealed a frustrated *kalimbubu,* Malem's WM felt compelled to reveal the quarrel. But, she added, addressing the medium, "You know I had forgiven *kèla* (DH). Indeed, I had forgotten the whole thing. It seems that even so my soul still feels injured, otherwise it would not come out in the reading."

Once an injury is revealed in this way and the *anakberu* apologizes in the way prescribed by the medium, the matter is completely resolved. So an elderly female *anakberu* asked him if the story was true. He admitted that it was and again expressed his regrets. She chided him, saying, "If you have another quarrel with your wife, please do not mention the names of her parents; that is very embarrassing." Another woman added, "I would rather be beaten." Yet another replied, "Neither is it good to beat a wife. The best thing is to have no quarrels. But if you must quarrel, avoid letting it become serious." All of this was said in Malem's presence and he found it quite embarrassing. The medium then advised Malem to hold a simple rite of reconciliation which would eliminate the frustration of the *kalimbubu* by "cooling" it. Preparations were made by putting some rice, onion, *kaciwer (kaempheria galanga), bunga sapa* (a kind of flower), a Dutch silver guilder, and cold water in a white porcelain bowl. Holding the bowl in his hand, Malem, accompanied by his mother, approached his WF and sat in front of him. He bowed his head and said, "I apologize to you *mama* (WF); I will never do it again." Then he handed the bowl to his WF who drank a little of the water. While he was drinking, the spirit medium and some other old women said, "May your heart be as cold as the water." Someone added, "Cold is the water and colder is your heart." After that, the ritual bowl was circulated and almost all of the *kalimbubu* present drank some of the water in turn.

In conclusion, it should be emphasized that although the condition of the soul of a man's *kalimbubu* by marriage does not directly affect his welfare, but only that of his wife or children, he is nonetheless implicated in this interfamily relationship. If, for any reason, social relations between the families are disrupted and the *kalimbubu* are thereby frustrated, this will necessarily result in injury to the woman or her offspring. Therefore, it behooves not only them and their mother, but also their father as well, to do everything within their power to maintain harmonious social relations between the families and their respective members. A man must therefore treat his WF and his WBs as he would his own MB, for the quality of his social relations with them profoundly effects the welfare of his children, just as the quality of his social relations with his MB effects his own welfare. None of this is to deny that a man is indebted to his WF and WBs for giving him their daughter and sister as a wife – yet, what is a wife for if not to bear him children?

Chapter Eight

Marriage

Every Karo marriage results in the formation of a new domestic family and household. Initially, the married couple are economically dependent on the husband's (sometimes the wife's) parents and usually reside with them for a time. But this dependence seldom exceeds one year and the couple soon move into their own house or apartment and cultivate their own gardens. The Karo do not expect one spouse to leave his or her parental home and to join the household of the parents of the other spouse. They expect *both* spouses to leave their parental homes and to establish a new one for themselves. This expectation is reflected in one expression for the married state, *erjabu,* to have a *jabu,* family or household, of one's own.

It should be clear enough by now that Karo do not regard a marriage as nothing more than a special kind of contract between two individuals, the spouses themselves. Certainly, such a contract is an essential part of any marriage. Recall that in the *sijalapen* described in Chapter 7 (pp. 124-126), the *anakberu* mediators are careful to note the necessity of asking the bride and groom whether they approve the contract for their marriage. While this is a formality – the kin of the bride and groom would not be assembled to transfer the brideprice if the couple had not already agreed to the marriage – it is not an empty formality. The Karo recognize that, whatever marriage may entail, it is first and foremost a union of two individuals for the purpose of creating a family, and the union should be the choice of those two individuals. It is all to the good if it is also the choice of their parents and other kin. It is all to the good because any marriage, whether arranged by the parents of the husband and wife or merely approved by them (perhaps under considerable duress), is also an alliance between families.

Moreover, the social implications of a marriage extend well beyond this interfamilial alliance. Through the extension of *kalimbubu-anakberu* relationships to the agnatic kin of the families most immediately concerned (ultimately to all of their lineage, subclan, and clan kin), and to the *kalimbubu* and *anakberu* of those families as well, a very large number of people necessarily have an interest in any marriage. Of course, their interest in the marriage itself is highly variable and diminishes greatly as their distance of genealogical relationship to the principals increases. Even so, each marriage generates a complex network of *senina-senina* and *kalimbubu-anakberu* relationships, none of which, no matter how distant, is without some potential social significance. Distant *senina, kalimbubu* and *anakberu* may be called upon by close ones to substitute for them; and when two or more Karo who have not hitherto had much to do with one another are thrown together and have to interact according to traditional social norms, the first thing they do is determine whether they are *senina* or *kalimbubu-anakberu;* thereafter they know, in very general terms at least, what to expect of one another. It is not necessary, in a situation like this, for two distantly related persons to know exactly how they are related and for them to be able to trace their relationship back to a specific marriage. It may be sufficient to determine that some of their respective agnatic kin or their *kalimbubu* or *anakberu* stand in a certain relationship to one another, without knowing why or how they do so. Because *kalimbubu-anakberu* relations are extended to members of the lineages, subclans and clans of the principal parties, the descent group system may facilitate this determination by providing a shortcut for the determination of the appropriate relationship. It needs to be emphasized, however, that marriage does not entail an alliance between the lineage segments, lineages, subclans, or clans of the principals. These are not corporate groups and they cannot enter into alliances as wholes.

PROHIBITIONS ON MARRIAGE BETWEEN RELATIVES

There are two basic prohibitions on marriage between relatives and from these most of the others may be deduced. These are: (1) familial kin may not intermarry, and (2) two individuals may not marry if an opposite-sex sibling of one has already married an opposite-sex sibling of the other.

Marriage or sexual intercourse between familial kin is virtually unheard of in Karoland, though marriage between siblings figures prominently in Karo mythology. Marrying a *turang,* a sibling or a classificatory sibling, is regarded as incest (*sumbang*). With the exception of the Sembiring and Perangin-angin clans, the prohibition on marriage between classificatory siblings within the clan is strictly observed. Needless to say, a marriage between classificatory siblings would hopelessly confound the basic categories of relationship, namely the *senina-senina* and *anakberu-kalimbubu* relationship, and the network of social relations based on them.

The second rule is based on this latter consideration: the first marriage between the two families establishes a *kalimbubu-anakberu* relationship between them, the second would not simply reverse that relationship but would thoroughly confuse the social relationships between the families and their relatives. The two sets of relatives would be both the *kalimbubu* and the *anakberu* of one another. In this situation it would be virtually impossible for the members of the two families to interact at all! Of course, the difficulties would be considerably less acute for persons who are only distantly related to the couple. For the most distant relatives, there would be no difficulty at all, or perhaps only some minor inconvenience if they happened to live in the same village as the married couple. Indeed, such distant relatives often stand as *kalimbubu* and *anakberu* of both spouses, even if the spouses are distantly related to one another. But for those who are more closely related to the spouses, the incompatibilities of their rights and duties in respect to one another, and the daily inconveniences, would be too great, and they would strongly argue against the marriage. Again, such incompatibilities may arise even if the prospective husband and wife are more or less distantly related to one another. To keep on good terms with their relatives, parents may find it necessary to oppose a marriage on these grounds.

Extensions

As Karo kin categories and terms are extended beyond their foci, so are the sexual and marital regulations associated with membership of the designated categories. But the marital prohibitions are not extended as far as the terms are. Thus, for example, the terms for father, mother, sibling and child are extended to clan mates of one's own parents, siblings and children. Of course, a person may not marry anyone so designated if that other person belongs to his or her own clan, because the clans are exogamous (with the exceptions noted above, p. 73); but if the other person belongs to another clan and is either a fairly distant relative or is not known to be a relative, then the kin-class relationship between the two is not necessarily a bar to their marriage. They may marry even if they are *turang sepemerèn,* i.e., classificatory siblings whose mothers belong to the same clan. Of the 112 married couples residing in Kuta Gamber and Liren in 1961, nine were related as *turang sepemerèn* because their mothers were clan "sisters." Strictly speaking, if their mothers belong to the same subclan, a couple should not marry, but such marriages sometimes occurred in the past and, according to my informants, are even more frequent nowadays. The Karo associate this and other forms of irregular marriage with drought and, in the past, ritually punished the parties to such marriages during times of drought by leading them to stream beds and throwing water on them. In 1961, one married couple in Kuta Gamber were related as *turang sepemerèn* because their mothers were subclan "sisters." There were no cases of marriage between persons whose mothers were lineage "sisters," and proposal of such a marriage would meet strong resistance today.

The exogamy of agnatic groups below the clan level is based on the notion that agnates are related by blood and should not mix their blood, and on the confusion of categories and their implied social relations that would inevitably result from a marriage between agnates. These ideas do not underlie clan exogamy, for as noted earlier, Karo do not suppose that persons who belong to the same clan necessarily are genealogically related. However, it is logically consistent with the extension of sibling-like social relationships to clan mates that members of the same clan may not intermarry. It is reasonably consistent also that the clan mates of one's own close kin are regarded as potential marital partners. After all, they are only classificatory relatives of one's own relatives and marriage with them may not create confusion in social relationships.

The prohibition on a marriage between two families that would be contrary to the established *anakberu-kalimbubu* relation between them also is extended to their respective agnatic kin. The reason, again, is that such a marriage would confuse social relationships by making some people both the *anakberu* and the *kalimbubu* of one another. But since not all *anakberu-kalimbubu* relationships are of equal significance to an individual and his close agnates, it follows that not all marriages of men to female *anakberu* and of women to male *kalimbubu* would be equally disruptive of established *anakberu-kalimbubu* relationships. Thus, it is not surprising that there is no flat prohibition on the marriages of men to female *anakberu* and of women to male *kalimbubu.* There is, rather, a prohibition on marriages of this sort that would disrupt established *anakberu-kalimbubu* relations and greatly inconvenience the people who are most immediately implicated in them. So although it is often said simply that a man should not marry a woman who is his *anakberu,* in this context the term is usually understood to refer to close *anakberu,* not to all *anakberu.*

One marriage that is plainly ruled out because of its certain disruptiveness of established *anakberu-kalimbubu* relations is that of a man to his FZD. Such a kinswoman is classified as *impal,* the same as MBD, but she is in addition *turang impal,* the cousin who is like a sister, because like a sister she is not marriageable. Her first and second agnatic parallel cousins (ego's FZHBD and FZHFBSD) also are not marriageable because their fathers and ego's FZD's father belong to the same "one grandfather" lineage segment. If a man were to marry his FZHBD or FZHFBSD, this would divide a "one grandfather" segment in two; some members of the segment would be that man's *anakberu* by birth while others would be his *kalimbubu* by marriage. Beyond the range of the "one grandfather" segment, however, social relations between agnates no longer exhibit – nor are they expected to exhibit – great solidarity, and so it is of considerably less consequence if more distantly related agnates find themselves divided in this way (some standing as *anakberu,* some as *kalimbubu,* to the same other persons). Some people say that it is not good for a man to marry a *turang impal* of the same subclan as his own FZD, but such marriages are not uncommon. I recorded two cases in Kuta Gamber in

1961. As can be seen from Tables 13 and 14, it is common for men of the same lineage to have both *kalimbubu* and *anakberu* in the same subclan. The men of Kuta Gamber lineage, Pinem subclan, stand as both *kalimbubu* and *anakberu* to the men of no less than eight other subclans. Most of these dual relationships cause little or no confusion and inconvenience in social relations because, for the most part, they are *kalimbubu-anakberu* relations only at the subclan level. Also, one relationship may be much closer than the other and the closer relationship usually takes precedence.

Table 13

The Kalimbubu of Kuta Gamber Principal Lineage[a]

Clan	Subclan		Total
1. Ginting	a. Munte	10	
	b. Tumangger	4	
	c. Jadibata	2	
	d. Babo	1	
	e. Suka	1	18
2. Tarigan	a. Gersang	9	
	b. Sibero	8	17
3. Sembiring	a. Milala	4	
	b. Keloko	3	
	c. Sinulaki	2	
	d. Busuk	1	
	e. G. Kinayan	1	11
4. Karo-karo	a. Sinuraya	2	
	b. Sinulingga	1	
	c. Ujung	1	4
Minangkabau (non-Karo)			1
			51

[a] The total number of married male members, both living and dead, is forty-four and these contracted fifty-one marriages. Table 13 shows the natal clan and subclan affiliation of their wifes.

Table 14

The Anakberu of Kuta Gamber Principal Lineage[a]

Clan	Subclan		Total
1. Ginting	a. Tumangger	8	
	b. Munte	5	
	c. Suka	2	
	d. Sugihen	1	16
2. Tarigan	a. Sibero	6	
	b. Gersang	2	8
3. Karo-karo	a. Manik	2	
	b. Sinulingga	2	
	c. Kaban	1	
	d. Kaciribu	1	6
4. Sembiring	a. Milala	3	
	b. Busuk	1	4
			34

[a] There are thirty-four married female members, both living and dead, in the genealogy of the principal lineage. Table 14 indicates the patrilineal affiliation of their husbands.

It is not strictly forbidden for a man to marry a woman who belongs to the lineage of his FZD. In Kuta Gamber there was one man who was married to his FZHFBSSD, a woman of his FZD's lineage who was his *anakberu* and his classificatory niece (*berébere*). In addition, there were two cases of men married to their FFBSDHZs, that is, to their classificatory sisters' HZ. In none of these cases did the marriage result in a division among the men of one "one grandfather" segment such that some stood as *anakberu,* others as *kalimbubu,* of the same other man or men.

In short, any marriage that would confuse categorical and social relationships by making some people both the *anakberu* and *kalimbubu* of one another may meet with disapproval from one quarter or another, but marriages that would so divide a "one grandfather" lineage segment are most strongly disapproved and, in fact, seem not to occur. This is readily understandable, for within this range agnates still have considerable influence over one another and are expected to exhibit solidarity in their social relations with outsiders. Even so, it should not be thought that the "one grandfather" segment operates as an "alliance group." To the extent that marriages are arranged (see below, pp. 155, 163), they are arranged by parents, especially fathers, not by the members of "one grandfather" segments acting as corporate groups. Furthermore, should a man marry a female *anakberu,* he and his brothers then regard his wife's family and her agnatic kin as their *kalimbubu,* but their agnatic parallel cousins do not; the parallel cousins maintain the old *anakberu-kalimbubu* relationship. This shows, once again, that the *anakberu-kalimbubu* relationship is primarily one between families, not agnatic groups of any scale.

CROSS-COUSIN MARRIAGE

Choice of a spouse among the Karo is not restricted to any one category of kinswoman or kinsman. As noted above, Karo sometimes marry classificatory fathers, mothers, siblings, children, nephews and nieces (*berèberè* or *permèn*), and classificatory FZDs. Such marriages are not considered wrong, provided that they do not greatly confuse established *senina-senina* or *anakberu-kalimbubu* relations. Of course, the marriages of men to their female *kalimbubu,* other than their close classificatory mothers (who are still *kalimbubu* until they marry) or their MB's wives, do not confuse established *anakberu-kalimbubu* relationships but reinforce or replicate them. Yet, as previously noted, the marriage of a man to a relatively distant *kalimbubu* must necessarily interfere with established *anakberu-kalimbubu* relationships by forcing him to pay less attention to his MB and his family in favor of his WF and WBs and their families. Clearly, the only way in which a man can marry and at the same time avoid having to neglect his MB and his family is to marry his own MBD, *impal.* In this way, his MB becomes his WF and is his *kalimbubu* by marriage as well as his *kalimbubu* by birth. Further, his MBS, who would otherwise become the WB of some other man, becomes his own WB and, for most of the rest of his adult life, the man who has the most immediate claims to his services as an *anakberu*. Of course, the Karo themselves are aware of all of this and frequently observe that the marriage of a man to his MBD preserves and renews established *anakberu-kalimbubu* relationships, while any other marriage is bound to interfere with them to some extent. In general, Karo strongly approve such marriages when they occur, for the marriage of a man to his MBD is a sure sign that the families of the spouses' parents are on good terms, as *anakberu-kalimbubu* should be. It is not true, however, that the marriage of a man to a woman other than his MBD is a sure sign that the families of the parents are on poor terms and wish to establish some social distance between themselves. A number of formal and informal considerations effect the frequency of MBD-FZS marriage and sometimes rule out the possibility of such a marriage even when a MBD is available and desired as a wife.

Before discussing these considerations in detail, it should be noted that Karo regard the marriage of a man to his MFBSD, also an *impal,* as nearly as effective as marriage to his MBD in maintaining or renewing an interfamily alliance. In this case MB and WF are first cousins and members of the same "one grandfather" lineage segment. Only these two kinds of marriage are regarded as "proper *impal*" marriages because their consequences for established *anakberu-kalimbubu* relations are quite different from the consequences of marriage between persons who are not MBD-FZS or MFBSD-FFBDS.

One of the formal considerations that effects the frequency of cross-cousin marriage is the rule that, should one of a set of brothers marry a MBD, the others may not do so; they may not marry the sisters of their BW even though those women are their *impal.* From the point of view of marital politics it would be wasteful for a man to marry several of his daughters to several brothers and thus deprive himself and his sons of the opportunity to acquire several sets of *anakberu.* Even so, should he wish to marry another of his daughters to another of his sister's sons, he is prohibited from this by the rule against it, and the rule is sanctioned by the belief that such an arrangement would unavoidably result in the death of one of the spouses. No one would imperil his child by permitting such a marriage. This prohibition applies even if a man marries a non-relative. A man is not allowed to marry his brother's wife's sister, even if she is not otherwise related to him.

Two full sisters, however, are allowed to marry their father's sisters' sons, as long as these men are not true siblings. In other words, a man who has two sisters and two daughters may marry both of his daughters to his sisters' sons who are parallel cousins.

Another formal consideration that effects the frequency of cross-cousin marriage is that there should be free choice in selecting a spouse. Consistent with this, there are neither infant betrothals nor child marriages. Of course, parents often do attempt to arrange marriages for their children, and a woman may encourage her son to consider his MBD. She usually does so if she and her husband are on especially good terms with her brother and if she is especially fond of her BD and would like to have her for a daughter-in-law. Other things being equal, a woman is likely to prefer her BD as a SW because they are close relatives and, therefore, the girl is more likely to feel obliged to look after her should she become a dependent widow. Moreover, a woman regards it as her duty to her brother to encourage her son to marry his daughter, or at least to consider the possibility. If she succeeds in promoting such a marriage, she may feel that she has met one of her principal duties in life. But it is her duty only to encourage her son to consider the girl, and he is under no obligation to marry his MBD if he does not wish to do so. Women often gently nag their marriageable sons about their eligible BDs when the sons return home for their evening meals, and a boy who wants nothing to do with his MBD will soon begin to avoid coming home for his meals.

In this context it should be noted that a woman's brother has no right to press her or her husband to arrange a marriage between their son and his daughter. He cannot demand that his ZS marry his daughter, nor should he even encourage his sister to encourage her son to consider the possibility. Even if he strongly resents the lack of attention given to his daughter by his ZS or suspects that his sister is not doing all she can to encourage her son to marry his daughter, he is obliged to say nothing about it to her or to anyone else. Interference on his part would be strongly resented by his ZH, who alone has the right to decide who his son should or should not marry – to the extent that his son will listen to him!

Yet another formal consideration is that, even if a young man should be willing to marry a MBD, he is not free to choose among them. He must marry the oldest available MBD or none at all. Thus a young man may be willing, even anxious, to marry a particular MBD but still be unable to do so because her elder sister "is still there." In one case I know of a young man wanted to marry one of his MBDs who had an elder sister who was a divorcee. His MB was insulted by the proposal to marry the younger girl and refused it. Later, the same young man proposed to marry an agnatic parallel cousin of these girls (his MFBSD), but this proposal also was refused. I was told that one should not pass over the daughter of an immediate *kalimbubu* in favor of a more distant one.

Demographic factors also must be taken into account. It occasionally happens that a woman has no son or her brother has no daughter, but more often, when a young man is ready to marry, none of his MBs has an eligible daughter. His MBDs may be married already, or they may be too young to get married, or he may not like the one or two who are available. So even if two men are of a mind to reinforce their *anakberu-kalimbubu* relationship by marrying the son of one to the daughter of the other, they may not be able to arrange it simply because the opportunity does not present itself.

Finally, as suggested above, the likelihood of a marriage between MBD-FZS depends in large part on the quality of social relations between their families, on a woman's opinion of her BD, and on a man's opinion of his ZS. A woman may think that her BD would not make a good daughter-in-law, and a man may think that his ZS is not the best possible son-in-law, so even if two may wish to marry, their parents may be less than enthusiastic. Conversely, a young woman may think that her FZ is likely to be too stern and demanding as a HM and a young man may have a similar opinion of his MB as a prospective WF.

Cross-cousin marriage, when it occurs, is generally regarded as a good thing because it renews and perpetuates established *anakberu-kalimbubu* relationships, because it entails no reordering of established relationships, and because it expresses satisfaction with those already established. But cross-cousin marriage is regarded also as a good thing in and of itself, and even though a particular marriage between cross-cousins may have some negative features, it is nonetheless a good thing because it conforms to the natural order of Things. This value placed on cross-cousin marriage is expressed in a ritual cross-cousin marriage which is supposed to have both curative and protective powers. Thus, a man living in Kuta Gamber had a dream in which he saw his young son in the company of a man who had recently died. The man was frightened by the dream and his wife went to consult a spirit medium. The medium interpreted the dream as a sign that the child's life was in danger and suggested that as a protective measure, the son should be ritually married to his cross-cousin. Such a ritual, when held for a boy, is called *tarohken kujabu kalimbubu,* bringing (him) to the *kalimbubu's* family; when held for a girl, it is called *tarohken kujabu anakberu,* bringing (her) to the *anakberu's* family. When performed for a girl, of course, the rite could not be intended to placate a frustrated *kalimbubu.* So far as I know, it was not intended to do that in this case, though the patient was a boy.

The rite itself is a miniature wedding ceremony. It is held in the morning and about twenty to thirty people attend. Four or five chickens are killed for a festive meal at midday. The procedure is that the "bride" and "groom" eat from a common dish. After the meal a nominal amount of "brideprice" (about Rp. 100) is handed to the relatives of the bride. The "marriage" is only symbolic; it has no jural entailments, except for the requirements that should the girl eventually marry someone else the "brideprice" must be returned. Even so, the "couple" may be teased about their "marriage." A relative might say to the boy:

"You have married, Siman, haven't you?"
"Yes, I have."
"Who is your wife?"
"Unjuk."
"Where is she?"
"At home."
"What is she doing there?"
"I don't know."

Bystanders may laugh and remark that it is strange that the "husband" has no idea what his "wife" is doing.

Frequency of Cross-Cousin Marriage

There are 115 married women in Kuta Gamber and Liren. Only 4 of these are the MBDs or MFBSDs of their husbands.

Thus, only 3.5 percent of the marriages in my sample are "proper *impal*" marriages. One other marriage, however, is regarded as equivalent to a "proper *impal*" marriage, though it is between a man and his MBSD, his *permèn.* The marriage is so regarded because the man is married to the daughter of an immediate *kalimbubu* by birth, and this has much the same effect on established *anakberu-kalimbubu* relations as does cross-cousin marriage – immediate *anakberu-kalimbubu* by birth are made also immediate *anakberu-kalimbubu* by marriage, and so their previously close social relations are not modified by the marriage. If we add this case to the previous 4, we have 5 marriages in which principal or immediate *anakberu-kalimbubu* by birth were also principal or immediate *anakberu-kalimbubu* by marriage. This amounts to about 4.4 percent of the total of 115 marriages.

There are in addition three instances of marriage to more distant kinswomen of the husband's mother's lineage. In one of these a man is married to his third cousin, MFFBSSD, *impal*; in another a man is married to the daughter of a third cousin, MFFBSSSD, *permèn;* and in the third the man is married to a classificatory *impal* (exact relationships unrecorded). None of these are regarded as "proper *impal*" marriages or as functionally equivalent to such marriages. I cannot be precise about the exact number of marriages to women within the range of the husband's mother's clan, but certainly they amount to less than 40 percent of the total. This is somewhat greater than the frequency expectable purely by chance, i.e., 25 percent.

Published data from two other studies in Sumatra suggest that these figures are not atypical of the region in general. Bruner (1959:120) found that, in a sample of urban Toba Batak, the frequency of marriage between actual MBD-FZS was 2.3 percent; an additional 15 percent of the wives were members of their husbands' mothers' clans. Tugby (1958:319) found 3.4 percent MBD-FZS marriage in a sample of Upper-Mandailing marriages.

I cannot say how the known frequency of cross-cousin marriage among the Karo compares with the maximum frequency that could be attained if Karo were to attempt to maximize the frequency of cross-cousin marriage (see Kunstadter, et al., 1963, for an attempt to estimate such frequencies for simulated populations), given the several jural constraints that Karo impose on contracting such marriages. But such a comparison, especially if intended as a measure of the degree to which Karo observe a rule of cross-cousin marriage (cf. Kunstadter 1966), would be sociologically irrelevant and misleading. The Karo have no rule of cross-cousin marriage; that is, men are under no jural obligation to marry MBDs if available. The figures noted above cannot reasonably be used to assess the degree of conformity to a rule which the Karo themselves do not know. Moreover, the figure of 4.4 percent represents not the frequency of marriage between actual cross-cousins (which is substantially lower), but the frequency of marriage to a daughter of an immediate *kalimbubu*, i.e., to the daughter of one's MB, MBS, or MFBS. It seems worth noting that the number of potential wives available to a man from within the range of his MBD's "one grandfather" lineage segment is necessarily much greater (on the average) than the number of his female cross cousins alone. Thus, if the Karo were jurally constrained to take their wives from among the daughters of their male immediate *kalimbubu* by birth, and if they attempted to conform to such a rule, the frequency could be much higher than 4.4 percent. Again, however, the Karo know of no such rule of marriage. Men are not jurally obliged to take their wives from among their immediate *kalimbubu* by birth.

Cross-cousin Marriage and Intergroup Alliance

Whatever may be the situation in other societies, cross-cousin marriage among the Karo is not a matter of perpetuating alliances between descent groups. It was noted above, but may deserve reemphasis here, that lineage segments, lineages, subclans and clans are not corporate groups, certainly not with respect to the marriages of their members. Certainly, the close agnatic kin of a man or woman have an interest in their marriage, for the marriage necessarily implicates them, at least by extension, in certain *anakberu-kalimbubu* relations which they may or may not wish to see established. But this is a very different matter from the corporate involvement of descent groups as such.

It follows, of course, that MBD-FZS marriage in Karo society is not an "expression" of relations of prescribed affinal or marital alliance between descent groups, and this is true even at the level of relations between lineage segments. Every marriage, even one between persons already related to one degree or another as *anakberu-kalimbubu,* establishes an *anakberu-kalimbubu* relationship between two families; this is necessarily a new *anakberu-kalimbubu* relationship because the *anakberu* family is itself a new one also established by the marriage. Nevertheless, marriage between MBD-FZS (or MFBSD-FFBDS) is regarded as perpetuating established *anakberu-kalimbubu* relations between "one father" and "one grandfather" lineage segments. Such a marriage does this, however, by recreating primary and immediate *anakberu-kalimbubu* relations for the immediate succeeding generation of agnates of families already so related.

PRELIMINARIES TO MARRIAGE

Courting begins for a boy between the ages of fifteen and seventeen, when he is described as a young bachelor (*anak perana*). For a girl it begins between the ages of thirteen and fifteen, when she is described as a young unmarried woman (*singudanguda*). Both are then regarded as having attained adulthood, but without as yet having acquired all of the attendant responsibilities. The Karo say that this is the happiest period of one's life. Boys and girls of this age are permitted to interact freely and to form close friendships with age-mates of the opposite sex, which may or may not include sexual relations, and which may or may not lead to marriage. A young man often has two or three girl friends in succession before getting married, and he may finally marry a girl by "proposal." She may or may not be the girl he has been courting. It is regarded as improper to have more than one girl friend or boy friend at a time, partly because the partners are supposed to love one another, and partly because one may get a reputation for promiscuity if he or she courts several others at once. Usually a boy meets his girl friend in the evening on the porch of her house. If she lives in a nearby village he may visit her there, spend the evening with her and return late at night to his own village. Nowadays, they write letters to each other and may meet at markets.

The period of courting lasts for several years and is ended by marriage. In the past, girls married at about the age of seventeen or eighteen and boys at about the age of nineteen or twenty. Nowadays many youngsters, especially boys, are sent to town for higher education and their marriages are postponed until completion of their studies. A man, it is said, "is never too old to marry," and nowadays the ages of twenty for a girl and twenty-five for a young man are regarded as respectable ages for marriage.

Getting married is regarded as an important goal in life. My informants emphasized this by saying, "What is the use of possessing everything if you do not get married?" Thus, parents encourage their children to get married, and if one of them does not, this is a serious matter for the family. It is embarrassing for them and it may become the subject of jokes in the community. There are no spinsters or bachelors in Kuta Gamber or Liren. In the past, it was customary to build a special commemorative house *(tungkup)* for a dead spinster, but not for a bachelor.

There are two legitimate paths to marriage, that is, two procedures are recognized by adat. One is called *arah rumah,* through the house, and the other *nangkih,* literally, to climb up. These are, in other words, marriage by proposal and marriage by elopement. In marriage by proposal, both the future partners and their parents consent to the marriage; the prospective spouses, unless they are cross-cousins, may have been courting one another but usually they have not. In marriage by elopement, the decision to marry is made by the prospective spouses, usually without the prior consent of their parents, and sometimes against the wishes of either or both sets of parents.

Marriage by Proposal

As noted above, the parents of a boy may encourage him to marry a particular girl. She may or may not be his cross-cousin or another immediate *kalimbubu,* and she may or may not be the girl he is courting at the time. She is not likely to be both at once because young men usually do not court their immediate *kalimbubu.* If he wishes to marry the girl, he appears to accept his parents' choice. If he does not want to marry the girl, his parents may then attempt to persuade him or they may look about for another girl to encourage him to consider.

When a young man and his parents finally agree on a girl, the procedure they then follow is the same whether or not the girl is an immediate *kalimbubu* of the family. The next step is to approach the girl and her parents. The boy's mother does this. She pays an informal visit to the girl's mother (who may be her BW) who is obliged to welcome her and not to exhibit a negative reaction to the proposal. The parents of the girl may privately criticize the suitor and his parents later on, and they may even suggest to their daughter that she refuse the proposal, but they must be polite to the suitor's envoy. It is conventional for the girl's mother, whether or not she approves of the proposal, to conclude the initial informal discussion with the observation that everything depends on her daughter's wishes. She remains polite but noncommittal by saying, "We (the parents of the girl) are honored by this proposal and would like to accept it, but it really depends on my daughter. We are like the drum, the child is our teacher." (The allusion here is to the two drums of the Karo orchestra. The small one, the "child," serves to mark the rhythm on which the variation played by the large "mother" drum is based.)

Shortly thereafter, the boy's mother approaches the girl informally. She is accompanied by one of her married female *anakberu,* either her HZ or her HBD. The girl's reply, like her mother's, should be polite but vague and noncommittal. Even if she is strongly in favor of the marriage, it would be immodest of her not to appear hesitant to accept the proposal. If she consents too readily, she may become the subject of gossip.

This is followed by a formal proposal. The boy's parents, again accompanied by an immediate *anakberu,* visit the girl's parents and ask directly but formally whether the girl has consented to the proposal. Usually the reply is much the same as before, but the boy's parents may be notified a few weeks later that the girl has consented. The people then say that she has changed her mind. Whether or not it is true, it is made to appear that the girl need not be in a hurry to accept the proposal. Of course, girls and their families who turn down too many proposals may acquire bad reputations for being too particular; and this little social game has to be played with care so that the boy's family is not kept waiting too long for the answer to their proposal.

Nowadays, as in the past, it is regarded as improper for parents to attempt to force their children to marry someone of the parents' choice. If a girl does not wish to accept a particular proposal, her parents may argue with her about it, but in the end they are not free to agree to the marriage without her consent. However, in the special case of a proposal from an immediate or close *anakberu* (FZS or FFBDS) of the girl's family, they were privileged to consent to the marriage without her approval. It must be emphasized, however, that they were under no obligation to consent to such a proposal. The *anakberu* had no right to demand that the girl consent to the marriage, or to demand her parents' consent if she refused, and they had no recourse should her parents not consent to force the marriage. It seems, then, that a girl had no right to block the renewal of an interfamily alliance with which the two families were particularly satisfied, and if she persisted in her refusal to accept the proposal despite her parents' strong wishes, they had the right to force her into the marriage. They could do this by secretly agreeing with the boy's parents that she should be caught by a party of his *senina* and *anakberu* and taken to his house. There a marriage ritual (*mukul*) was immediately performed and she was expected then to accept her status as his wife. The meeting to determine the brideprice and the formal wedding were both held later on.

The last such forced marriage occurred in Kuta Gamber in 1933 and the villagers now say that no such marriages are likely to occur in the future. The girl in this instance lived in a village about 10 kilometers from Kuta Gamber where her *impal* lived. A few weeks after she refused his proposal, she was caught near her village by four people, two men and two women. They bound her hands and forced her to go to Kuta Gamber. She wept all the way, refused to walk, and had to be jogged along or carried. She was married to her *impal* that evening. According to my informants, forced marriages were rare even in the past because most parents were reluctant to take such extreme measures; in so doing, they ran the risk of the girl committing suicide, and I was given several accounts of situations in which this actually happened. The marriage mentioned above, however, has been successful.

Marriage by Elopement

A young man may decide that he wants to marry the girl he is courting and she may be willing. He then makes it known to his parents that he is ready to marry and hopes that they will make the proposal for him. If his parents refuse to cooperate or if the girl's parents are strongly disposed not to accept the proposal, he and the girl may elope. Also, if a boy is courting a girl whom he knows his parents dislike, the couple may elope without ever consulting the parents of either about the possibility of their marriage. Moreover, young people who wish to marry one another tend to be impatient with their parents and the whole complicated business of arranging a marriage, so some couples elope even if they are not likely to encounter strong objections to their marriage. Young men, it is said, are especially likely to favor this course of action, if only to assert their independence by proving that they are able to find wives by themselves without the assistance of parents and other relatives. A girl may find herself forced to elope with her boy friend if her parents are pressing her to accept the proposal of a cross-cousin whom she does not want to marry.

The usual procedure in elopement is for the young man, on an auspicious evening and accompanied by three of his friends (an even number would be inauspicious), to take the girl to the house of one of his *anakberu*. The *anakberu* who so cooperates in an elopement is not usually an immediate *anakberu* of the boy's family but usually a classificatory FZH. Strictly speaking, the elopement starts when the girl has arrived at the *anakberu's* house, but they are not considered married at this point.

The period of elopement usually lasts for four or five days. During this period the girl stays in the house of the boy's *anakberu* and the boy takes his meals there but sleeps in a rice barn. Sexual intercourse in the house of the *anakberu* is forbidden, but the couple may meet on the porch at night and have intercourse there. The first few days are a period of uncertainty, for it is during this time that the girl or the boy may be persuaded by her or his parents or other close kin to give up the attempt to marry. The girl's parents, however, have no right to compel her to leave the house. While there, she is under the protection of the boy's *anakberu* and "no one can do her harm" as long as she stays in the house. If she ventures out, she may be captured by a party of her parents' *anakberu* whom they have sent for the purpose. If a girl has eloped to avoid marrying a cross-cousin, the *anakberu* who issued the proposal may not interfere and attempt to capture her on their own; they may act only if asked to do so by the girl's parents. Nowadays, very few elopements are foiled in these ways and the couple almost always emerges from the situation as husband and wife and with, at least, the grudging consent of their parents. Nevertheless, I did witness one elopement that failed. The marriage was strongly opposed by the girl's FB who was also the boy's MBSS. That is, the boy wanted to marry his FFZSD, one of his *anakberu*. Although the girl's family was not the immediate *anakberu* of his own family, her FB felt strongly that the marriage would greatly confuse established *anakberu-kalimbubu* relationships. He told the girl, "I am no longer your father if you marry him." The girl then terminated the elopement.

After a day at the house of the boy's *anakberu,* a party of these *anakberu* visit the girl's parents and tell them what has happened. Together they fix a date for the girl's parents and her father's close agnates to visit the couple. If the girl's parents do not oppose the marriage, they may agree at this time to make the visit a *kalimbubu ngembahken nakan,* the *kalimbubu* bring food. The occurrence of this visit a few days later signifies that the girl's parents have consented to the marriage. At this point the elopement period ends and that evening the girl moves to the boy's father's house. They are then *de facto* husband and wife, though the marriage rite may not be held until a few days later.

Finally, on the subject of elopement, it should be noted that cross-cousins are not supposed to do this and the adat provides for a fine in the event that they do. The fine is called *pengeruhak dingding* (damage of the wall) and amounts to Rp. 100 or Rp. 200; it is paid to the father of the bride. As one informant remarked, "Why come through the window if you are welcome through the door?" That is, why bother to steal a woman if her parents surely will give her to you? Why insult your *kalimbubu* by failing to ask politely for something they are not likely to refuse? Elopement by cross-cousins does not occur, not simply because it is forbidden by customary law but also because only courting couples elope and men do not court their *impal* or other close *kalimbubu*. Courting an *impal* is regarded as improper and would be ridiculed. When I inquired about this I was told, "Your *impal* is much like your sister; the difference is that you may marry your *impal* but not your sister." That is to say, MBD (like FZD) is regarded as similar to a sister; she is a close kinswoman of one's own generation and as such she is not properly an object of sexual desire. So there is something at least vaguely incestuous about courting a MBD, for it is fairly safe to assume that a courting couple is having sexual relations. Even so, a man may marry a MBD, but not a sister or a FZD. The reason for this apparent inconsistency in attitudes toward purely sexual as opposed to marital relations between MBD-FZS is, of course, that courting is by and large a matter of casual sexual relations and may or may not end up in marriage, while marriage involves a great deal more than sexual relations. Thus, despite the vaguely incestuous aspects of sexual relations between MBD-FZS, the society permits marriage between them for the social advantages it may have for their families. In contrast, the social disadvantages of FZD-MBS marriage would only add to the incestuous nature of such a marriage, and so it would be doubly bad.

MARRIAGE CEREMONIES

Ideally, marriage is legitimated through a wedding ceremony which has three main parts, the payment of a provisional brideprice, the marriage rite (*mukul*) itself, and the transfer of the full brideprice. It often happens, however, that the marriage is consummated and the marriage rite performed long before the full brideprice is transferred. The ceremony of transfer must be attended by a large number of relatives of both parties and they must be fed. The groom's parents, unless they are wealthy, are not likely to have the necessary amount of food on hand until immediately after the harvest. Another convenient time for a wedding is just before the harvest when people have plenty of leisure time and relatives living some distance away are able to attend. To have a wedding at this time, the family of the groom usually has to borrow rice from relatives and repay them after the harvest. In any event, it is not considered necessary to postpone cohabitation until the brideprice has been transferred, and so the marriage rite may be performed as much as a year before the major wedding ceremony. It occasionally happens that the "bride" – already legally a "wife" – is pregnant or has already given birth to a child when her wedding ceremony is held.

Couples who elope are married in a small ceremony held at the girl's parents' house a few days after the couple have begun to live together in the house of the boy's parents. In the case of marriage by proposal, the same ceremony may be held soon after the proposal has been accepted.

The Provisional Marriage Payment

On this occasion the *anakberu* and *senina* of the bride's and groom's parents meet and come to an agreement about the amount of the brideprice and the date of the wedding ceremony. When this is done the marriage is legitimated by the bride's village chief. The usual procedure is for the groom's parents to give Rp. 300 to the chief who then hands the money to the bride's parents. The payment is called *si arah raja,* through the king, and it serves as a provisional marriage payment until the whole sum is transferred at the wedding ceremony. The chief usually makes a brief speech, addressing first the bride and then the groom. He reminds them that the payment just made has altered their social statuses, the bride is no longer a girl but a married woman, and the boy is no longer a young bachelor but a married man. They now have the duties and responsibilities of adults and they must try not to remember or long for the carefree days of their youth. He may say that they are like the maize that has been placed on the drying rack in the kitchen; though they may be young, they are "old" and must behave accordingly.

A further Rp. 500 is paid by the groom's parents as *penindih pudun,* literally, a thing to press the knot, but figuratively a deposit to keep the appointment. This serves as a guarantee that the wedding will be held at the agreed time. This money is kept by the *anakberu* of the bride's parents. Should the groom's parents fail to hold the wedding, they forfeit the *penindih pudun.* Both the *si arah raja* and the *penindih pudun* are returned at the wedding ceremony.

Soon after this, the marriage rite (*mukul*) is held on an auspicious evening. It is a simple rite in which the couple eat from a common dish. The Karo say that this rite unites the souls of the bride and groom.

The Wedding Ceremony

On the evening before the wedding a formal meeting is held between the bride's and the groom's parents and their respective *anakberu* and *senina.* This meeting is termed *ngembah manok,* bringing a chicken. The main purpose of the meeting is to make certain that the arrangements for the ceremony have been completed and that it will proceed smoothly. To avoid any misunderstanding, the sum of the marriage payment is again announced. Also, so that sufficient food will be prepared, both sides make estimates of the number of their respective guests.

The wedding ceremony itself is the culmination of the process of marriage, for it is on this occasion that the brideprice is transferred and the adat debt (*utang adat*) of the *anakberu* to the *kalimbubu* is paid. The ceremony is held in the bride's village (if different from the groom's) and both the bride's and the groom's parents are recognized jointly as the feast-givers, despite the fact that the groom's parents are responsible for all expenditures. Both parties send written, usually stencilled but sometimes printed, invitations to their respective relatives. Co-villagers, regardless of their relationship to the feast-givers, are orally invited by the wives of the feast-givers who go from house to house.

The average number of guests at a wedding ceremony is about 300. One or two pigs, occasionally a cow, are killed for the occasion. Two simple rectangular booths are erected and mats are spread on the ground under them. These form two separate seating areas, one for the groom's and the other for the bride's party. Each of these areas is divided into three sections: the middle part is for the feast-givers and their *senina,* on their left are their *anakberu,* and on their right are their *kalimbubu* (see Figure 11). (As might be expected, the left side is associated with inferiority, the right with superiority.) The two major groups face each other with an open space in between.

Figure 11. Seating arrangements at a wedding ceremony.

Groom's party

kalimbubu	*senina*	*anakberu*

Bride's party

anakberu	*senina*	*kalimbubu*

Both the bride and groom are dressed in ceremonial attire. Often they alone are seated on chairs, at a table, and in front of the groom's party. The bride and groom should be calm and reserved, but excessive shyness is ridiculed.

The wedding ceremony is divided into four parts: (1) presentation of the marriage payment; (2) delivery of *kalimbubu* gifts (*luah kalimbubu*); (3) a meal; and (4) a formal visit to each group of relatives by the bridal couple. About 11 A.M. the guests assemble and seat themselves in the appropriate places. When the guests are seated, a number of mats are unfolded between the two booths where the first part of the ceremony takes place. The transfer of the brideprice usually takes about an hour to complete. Then the *kalimbubu* who receive the *berébere* and the *kalimbubu* who receive the *perkempun* simultaneously deliver their respective gifts to the couple. These usually consist of kitchen utensils – a cooking pot, a small kettle, two porcelain dishes and two porcelain bowls. In addition, a chicken, a mat and two pillows may be given. The bowls are filled with rice, and an egg, symbolizing fertility, is placed on top. Presentation of these gifts may take up to twenty minutes.

Immediately after this the food is served. The meal takes about an hour. It was not the custom in the past to make speeches at this time, but it is now, especially in cities and towns. After the meal, the bride and groom are introduced to the guests. A female relative leads the bride and a male relative leads the groom as they go from one group of relatives to another. Meanwhile, other guests also move about and exchange words with their relatives. Cigarettes and betel are exchanged and this marks the conclusion of the wedding ceremony. About two P.M. the guests begin to depart.

The wedding ceremony is highly significant because it "completes" the marriage. As already noted, the marriage may have been contracted and consummated long before the wedding ceremony, but the marriage is not considered complete until the adat debt has been paid. Prior to the wedding, a man may say, "Yes, my son has gotten married, but only *si arah raja* has been paid. It has not been ceremonialized (*ikerjaken*); the adat debt has not been paid."

The expression "adat debt" refers specifically and exclusively to the brideprice and to the ceremonial feast that must be held when it is transferred; and it is easy to see why no marriage is regarded as "complete" until this debt has been paid. Marriage establishes an alliance between two families and (by extension) their respective agnatic kin. At the wedding ceremony all of these relatives are brought together to witness the marriage and to signify their acceptance of it and of its implications for the wider ranges of the kin of the bride and groom. This they do simply by attending the wedding and participating in the feast. For the Karo, sharing food is a sign of social solidarity. To accept another man's food is to accept his friendship. The presentation and sharing of food is a nearly universal feature of Karo rituals, especially those in which relatives participate together. Thus, taking food with the other relatives of the bride and groom signifies acknowledgment and acceptance of one's position in the network of *senina-senina* and *anakberu-kalimbubu* relationships implied by the marriage. Prior to the wedding ceremony, the bride's relatives are not obliged to regard the groom and his relatives as their own relatives, and conversely for the groom and his relatives. Afterward, however, a relative of the bride may not say of the groom, "I do not know him because I have not eaten his food." At the wedding ceremony new relatives meet one another, and besides sharing a meal, they exchange cigarettes and betel and discuss the new relationships that have been established. The bride's father, for example, goes to the groom's mother's brother and introduces himself by saying, "I am the father of the bride. I have heard that you are the *mama* of my son-in-law, so we are *senina*."

Of course, there is also the matter of the brideprice. It is not without special significance that the several sets of *kalimbubu* are identified in the context of wedding ceremony, and in other contexts as well, in terms of the portion of the brideprice they receive (see above pp. 140-142, and below pp. 174-177). The implication is that these relationships are not established until the appropriate payments have been made. Thus, I was told by one man whose daughter's wedding had been delayed more than once, that he was quite embarrassed by the failure of her husband's family to meet the obligation promptly. He said most emphatically, "My own *kalimbubu* and other relatives have not received their share of the brideprice. Nor have they eaten the wedding feast. This means they do not know my son-in-law. I know there is gossip about it now." If the brideprice is not paid promptly when promised, the embarrassment and concern is not only on the part of the bride's family and relatives. Certain relatives of the groom are entitled to a portion of payment, and payments are made to the village chiefs on both sides, to coresidents of the house in which the couple will live, and to the *guru* who selected the auspicious day for the ceremony. Protracted delay in making these payments can become a public scandal.

MARRIAGE PAYMENT

The marriage payment is known as the *emas,* gold or money. It is divided into three parts: the *ulu emas,* the *tukor,* and the *si mecur.* Payment is said "to go three times" (*telu kali erdalan*) because each of the three parts is separately delivered. In Kuta Gamber and surrounding villages in 1961, the total amount of money transferred in the marriage payment varied from Rp. 2,500 to Rp. 3,000, divided as follows: *ulu emas* Rp. 15; *tukor* Rp. 1,500 or 2,000; and *si mecur* Rp. 1,000. Nowadays the total is not regarded as a substantial amount of money. The size of the marriage payment has not increased in direct proportion to the scale of inflation in the general economy. In the Dutch period the marriage payment varied from 40 to 60 florins. According to one of my informants, this sum would then purchase eight or twelve buffalo, the price of a buffalo then being about f.5. He pointed out that a buffalo is now worth about Rp. 4,000, so that today the marriage payment is not sufficient to purchase even one. This discrepancy has given rise to the popular notion that "women are very cheap now." One implication of the change is that nowadays only a poor family has any difficulty raising the money on its own, but in the past most families had to call on their relatives, especially their close *anakberu* and *sembuyak,* for assistance.

Ulu Emas

Ulu emas may be translated literally as the source or head of the gold, i.e., the marriage payment. This is the payment due to the family and agnatic kin of the groom's MB. In other words, it is allocated to the *kalimbubu* by birth of the groom, and they are described as the *kalimbubu* who receive the *ulu emas.* In the event of a cross-cousin marriage, this payment is not required. It should not be thought, however, that *ulu emas* is a fine payable in the event that a man does not marry a cross-cousin. It is rather a token sum, presented before the other parts of the payment, and it is intended to honor the groom's *kalimbubu* by birth, to signify that the bride becomes the classificatory daughter of the groom's MB, and that his agnates and the bride's become the *senina* of one another. Similarly, if a man marries a woman who is not his cross-cousin, a small payment may be made to the bride's immediate *anakberu.* Again, this is not a fine or compensation for depriving the bride's *anakberu* of a woman over whom they have a marital claim, for they have no such claim. The people say that, just as *ulu emas* unites the old and the new *kalimbubu,* this payment unites the old and the new *anakberu.*

Adat prescribed Rp. 15 for the *ulu emas,* but this sum is generally regarded as too small; it is commonly supplemented by contributions from both the groom's and the bride's fathers. Indeed, Rp. 15 is the price of a pack of cigarettes, and if the *ulu emas* were not increased, its distribution among a large number of people would pose a problem. At a wedding I witnessed in Kuta Gamber in 1961, the groom's father donated another Rp. 50 and the bride's father another Rp. 200. The *ulu emas* total Rp. 265. As prescribed by custom, it was distributed as follows:

1/3 x Rp. 265, rounded to Rp. 80 was given to the groom's MBs.

4/9 x Rp. 265, rounded to Rp. 120, was divided equally among the groom's MB's agnates who were present at the ceremony.

2/9 x Rp. 265, rounded to Rp. 65, was presented to "the four *kalimbubu*" of the groom. These were the residents of Kuta Gamber who are not members of the groom's clan, but of the other four clans. Each person received an equal share.

Tukor

The *tukor* is the main part or "trunk" of the marriage payment and it may be regarded as the brideprice proper. It is the only part of marriage payment refundable in case of divorce. *Tukor* itself means purchase, but this part of the payment is also called *batangna* or *unjuken. Batangna* means trunk, but the meaning of *unjuken* is obscure. This part of the payment goes to the bride's agnatic kin and to any of her kin who are classified under the same kinship terms as her agnates, e.g., her parent's uterine classificatory same-sex siblings (*senina sepemerèn,* FMZS and MMZD). Any of these who attend the wedding receives a share of the *tukor,* usually about Rp. 5. A distant agnate of the bride receives Rp. 10 to Rp. 20, a close agnate about Rp. 50, and her father keeps the remaining few hundred *rupiah.* There are no fixed rules about the distribution of the *tukor,* but there is some correlation between the size of the share and distance of the agnatic relationship.

Si Mecur

Si mecur may be translated literally as the tiny ones. This payment is divided into five parts: *rudang-rudang, berėberė, perkempun, perkembaren* and *perbibin.* In the wedding I witnessed in 1961 the *si mecur* totalled Rp. 980; the five subparts amounted to Rp. 150, Rp. 430, Rp. 220, Rp. 120, and Rp. 60, in the same order.

The *rudang-rudang* is for the clansmen (of different subclans) of the bride's father. The bride's father's lineage and subclan mates share in the *tukor.* According to my informants, this distinction among the bride's father's relatives was not made in the past; it is a recent development. Since to make the distinction is to imply that those who are only clan mates are less important relatives than those who are more closely related, the bride's father, when distributing the *rudang-rudang,* may refer to it as *tukor.* In this way he honors his clan mates by treating them as closer relatives than they really are.

The principal recipients of the *berėberė* are the bride's MB and his agnates, but the bride's FMB and his agnates are entitled to a share. Thus, from the point of view of the bride's father, who is the principal recipient of the marriage payment, the *berėberė* goes to his *kalimbubu* by marriage (the bride's MB, etc.) and to his *kalimbubu* by birth (the bride's FMB, etc.). "The four *kalimbubu*" of the bride's father also receive a share. At the wedding I witnessed, the *berėberė* was Rp. 430. Prior to its distribution by the bride's *anakberu,* Rp. 140, the value of two chickens, was set aside because these *kalimbubu* had an obligation to provide two chickens for the bride's first pregnancy rite. The remainder, Rp. 290, was divided as follows:

1/3 x Rp. 290, rounded to Rp. 100, for the bride's MB and his agnates.
2/9 x Rp. 290, rounded to Rp. 60, for the bride's FMB and his agnates
4/9 x Rp. 290, rounded to Rp. 130, for "the four *kalimbubu*" of the bride's father.

Each part of the marriage payment is handed over by one of the groom's agnates, for example his FB, to his *anakberu* who passes it on to the *anakberu* of the bride, who finally hands it over to the intended recipient. No part of the marriage payment can be directly given by the groom's father to the bride's kin. The principal recipient of some portion of the marriage payment normally discusses with his agnates present at the ceremony how the money should be distributed. For example, the bride's MB, after receiving Rp. 100 as part of the *berèberè,* says to his agnates, "As you see we have received Rp. 100; please advise me how to distribute it." Normally about half the money is distributed to distant agnates (subclan and clan) and the rest to close agnates of the MB. If the MB is unable to attend the wedding, his close agnates will take his place and his share will be sent to him.

The *perkempun* is for the bride's MMB and his agnates. They are the *kalimbubu* of the *kalimbubu* who receive the *berèberè,* and they are the bride's father's *puang kalimbubu* by marriage. They are entitled to a sum equivalent to half of the *berèberè,* they are obliged to donate only one chicken to the bride's first pregnancy rite. At the 1961 wedding, the *perkempun* was Rp. 220. Rp. 70 was set aside for the first pregnancy rite and the remainder, Rp. 150, was divided as follows:

1/3 x Rp. 150, rounded to Rp. 50, for the bride's MMB.
2/9 x Rp. 150, rounded to Rp. 30, for the lineage and subclan mates of the bride's MMB.
4/9 x Rp. 150, rounded to Rp. 70, for the clan mates of the bride's MMB.

The *perkembaren* is for the *anakberu* of the bride's father. At this wedding it totalled Rp. 120 and was divided as follows, and distributed in this order:

a. for the groom	Rp. 10
b. for the *anakberu* who open the *baka*	10
c. for the *anakberu menteri*	10
d. 1/3 of the remainder for the *anakberu tua*	30
e. 2/3 of the remainder for "the four *anakberu*"	60
	Total Rp. 120

It may seem paradoxical that the groom himself receives a portion of the marriage payment. However, as noted above, receipt of a share of the marriage payment signifies acceptance of certain rights or duties. This payment to the groom formalizes his status as the *anakberu* of the bride's father and brothers; the payment is called *upah erduhum,* the wage for taking the oath (as guarantor for the *kalimbubu*). The *anakberu* who open the *baka* (a container for storing valuables) are the bride's FZs and FZHs; the designation alludes to their knowledge of and involvement in the bride's father's family affairs (as the closest *anakberu* of his family). The *anakberu menteri* are the bride's FFZDs and their families. The *perbibin,* the last part of the *si mecur,* is given to the bride's MZs (cf. *bibi,* MZ, FZ).

Table 15 summarizes the data presented above on the composition and distribution of the marriage payment.

Nowadays, after transfer of the marriage payment, a form (marriage contract) supplied by the national government is completed. On this form the amount of the *tukor* is stated but no other part of the marriage payment is mentioned. (In customary law, too, the *tukor* is the most important part of the payment.) The contract is signed by five people, the bride's and groom's fathers and one each of their *anakberu,* and the bride's village chief. A special payment of Rp. 50 called *perpengulun* is made to the chief for legalizing the contract. Thus, in many cases the marriage is legalized twice, but the first time (when the marriage rite is performed by the chief before the wedding ceremony) has no status in national law. Before a marriage is legalized by a wedding ceremony and before submission of the contract signed by the chief, the marriage may be dissolved by negotiation between the parties concerned; afterward, it can be dissolved only in the courts at the regency level.

The marriage payment is concluded by distributing 100 or 120 cakes of gambier. At the Kuta Gamber wedding I attended, 100 cakes of gambier were distributed as follows:

a. *tastas namor*	3
b. *si niktik wari*	6
c. *si nangket amak*	10
d. *bukabuka rumah*	10
e. *si nggulé*	12
f. *gamber ingetinget*	59
Total	100

Tastas namor, literally, clearing the dew, is payable to the person who initiated the marriage agreement, namely someone who was involved in the early stages of the arrangement. *Si niktik*

Table 15

The Distribution of Marriage Payment

Part of the marriage payment	Allocated to
I. *Ulu emas*	1. groom's mother's agnates, i.e., his *kalimbubu* by birth
	2. groom's 'four *kalimbubu*'
II. *Tukor*	bride's natal agnatic group
III. *Si mecur,* 'the small ones':	
a. *rudang-rudang*	bride's distant agnates (clansmen)
b. *berébere*	1. bride's mother's natal lineage, i.e., the bride's F's *kalimbubu* by marriage
	2. bride's FM's natal lineage, i.e., her father's *kalimbubu* by birth
	3. bride's father's 'four *kalimbubu*'
c. *perkempun*	bride's MM's lineage, subclan and clan, i.e., the bride's F's *puang kalimbubu*
d. *perkembaren*	1. the groom, i.e., the new *anakberu*
	2. the bride's F's married sisters, i.e., 'the *anakberu* who open the *baka*'
	3. the bride's FFZD, i.e., the *anak-beru menteri*
	4. *anakberu tua*
	5. the bride's F's 'four *anakberu*'
e. *perbibin*	married sisters of the bride's mother

wari refers to the person who, through divination, chose an auspicious day for both the wedding and the marriage rite. This is usually a *guru.* Those who prepare the bridal suite are called *si nangket amak,* literally, those who hang the mats, i.e., the mats that divide the apartments in an adat house. *Bukabuka rumah,* opening the house, goes to the residents of the adat house in which the couple will live and symbolizes their incorporation in the house community. One informant remarked that the residents of the house will then be prepared to open the door in case the husband comes home late after the doors are shut and barred. The fifth part, *si nggulė,* is for those who prepare the food for the wedding. The last, *gamber ingetinget,* the gambier to remember, is given to those who are expected to remember the amount of the *tukor.* It is divided into three equal parts. One part is for the village chiefs of the bride and groom, another for the groom's party, and another for the bride's party. The presentation of each part is preceded by a formal explanatory speech, e.g., "Here is the gambier to remember. It will remind you of the amount of the *tukor.* Of the *tukor* amounting to Rp. 2,000, Rp. 1,500 has already been paid here today; the remainder will be paid in the future."

RESIDENCE AFTER MARRIAGE

As explained in Chapter 3, a newly-married couple usually does not establish a household of its own but join the household of the husband's parents. After a year or so, usually after reaping the first harvest from their own gardens, the couple becomes economically independent. "They kindle their own hearth," that is, they prepare their own meals from food they have grown. They may or may not continue to live in the same house as the husband's parents, but if they do, they acquire an apartment of their own as soon as possible. The usual dependence of the couple on the husband's father's family is a function of the obligation of the husband's father to provide for them until they are able to feed themselves from their own gardens. Thus, other arrangements are permitted under the adat and frequently occur.

In a sample of seventy-six marriages (all couples residing in Kuta Gamber in 1961), thirty-eight (60 percent) of the couples joined the household of the husband's parents immediately after marriage (see Table 16). The duration of their economic dependence ranged from three months to three years, though in the majority of cases (69 percent) it was one year (see Table 17). In some cases the couple did not reside with the husband's parents but did take their meals with them. One couple I knew immediately acquired an apartment in another house but, at first, took their meals with the husband's parents. After about three months, the husband's parents supplied the couple with a year's supply of rice which they cooked and ate in their own apartment. After that they were fully independent of the husband's parents. Such economic assistance given by the husband's (or wife's) parents is called *penjayon.* In this case, the HM explained, "My apartment is too small for two families, but I wanted them (her son and his wife) to take their meals with us for a while because, otherwise, people might say I am reluctant to have my daughter-in-law in the house." This case is included in category 6 in Table 16. In the other case included in that category, the couple lived in the wife's parents' village but in a different house and the *penjayon* was provided by the husband's parents.

Table 16

Temporary Residence After Marriage

Residence	No. of Couples
1. Household of HP	38
2. Household of HB	2
3. Household of HZ	1
4. Household of HFZ	1
5. Household of WP	8
6. Neolocal but *penjayon* from husband's parents	2
7. Neolocal without *penjayon*	24
Total	76

Table 17

The Duration of Residence in the Household
of the Husband's Parents After Marriage

Length of Stay	No. of Couples
3 - 9 months	6
1 year	25
1 ½ years	1
2 years	4
3 years	2
Total	38

In twenty-four cases (31.6 percent) the couple became residentially and economically independent immediately after marriage (category 7, Table 16). In five of these cases, the husband's parents were dead or they were in economic difficulty themselves and could not offer to help the couple. In two cases, the husbands had worked hard and saved money before getting married and so the couple did not require parental assistance. Five men who had regular cash incomes when they married (two teachers and three men engaged in trading in town) did not require parental assistance either. Of the twelve other couples in this category, eight (10 percent) joined the wife's parents' household. This is called *kekěla,* having a *kěla* (DH) in the household, and it usually happens when the couple intend to settle in the wife's village. Two couples joined the households of HBs. This happens when the husband's parents are dead when he marries. Residence is usually with an elder brother of the husband. In one case, the couple took up residence in the HZ's household, and in another, in the HFZ's household, in both cases with one of the husband's immediate *anakberu.* In these cases the husband's parents were dead and the husband was an eldest or only son.

LATER RESIDENCE

So far I have discussed immediate post-marital residence at the level of the household. We may now consider longer-term residence at the village level.

All Karo villages are compact settlements. The average village is no more than 150 meters long. Except for those larger villages which are divided into wards (see p. 13), no village is divided into socially significant clusters of houses. There is no section, for example, where the houses of members of one lineage are grouped together. Thus, in the case of an intravillage marriage, it is not considered significant that the couple may eventually reside closer to the husband's parents than to the wife's parents or vice versa. Moreover, it is not considered significant that the couple may or may not choose to remain in the same house as the husband's (or the wife's) parents, if the couple resided with them immediately after marriage. This depends, in large part, on the availability of an apartment. Wherever the couple choose to reside within the village, both sets of relatives will see them quite often, be able to offer them help when it is needed, and be able to get help from them. So, the Karo say, it matters only which village a couple choose to reside in, the husband's or the wife's, if theirs is an intervillage marriage. In my sample of seventy-six marriages, twenty-six (34.2 percent) were intravillage, fifty (65.8 percent) were intervillage.

Intravillage Marriage

A number of factors favor intravillage marriage. Villages are heterogeneous in terms of the descent group affiliations of their inhabitants and it is usually not difficult to find courtable and marriageable girls within one's own village. Moreover, parents prefer that their children marry into families they know fairly well, for as one informant put it, "We do not know the secrets of people who live far away." Also, it is easier to court a girl of the same village, not only because it is less difficult to arrange liaisons with her and to see her often, but also because the boys of other villages may resent a stranger coming to court their girls. A jealous or resentful resident of the village may stone the courting couple at night and drive the visitor home to his own village.

For the most part, the ancestors of the twenty-six couples who married within Kuta Gamber also resided there. The families with the longest histories of residence in the village are those who belong to the ruling lineage. Of the twenty-six husbands, four are members of this lineage, and another is a member of the same subclan as this lineage. His ancestors are said to have lived in the village since it was founded. Of the twenty-six wives, six are members of the ruling lineage and another two are sisters of the subclan mate just mentioned. Most of the husbands and wives who do not belong to the ruling lineage explained that their ancestors had lived in Kuta Gamber for the past three or four generations. One man's FFF married into Kuta Gamber and died there; his FF and his F also married Kuta Gamber women, and so has he. In two cases, the sons of families who recently migrated into Kuta Gamber have married girls who were born in the village.

Intervillage Marriage

Of the fifty intervillage marriages, twenty-seven (54 percent) were virilocal, twenty (40 percent) uxorilocal, and three (6 percent) neolocal (see Table 18). The first two categories may be subdivided according to whether the HF or WF was or was not a member of the ruling lineage of the village. In sixteen cases (32 percent of the cases of intervillage marriage), the couple chose to reside in the village of the HF where he was a member of the ruling lineage. In four cases, the couple chose to reside in the village of the husband's parents but where the HM was a member of the ruling lineage. In some of these cases, the ancestors of the HF had been residents of the village for two or more generations. In four of the seven other cases, the parents of neither spouse lived in the village but the sponsors of the couple were kin of the husband. Among these seven cases are two in which the husbands are sons of men who migrated to Kuta Gamber when the village in which they were living became depopulated. In two cases, the couples migrated to Kuta Gamber in order to establish tobacco plantations there. They were

Table 18

Types of Residence in Intervillage Marriage

Virilocal			
a.	HF's village	16	
b.	HM's village	4	
c.	Other	7	
			27
Uxorilocal			
a.	WF's village	10	
b.	WM's village	8	
c.	With WMM's patrilineal kin	1	
d.	Other	1	
			20
Neolocal			3
	Total		50

sponsored by kin of the husband, in one case a FFBS, in the other a distant classificatory brother. In two other cases, the couples settled where the husband's FZs had married before them. A son of one of these couples married and brought his wife to live in Kuta Gamber.

Among the twenty couples who chose to reside in the wife's village, ten resided where the WF was a member of the ruling lineage, eight where the WM was a member of that lineage, and one where the WMM was. In the one "other" case the couple moved to Kuta Gamber to grow tobacco and were sponsored by the WFB who happened to live there.

In the category of neolocal residence, I include only those couples who settled in Kuta Gamber without close or specific distant relatives as sponsors. In two of these three cases, the couple migrated to Kuta Gamber, again to grow tobacco there, and they chose this village because they were members of the same clan as the ruling lineage. In the third case, the couple came from a town where they had been living neolocally. Both husband and wife were engaged in petty trading in town and were not succeeding in making a living by this means. They were sponsored in Kuta Gamber by a friend to whom neither spouse was related.

The central tendency in intervillage marriage is for the couple to reside in the village of the HF. This is consistent with the patrilineal aspects of Karo culture, especially the value placed on solidarity among close agnates; and if a man resides in the village where his is the ruling lineage, this is felt to be a good thing because it helps to maintain the influence of that lineage in village affairs. The Karo are fully aware that if close kin and relatives by marriage do not live together in the same village, the social significance of their relationship cannot be fully realized. It should be clear, however, that the Karo value solidarity among *anakberu-kalimbubu* as well as *senina,* and it is difficult if not impossible to say which they value the most. Therefore, residence in the wife's village also is consistent with Karo kinship values and no stigma attaches to it. Indeed, in some circumstances – for example, if the wife has no brother to care for her parents in their old age – the choice may be backed by strong social approval. Understandably, in a number of cases the motive for uxorilocal residence is said to be strictly personal; for personal reasons the wife is reluctant to leave her natal village. One man who had married uxorilocally for this reason suggested that his wife was reluctant to leave home because she was strongly attached to her mother: "There seems to be no end to the business that links a daughter to her mother," he said. Sometimes a girl demands it as a condition of her consent to marry that she should not be forced to leave her own village, and occasionally a proposal (or a courtship) fails because the parties cannot reach agreement on the matter of postmarital residence. It is generally explained that a couple cannot expect to receive economic assistance from the wife's parents even if they choose to reside with them. It is true enough that the couple has no rightful claim to such support; but having a married daughter and her husband close at hand is a great advantage, so the wife's parents may offer some support even though not obliged to do so. They may be better able than the husband's parents to provide food for the newlyweds, and they may have an extra apartment for them to use. Since land is the corporate property of the village as a whole, access to land is not controlled by the parents of a couple. If a man chooses to reside in his wife's village, he enjoys full usufructuary rights there over any land that is not already in use. It follows that the wife's parents cannot entice a couple to settle with them by promising the couple some land. However, their village may have more or better land suitable for cash crops that the husband wants to plant.

The ready availability of land, at least for subsistence purposes, makes it possible for couples to migrate to villages in which they have distant kin or even no real relatives at all. A migrant must declare that he relinquishes membership of the village community from which he came and register himself as a member of the village community he wishes to join. Also, he must pay a formal visit to his new village chief and present him a liter or so of rice, an egg and a chicken. Having done this, the immigrant is one of the *anak kuta,* people of the village, and he too has full usufructuary rights over the village land. Those who have no close or distant kin in the villages in which they settle are not necessarily greatly disadvantaged. For them, relations of clanship and extended *anakberu-kalimbubu* relations gain an added significance and give them a place in community life. Similarly, if a man moves to his wife's village, he does not cut himself off completely from his agnatic relatives. He is almost certain to find subclan and clan mates there and the potential value of these *senina* relationships will be realized. A man living away from his natal village and his close agnates may be nominated to serve for them as an *anakberu* or *kalimbubu* in situations where their participation is required.

DIVORCE

Of the seventy-seven husbands in Kuta Gamber in 1961, nine had already experienced divorce; one of them remarried his former wife and another had divorced three wives. Most of these divorces occurred during the first or second year of marriage and before the couples had produced offspring; in two cases, however, divorce occurred after the couples each had one child. Of the seventy-eight wives (including one case of polygyny), seven had been divorced. One had remarried her former husband and one had divorced three husbands without having produced a child by any one of them. One had produced a child from her first marriage.[1]

The Karo expression for divorce is *mulih,* literally, to return, and the emphasis is on the return of the wife to the jural, if not physical, custody of her parents or brothers or other close agnates if the former are deceased.

The process of divorce is initiated by desertion; either spouse may be deserted by the other. According to adat, a woman should lodge her complaints with an *anakberu* (HZ, HFZ, etc.) and when she deserts her husband she should stay with these *anakberu.* In practice, however, a woman usually goes to her parental home, especially if it is nearby, when she decides to leave her husband. Her parents then report her action to a close *anakberu* of her husband (his married FZ, FZH, married Z, ZH, etc.). The *anakberu* then organize a family meeting which is attended by the husband and wife, the husband's brothers, and a few immediate *anakberu* of the husband. The matter is openly discussed and the woman's complaints are disclosed. On one such occasion, a woman said, "My intention to desert my husband this morning has been made clear. I want to divorce him. His laziness is intolerable and I am sick of nagging him about it. He promises to come and work in the field but does not show up. Instead he plays cards in the *jambor.* This has happened many times." The husband's elder sister also chided him and told him that he should assume more responsibility for his family's welfare in the future. As usual, the husband was given an opportunity to speak, and on this occasion he pointed out some exaggerations in the accusations of his wife but admitted that he was partly to blame. Sometimes these family meetings lead to reconcilation; after one or the other spouse or both of them

[1] The records on divorce obtained from the Karo Regency Court in Kabanjahe were unfortunately for one year only, January – December, 1959. In that year the total number of divorces was 58 for a population of about 140,000, a proportion much lower than in Java. In Sriharjo subdistrict, Central Java, for example, where I did demographic research in 1969-70, the average annual number of divorces for the years 1955-64 was 55 in a population of about 7,000 (see also Koentjaraningrat 1967:258-9, and *Statistical Pocketbook of Indonesia* 1963, p. 25).

have been reprimanded, and after he or she has promised to mend his or her ways, the deserting spouse may agree to return to his or her partner.

If the first family meeting fails to achieve a reconcilation, several further meetings must be held before the wronged and deserting spouse may bring the matter before the village chief and thereafter before the district chief (*camat*). The village chief and the district chief must be satisfied that the families concerned have seriously attempted to achieve a reconciliation, and so when a case is brought before them they ask, "Has the matter been fully discussed with the *anakberu* and *senina* of both sides?" When the village chief and then the district chief are satisfied that reconciliation is not possible, the district chief gives his permission for a divorce petition to be lodged before the court at the regency (*kabupaten*) level where the marriage is legally dissolved.

Divorce is strongly stigmatized but there are no set rules regarding the permissable grounds for divorce. Adultery by the wife or the husband's intention to take another wife are regarded as strong grounds for divorce. Other grounds commonly cited are: laziness, irresponsibility with the family income, ill-treatment of the spouse or the spouse's relatives, and incompatibility in temperament. Tamboen (1952:152) mentions childlessness, or having no son, as substantial grounds for divorce; but in such a situation the husband is more likely to look for a second wife than he is to divorce the first one for this reason alone.

Divorce not only terminates the jural relationship of husband and wife, it also dissolves the *anakberu-kalimbubu* relationship by marriage that was established by the union. As previously noted, the *kalimbubu-anakberu* relationship by birth is indissoluable; it is not affected by the divorce of the mother. The mother's brother remains "the visible god" of the offspring of the union, and the *impal* (cross-cousin) relations are not affected either. Even so, the quality of the social relations between these *kalimbubu-anakberu* by birth may suffer as a consequence of the social distance that arises between them. Jurally, and usually physically, the offspring remain in the custody of their father. Because their father is no longer the *anakberu* by marriage of their MB, etc., and no longer renders them services as such, the offspring may cease to have much to do with their *kalimbubu* by birth. Moreover, when their mother remarries and has other children by the subsequent marriage, the *kalimbubu-anakberu* relationship by birth established by this marriage largely supercedes the old one; her brothers take a greater interest in the offspring of her current marriage than they do in the offspring of her former marriage.

The general rule is that in the case of divorce, the husband has the right to demand repayment of the trunk (*tukor*) of the marriage payment. Indeed, in some circumstances, he has the right to demand repayment of twice the amount of the original *tukor*; for example, if his wife persists in demanding a divorce, but without sufficient grounds, he may do this. Conversely, however, if the husband persists in demanding a divorce without sufficient grounds, he may be granted the divorce but required to forfeit repayment of the *tukor.* Other parts of the marriage payment are not returnable in the event of divorce. In any event, the wife is fully entitled to the *kalimbubu's* wedding gifts – a cooking pot, a kettle and some porcelain bowls and dishes. Other family properties acquired during the marriage are divided equally between the parting spouses.

For a woman one of the most serious jural implications of divorce is that she has no permanent right of custody of her children. If a child is still nursing, she may keep it until it is weaned, but a child should join its father or other close agnates as soon as it is no longer physically dependent on its mother. I know of no instances in which a child of divorced parents in time became recognized as a member of his or her mother's lineage. However, I was told of one instance in which a girl was neglected by her close agnates who took custody of her; she joined her mother's household and subsequently became identified with her stepfather's (MH) lineage, subclan and clan.

Chapter Nine

Summary

It is not too much to say that Karo conceive of human social relations in general as social relations between relatives (*kadé-kadé*). It is said that for a Karo no other Karo is a non-relative, because everyone is a member of one of the five clans and because members of each of the five clans intermarry with members of the other four. Thus, the Karo sometimes describe or speak of their society as a whole as *merga si lima,* the five clans. This, however, is a manner of speaking, and it should not be taken to imply that Karo society is best understood as a "segmentary lineage system" (cf. Fortes 1953, 1969) or as an "asymmetric prescriptive alliance system" (cf. Needham 1962, 1966a; Dumont 1968). Also, the Karo recognize that in particular instances it may be virtually impossible for two persons to find a "meeting point" in their respective genealogies, though perhaps in principle they should be able to do so. They recognize too that, although it may be that all Karo are related in one way or another, many Karo are relatives of one another in name only.

Karo clans are not corporate descent groups; indeed, strictly speaking, they are not even descent groups (see p. 72). Moreover, Karo subclans and lineages, though they are descent groups, are not jointly liable for one another's actions or debts. Consistent with this, Karo lineages and subclans are not maritally allied to one another, though the Karo sometimes speak of such groups as though they were so allied. But again, this is only a manner of speaking, an idiom that is not inconsistent with the fact that the set of interpersonal and interfamilial relationships established by marriage is extended, in an attenuated form, to the agnatic relatives of the principal parties to the marriage. Nor is it inconsistent with the substitutability of agnatic kin for one another in those situations in which it is not possible for the principal or close *kalimbubu* or *anakberu* directly to fulfill their duties as such.

So when the Karo speak of descent groups A and B as related as *kalimbubu-anakberu* – as they may do in the context of a ritual or ceremony when numerous (but not all) members of groups A and B are gathered together and participate by virtue of their agnatic relations to the principal parties – they do not intend to assert that all members of these groups are equally related as *kalimbubu-anakberu.* They assert only that individuals who happen to belong to groups A and B stand as *kalimbubu-anakberu* of one another (though in varying degrees), and this because they are agnatic relatives of the principal parties. The idiom of lineage or subclan affiliation serves in these contexts as a convenient kind of verbal shorthand, as a summary indication of the identities of the sets of participants, but not as an assertion of the jural basis of their participation. It is true that the parties to a ritual or ceremonial transaction are for the most part members of two or a few lineages or subclans. However, it is not true that their lineage or subclan affiliations are the jural basis of their participation – except for members of those groups who are not close kin of the principals but who happen to reside in the village where the ritual or ceremony is held; and these people are invited to participate only as a matter of courtesy.

It is worth emphasizing that these observations apply to lineage segments, "one father" and "one grandfather," as well as to lineages and subclans. These are non-corporate groups and they do not enter into marital alliances. Of course, the close agnatic kin of a couple who propose to marry have a much greater interest in the marriage than do the more distant agnatic kin, for as close kin they are more directly implicated (by extension) in the *kalimbubu-anakberu* relationship established by the marriage. Even so, arranging a marriage is primarily the business of the domestic families of the prospective spouses. In arranging a marriage they have the responsibility to avoid creating a *kalimbubu-anakberu* relationship that would run counter to those already established among the close kin of the would-be spouses. Thus, close kin of the would-be spouses may raise this objection to their marriage, but these close kin (agnates or not) have no joint right to determine who marries whom. In other words, individuals are obliged to consider the feelings and interests of their close kin when they are about to marry or to consent to the marriages of their children, but these close kin are not jurally entitled to interfere, except in the special circumstance noted above.

If Karo sometimes describe their society as a whole as *merga si lima,* the five clans, they describe the foundation of their adat (custom) as *sangkep si telu,* the three intact, i.e., the three categories of relationship, *senina* (or *sembuyak*), *kalimbubu* and *anakberu.* The primary meaning of *senina* is sibling (of the same sex) but the expression serves also as the designation for the category agnate. *Sembuyak,* literally, of the same womb, also means agnate but its use is restricted to members of the same lineage or subclan; clan mates are not assumed necessarily to be agnatically related. Thus, members of the same lineage or subclan refer to one another as *sembuyak* or *senina,* and members of the same clan refer to one another as *senina.* Also, individuals who share the same *kalimbubu* or *anakberu* but who are not members of the same lineage, subclan or clan refer to one another as *senina* or by another more specific kinship term. The prototype for social relations between such persons is the same-sex sibling relationship with its emphasis on amity and solidarity. By extension, *senina* are implicated (though in varying degrees) in one another's *kalimbubu-anakberu* relationships. Of course, the norm and the expectation is that closely related *senina,* especially those of the same "one father" and "one grandfather" segments, will support one another and substitute for one another in their respective *kalimbubu-anakberu* relations. More distantly related *senina* also are potential substitutes in these relationships, and they owe one another hospitality and other minor courtesies.

The expressions *kalimbubu* and *anakberu* designate the parties to an interfamilial relationship, the relationship of a woman's family of orientation (*kalimbubu*) to her family of procreation (*anakberu*). An unmarried woman, like her unmarried brother, is a member of her father's domestic family (*jabu*) and of his lineage, subclan and clan. When she marries, she leaves her father's domestic family and, with her husband, forms a domestic family of her own. Although she remains a member of her father's descent groups, she is associated also with the descent groups of her husband; she is not spoken of as "a woman of" these groups but they are described as her *jé,* and members of these groups include her among their *senina.* Because the *kalimbubu-anakberu* relationship is one between domestic families, a married woman is regarded as one of the *anakberu* of her natal family, and the members of her natal family are her *kalimbubu.* Her husband and offspring also are the *anakberu* of her natal family, and, conversely, the members of that family are their *kalimbubu.* Of course, designation of a married woman (by her father and brothers) as *anakberu* does not imply that she is no longer regarded as an agnate but rather as an affine; it is her status as a *married* daughter or sister and, therefore, as a link between two families that is marked by her designation as *anakberu.* Both consanguineal and affinal (marital) relatives are included in the *kalimbubu* and *anakberu* categories, and Karo distinguish between *kalimbubu* and *anakberu* by birth and by marriage (see pp. 97-98).

Social relations between *kalimbubu-anakberu* are dominated by the jural inferiority of the *anakberu* with respect to the *kalimbubu.* Just as a woman is jurally inferior to her father and brothers, so her family is jurally inferior to the families of her father and her brothers. Consistent with this jural relationship, a man may marry his MBD for she belongs to a family that is already his *kalimbubu.* The interfamily relationship created by this marriage parallels the one already established between the families of his father and mother's brother. Conversely, a man may not marry his FZD because such a marriage would thoroughly confuse social relations between close relatives. His FZS, for example, would be both his *kalimbubu* (by marriage) and his *anakberu* (by birth). For this reason (and because she is a close kinswoman of his own generation), a man's FZD is regarded as like a ZH, an *anakberu.* It follows that the *anakberu* of one's *anakberu* also are one's *anakberu (anakberu menteri)* and, conversely, that the *kalimbubu* of one's *kalimbubu* also are one's *kalimbubu (puang kalimbubu).*

These categorical relationships are extended along agnatic lines to numerous individuals, families and even descent groups, so that ultimately every Karo individual should in principle be able to trace a *senina, kalimbubu* or *anakberu* relationship with every other Karo. It is, of course, this *extension* of *senina, kalimbubu* and *anakberu* relations ultimately to relatives of the same clans as the principal parties, that informs the notion that all Karo are relatives of one another, because each Karo belongs to one of the five clans and because the five clans intermarry with one another.

It is hardly adequate to say only that a man *may* marry his MBD but not his FZD, for there is much more to MBD-FZD marriage than that. The Karo do not assert that a man must or should marry a MBD if one of marriageable age is available when he chooses to marry; indeed, they quite definitely forbid some men from marrying their MBDs, if for example one of their brothers has already married a MBD. Nor do they assert that a man should or must marry an *impal,* a kinswoman designated by the same term as MBD. In short, the Karo do not prescribe or enjoin MBD or classificatory *impal* marriage, nor do they prescribe or enjoin marriage between men and their female *kalimbubu.* Conversely, they do not prohibit marriages between men and women who are not their *impal* or other kinds of *kalimbubu.* Furthermore, they permit marriages (without stigma) between men and their female *anakberu*, provided that the individuals concerned are distantly enough related that the *kalimbubu-anakberu* relation created by their marriage will not confuse social relations among their relatives. In general, a proposal to marry a female *anakberu* who is a third or more distant cousin or some other equally distant relative will not meet strong objections.

If the Karo do not "prescribe" MBD or classificatory *impal* marriage, neither do they "prefer" these forms of marriage, if by "prefer" we mean that they value and encourage these forms of marriage above all others. As already noted, they even prohibit marriage between MBD-FZS in certain circumstances. The numerical data presented in Chapter 8 indicate that there is no marked preference in practice for marriages between men and their MBDs or classificatory *impal.*

Of course, this is not to suggest that Karo do not value MBD-FZS marriage, though they value this form of marriage as one example of marriage between immediate *kalimbubu* and *anakberu.* The Karo say that such marriages prevent immediate *kalimbubu-anakberu,* especially MB and ZS, from becoming socially estranged from one another, as would necessarily happen if a man (the ZS) were to marry a woman other than his MBD, MBSD, or MFBSD. Thus, although a man is free to marry any woman he calls *impal* (provided that his brother is not already married to her sister) and, for that matter, free to marry many other kinds of kinswomen as well, if the woman he marries is not his immediate or close *kalimbubu,* the Karo say that their's is not a genuine or proper *impal* marriage or equivalent to such a marriage in its social implications.

It is not difficult to understand why it is that, despite the value placed on maintaining close social relations between primary and immediate *kalimbubu-anakberu* and on not allowing these social relations to become compromised by the fact that one's *kalimbubu* by marriage are not also one's *kalimbubu* by birth, the Karo nevertheless prohibit two brothers from marrying two sisters. If one of a set of brothers marries a MBD, this in itself is sufficient to maintain close social relationships between the whole set of brothers and the MB and his family (or the MBs and their families). It is sufficient because brothers are strongly implicated in one another's *kalimbubu-anakberu* relationships. Thus, the marriage of one of his ZSs to one of his daughters is sufficient to assure a man that all of his ZSs will remain socially close to him, though not all will remain equally close. The remaining ZSs are free (indeed jurally compelled) to contract marriages with women other than MBDs and thereby to diversify their marital alliances and commitments. It should be emphasized here that not even one of a set of brothers is duty-bound to marry one of their MBDs. The relevant obligation in this context is the moral obligation of a woman to do her best to get one of her sons to marry one of her brothers' daughters. This she can do only by encouraging her son, perhaps to the point of nagging him, to consider proposing to an eligible MBD.

Should a woman succeed in these efforts, the consequence is that the offspring of two families related as primary *kalimbubu-anakberu* are themselves related as primary *kalimbubu-anakberu* also; the WB-ZH relationship between two men is replicated between their respective sons. Strictly speaking, this does not amount to perpetuation, maintenance or even reinforcement of an interfamily alliance, for the allied groups are merely domestic families; since these are transient entities that do not endure from generation to generation, there can be no transgenerational perpetuation of the alliance between them. Even so, the families of a man's sons (especially that of his eldest son) are said to replace his own family, if only in a figurative sense. Thus, it makes sense to the Karo to speak of marriage between immediate *kalimbubu* and *anakberu* as perpetuating an established *kalimbubu-anakberu* relationship. They mean of course only that men who stand as primary and immediate *kalimbubu-anakberu* are not thereby drawn apart by new and necessarily conflicting rights and duties to other men. So much then for "perpetual alliance" in Karo society.

It needs to be added that, although Karo in general value marriage between immediate *kalimbubu* and *anakberu* and regard it as a good thing in and of itself, particular Karo in particular circumstances recognize that it may be just as well for particular immediate *kalimbubu* and *anakberu* not to intermarry. If social relations between two families are already strained, the heads of these families may not want their offspring to marry one another, and it would be best for them not to do so. In short, it is essential to distinguish between cultural and individual preferences and values in this area of social life as in others.

It should be clear enough by now that Karo society is not ordered as an "asymmetric prescriptive alliance system" in Needham's (1962) holistic sense. Even so, it seems appropriate to comment, from the perspective of the data and analysis presented here, on Needham's claim that the categories of such a system are "defined by descent and alliance" rather than by relations of genealogical connection (Needham 1962:83). Needham's argument refers specifically to systems of kin classification, and it is evident that the data on Karo kin classification (see Appendix II) would require him to argue that that system has the structure of an "asymmetric prescriptive alliance system of social classification." Also, he has argued (1966, 1971) that, although the available ethnographic data on the Batak leave much to be desired, these data demonstrate beyond a reasonable doubt that societies ordered holistically as "asymmetric prescriptive alliance systems" do in fact exist. If the situation among other Batak is much the same as it is among the Karo – and I am reasonably certain that it is – then Needham's model of "asymmetric prescriptive alliance systems" is a factitious type which has no counterpart in ethnographic fact (cf. Needham 1966a:1266), at least among the Batak.

The evidence provided by the Karo system of kin classification is considered in Appendix III, and so we need not consider it here. We may inquire, however, into the additional possibility that the Karo categories *senina, kalimbubu* and *anakberu* are "defined by relations of descent and alliance" rather than by relations of genealogical connection. It is important to note before doing so that this tripartite classification and the more differentiated system of kin classification are not simply isomorphic. In particular, it is not the case that the Karo system of kin classification consists in a further partitioning of the three major categories of *kadèkadè* (again see Appendix III).

In the preceding chapters much emphasis was put on the fact that the *kalimbubu-anakberu* relationship is primarily between domestic families, not between descent groups of any scale. This in itself makes it difficult to see how it could reasonably be argued that the relationship is "defined by descent and alliance," if by that expression we intend something more than relations of genealogical connection and marriage. It is true, of course, that because the *kalimbubu-anakberu* relationship is primarily between domestic families, both consanguineal and affinal relationships are equally basic elements in the relationship; the WF-DH relationship, for example, is just as basic or nuclear as is the MB-ZS relationship, at least in this context. (The arrangement in the system of kin classification is somewhat different; see Appendix III.) That is to say, certain affinal relations as well as certain consanguineal (genealogical) relations are included in the primary ranges of the terms *kalimbubu* and *anakberu*. These ranges are so narrow, however, that it is hardly appropriate to describe them in terms of "descent" and "alliance." Clearly, the most central relation is that of a married woman to her father – little more than a simple parent-child relation, and "little more" only in that the child must be, in addition, a married woman.

Relations of descent – if by this we mean either genealogical continuua greater than parent-child relations or membership of descent groups – enter into the definition of *kalimbubu-anakberu* relations only as criteria for their *extension* to broader ranges of relatives, and so only as criteria for the definition of structurally derivative categories of *kalimbubu* and *anakberu*. All families whose heads are agnatically related to the heads of the primary *kalimbubu-anakberu* families stand as *kalimbubu-anakberu* to one another as well.

The marital relations of parent-in-law to child-in-law and of sibling-in-law to sibling-in-law are by definition part of the *kalimbubu-anakberu* complex of relations, and again these are extended by reference to relations of common descent. Individual relations by marriage are not normatively entailed by previously established *kalimbubu-anakberu* relations between descent groups. Descent group affiliation is not normatively irrelevant to who marries whom – there is the rule of clan exogamy and the (not rigorously enforced) rule prohibiting marriage between men and their female *anakberu* of their FZDs' lineages and subclans – but there are no positive rules that enjoin marriage between persons solely on the basis of their respective descent group affiliations and the established *kalimbubu-anakberu* relations between those groups. Indeed, there are no positive rules of marriage of any kind.

Furthermore, the *puang kalimbubu-anakberu menteri* relationship by marriage is not a relationship between the wife-giving group of one's own wife-giving group and, conversely, the wife-taking group of one's own wife-taking group, such that, if it were, we might say that relations of marriage serve also as a basis for the extension of *kalimbubu-anakberu* relations. As noted above, the *puang kalimbubu-anakberu menteri* relationship follows from the requirement not to confuse social relations between close relatives by contracting marriages that would make them both the *kalimbubu* and *anakberu,* or *kalimbubu* and *senina,* or *anakberu* and *senina* of one another. It follows, that is, from the prohibition on marriage between FZD and MBS, the sister-like status of a man's FZD, and consequently the classification of FZDH as *anakberu.* Further still, the fact that persons who share the same *kalimbubu* or *anakberu* by marriage or by birth regard themselves as *senina* is not a consequence of extension of such relations by reference to relations of marriage. This follows from the rule of agnatic extension of *kalimbubu-anakberu* relations, for by this rule a man's BW's family, like his own wife's family, is a *kalimbubu* family; conversely, men who share the same *kalimbubu* (or *anakberu*) are like brothers.

In short, the principal *kalimbubu-anakberu* are certain close relatives, persons related as the members of a woman's families of orientation and procreation. The terms, and to a degree the social relations they connote, are extended to all families whose heads are agnatically related to the heads of those families. Descent is not a principle which defines these categories of relationship, certainly not the prime categories, but it is the major principle that governs their extension and therefore the definitions of their broad and derivative ranges and senses.

Finally, we may note the interesting fact that the Karo classify all subclans into five major categories herein described as clans, and they recognize five categories of relatives, *senina, kalimbubu, anakberu, puang kalimbubu,* and *anakberu menteri* (though these are reducible to three, since *puang kalimbubu* are special kinds of *kalimbubu* and *anakberu menteri* are special kinds of *anakberu*). Similarly, the Kachin, whose social structure resembles in many ways that of the Karo, assert that they are divided into five clans. Leach (1945 [1961:51], 1958:141) has argued that the number of Kachin clans is not simply an historical accident. He argues that the Kachin assertion that they "have five clans" is a "fiction," that "the Kachin need five patrilineal categories if they are to explain to themselves the workings of their own society, and the fiction that there are only five clans altogether serves just this purpose" (Leach 1958:141). Leach's argument is predicated on the assumption that Kachin "kinship terms" designate socially, rather than genealogically, defined categories, and that these categories are parts of a system of asymmetric prescriptive alliance between local unilineal descent groups. In his view, when the Kachin say that they have five clans, they are making an oblique statement about the "ideal" form of their social order, an order predicated on a distinction between five kinds of local descent groups (this from the point of view of the members of any particular local descent group).

The validity of this interpretation of the Kachin case is open to question, especially because there are good reasons to believe that the Kachin system of kin classification is just that, a system of *kin* classification (see Scheffler and Lounsbury 1971, especially pp. 199-206). It may be, nevertheless, that the Kachin claim to "have five clans" is, as Leach argues, not a mere historical accident. The Karo division of their numerous subclans into five clans, and only five clans, certainly permits them to *extend* *senina-senina* and *kalimbubu-anakberu* relations throughout the entire society, and to do so in a systematic fashion that would not be possible if they were to posit the existence of more than five clans. This limitation of the number of clans makes it possible to conceive of each Karo as necessarily related in one way or another to every other Karo, even if it does not make it possible for each and every Karo to specify exactly how he is related to every other Karo. Thus, by extending *senina-senina* and *anakberu-kalimbubu* relations along agnatic lines, ultimately to the clans of the principal parties, and by limiting the number of clans to five, the Karo manage to one degree or another to order all social relations among Karo as though they were social relations among the members of closely related domestic families.

Appendix I

The Siwah Sada Ginting Myth: A Summary

A Ginting man in Pakpak country moved from Kalasen to Tinjo where he became the village chief. His wife gave birth to a son on an inauspicious day. A *guru* said that the birth was *nunda,* meaning that it would cause the death of the child's father. To avert this, the son would have to be killed. The chief's younger brother, however, kept the baby alive in a field. There the child was fed on the sap of a *mbetung* tree and later on the milk of a white buffalo which was kept tethered close by under a banana tree. The baby was named Mantangken (to abstain from) with the implication that he and his descendants should abstain from eating white buffalo and the *galoh si tabar* (*pisang kapok,* I) variety of banana. They had also to avoid using the *mbetung* tree for firewood.

The child and his paternal uncle went to Karoland and founded a village, Layo Lingga. One day, when Mantangken was a young man, he went to the forest to snare game and to his astonishment caught a beautiful fairy who happened to fall from heaven. He married her and the place where they met is called Deleng Sibolangit (*deleng,* mountain; *sibolangit,* which smells like heaven).

Mantangken's oldest son, Tindang, was a wanderer and founded the village of Gurubenua. Tindang's wife gave birth to an unusual child who resembled a gourd (*gundur*) because it was covered by a membrane. The baby was kept in a jar (*guci*). Altogether ten children were born of this union and they all resembled gourds and were kept in jars.

Fortunately a band of seven Pakpak priests of great distinction (*guru* Pakpak *pitu sendalanen*) happened to visit Gurubenua and took their meal at the house of Tindang, the village chief. Tindang consulted the priests about the peculiarity of his children. "Give us a white cloth and seven layers of mats," said the priests. Then Tindang's *anakberu* and *kalimbubu* (not specified) came and put the babies on the cloth.

The priests in turn uttered their spells while their heads were covered with the white cloth. The membranes split one by one and the ten children, one girl and nine boys, were "hatched" (*naper*). The girl was called Bembem, the boys Babo, Gurupatih, Suka, Beras, Jadibata, Sugihen, Garamata, Bukit and Ajartambun.

When Bembem married, the distribution of her brideprice caused bitter conflict among her brothers. Jadibata intended to take the whole brideprice for himself without giving any of it to his eight brothers. They quarrelled. "Do not quarrel, my beloved brothers," said Bembem, "hear me, for all of you will win, all of you will gain." She conducted a ceremony on a hill and many people gathered, including her nine brothers. While an orchestra played, Bembem danced in full ceremonial attire in the midst of all the people. While dancing she said: "My brothers, this place will be the gathering place of people from the east and west; if you trade here, all of you will enjoy the market tolls." She then stamped her feet and vanished. At that place a market, Tiga Bembem (*tiga,* market), was founded. Her distressed brothers scattered. Suka went to Suka village; Bukit went and founded Raja Merahe village; Gurupatih went and founded Sarimunte village; Garamata founded Tobaland; Sugihen founded Sugihen village; Jadibata went to Juhar village where he founded a ward; Beras went to Juhar; and Ajartambun went back to Layo Lingga, the ancestral village.

Appendix II

Karo Kin Classification

Karo kinship terms are polysemic; each designates two or more semantically related categories of kin or affines. In addition, each term connotes those social and affective relations that are normatively ascribed or otherwise expected between ego and the category of relative designated by the term. These social and affective relations are ascribed primarily between ego and the principal (closest) types of relative denoted by the terms, but as the terms are extended so are some aspects, at least, of the social relations they connote (but see p. 149). In this Appendix, however, I am concerned only with the genealogical and affinal denotata of Karo kinship terms. A structural semantic analysis of these data follows in Appendix III.

A relatively full list of the denotata of Karo kinship terms is presented in Table 19 and Figures 12-15. The principal or structurally primary denotata of the terms are listed in column 2 and their derivative denotata are listed in column 3. The principal or structurally primary category designated by each term may be designated not only by the simple term but also by that term suffixed by the form *kal*. In other contexts, as in this one, *kal* means much the same thing as English "real." Thus, for example, Karo *bapa* means father, in the sense of genitor, and the term is extended to a variety of other kintypes. To distinguish his own or actual father from classificatory fathers (other relatives called *bapa*), a Karo may say *bapa kal,* real father, and the various classificatory fathers may be designated by relative product expressions which describe the genealogical relationship between ego and the designated kinsman, e.g., FB may be referred to as *senina bapa,* same-sex sibling (of) father. Alternatively, a parent's same-sex sibling may be distinguished from the parent with whom he or she is otherwise terminologically identified by referring to birth order in the sibling set. This is done by adding the expressions *tua,* senior, *tengah,* middle, and *nguda,* junior, to the appropriate kinship term. Thus, for

Table 19

Karo Kin Classification

	1 Term	2 Focus	3 Other Denotata
1.	*nini*	PP	All G+2 relatives
2.	*kempu*	CC	All G-2 relatives
3.	*bapa*	F	FB, FFBS, FMZS, MFZS, MH, MZH, HMB, WFZH, FZSWF
4.	*nandé*	M	FW, FBW, HMBW, FMZSW, FZSWM
5.	*bibi*	MZ, FZ	MFBD, MMZD, FMBD, FFBD, FMZD, MFZD, FFZD, WFZ, HFZ, HM, HMZ, HFBW
6.	*simetua*	HM	None
7.	*mami*	MBW	MMBD, WM, WMZ, WFBW, WMBW, MMBSW, WMMBD, WMMBSW
8.	*bengkila*	FZH	FFZS, FFZDH, HF, HFB, HFZH, HMZH, ZHF, FZDHF
	ajinta	HF	None
9.	*mama*	MB	MFBS, MMZS, MMBS, FMBS, WF, WFB, WMB, WMZH, WMMBS, WMMBDH
10.	*senina*	♂B, ♀Z	♂FS, ♂MS, ♀FD, ♀MD, ♂FBS, ♂MZS, ♀FBD, ♀MZD, ♂FMBDS, ♀FMBDD, ♂MFZSS, ♀MFZSD, ♂MMZDS, ♂FFBSS, ♀MMZDD, ♀FFBSD, WFZS, HMBD, ♂MBDH, ♀FZSW
11.	*senina sepemerén*	♂MZS, ♀MZD	♂MFBDS, ♀MFBDD

Table 19

Karo Kin Classification (Contd)

12.	*senina siparibanen*	WZH	H of any clan 'sister' of one's wife
13.	*cimbang*	HBW	W of any clan 'brother' of one's husband
14.	*turang*	♂Z, ♀B	♂FD, ♂MD, ♀FS, ♀MS, ♂FBD, ♂MZD, ♀FBS, ♀MZS, ♂FMBDD, ♂MFZSD, ♀FMBDS, ♀MFZSS, ♂MFBDD, ♀MFBDS, ♂FFBSD, ♀FFBSS, WFZD, HMBS, ♂MBDH, ♀FZSW
15.	*turang sepemerén*	♂MZD, ♀MZS	♂MFBDD, ♀MFBDS
16.	*impal*	MBC, FZC	MFBSC, FFBDC, MMZSC, FMZDC, MMBSS, FFZDC, FMBSC, FFZSC, WZ, WB, WFBC, WMZC, HZ, HB, HFBC, HMZC, HFZD
17.	*turang impal*	♂FZD, ♀MBS	♂FFBDD, ♀MFBSS
18.	*éda*	♀BW	♀FBSW, ♀MBSW, ♀MZSW, ♀SWM
19.	*beru*	HZ	HFBD, HFZD, HMZD, ♀DHM
20.	*silih*	WB, ♂ZH	WFBS, WMBS, ♂FBDH, ♂FZDH
21.	*turangku*	WBW, HZH	WMBD, HFZS, ♀DHF, ♂SWM, ♀DBWBD, ♂FZHZS, ♂MMBSD
22.	*anak*	C	♂BC, ♂MZSC, ♂FBSC, ♂MBDC, ♂ZSW, WZC, WBDH, ♀ZC, ♀MZDC, ♀FBDC, ♀FZSC, HBC, HZSW

Table 19

Karo Kin Classification (Contd)

23.	*berébere*	♂ZC	♂MZDC, ♂FBDC, ♂FZDC, ♂FZSC, ♂FZDC, DH, ♂BDH, ♀ZDH, WZDH, HZC, HZDH, HBDH
24.	*kéla*	DH	♀ZDH, HZDH, WZDH
25.	*permén*	♀BC	♀FBSC, ♀MZSC, ♀MBSC, ♀MBDC, ♂MBSC, ♀SW, WBC, WBSW, WZSW, HBSW ♀BSW
26.	*permain*	♂SW	♂BSW, ♂MZSSW, ♂FBSSW, WZSW, ♂SWBW
27.	*silangen* (*diberu,* colloquial)	W	♂BW, wife of any 'brother' of male ego's clan
28.	*perbulangen* (*dilaki,* colloquial)	H	HB, HFBS

Figure 12. Man's terms of reference for cognates.

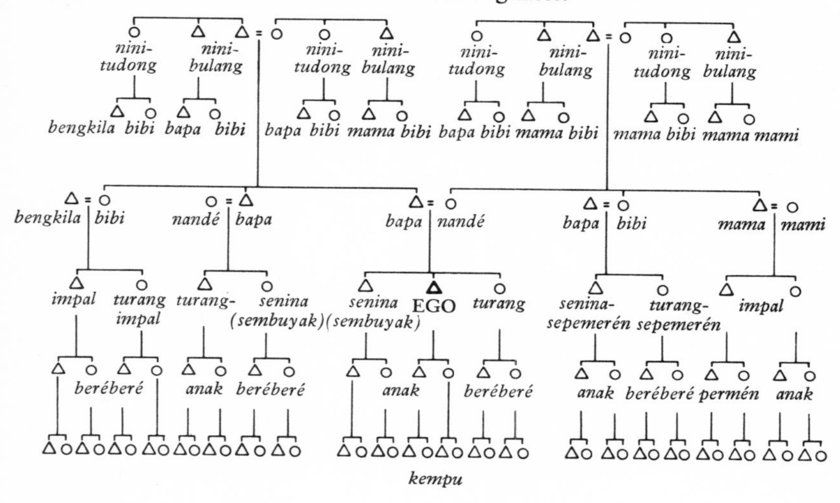

Figure 13. Woman's terms of reference for cognates.

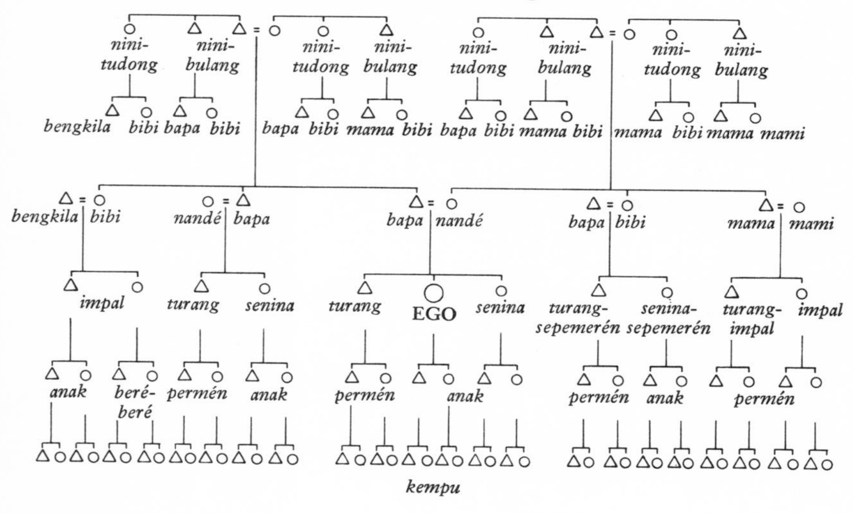

Figure 14. Man's terms of reference for affines.

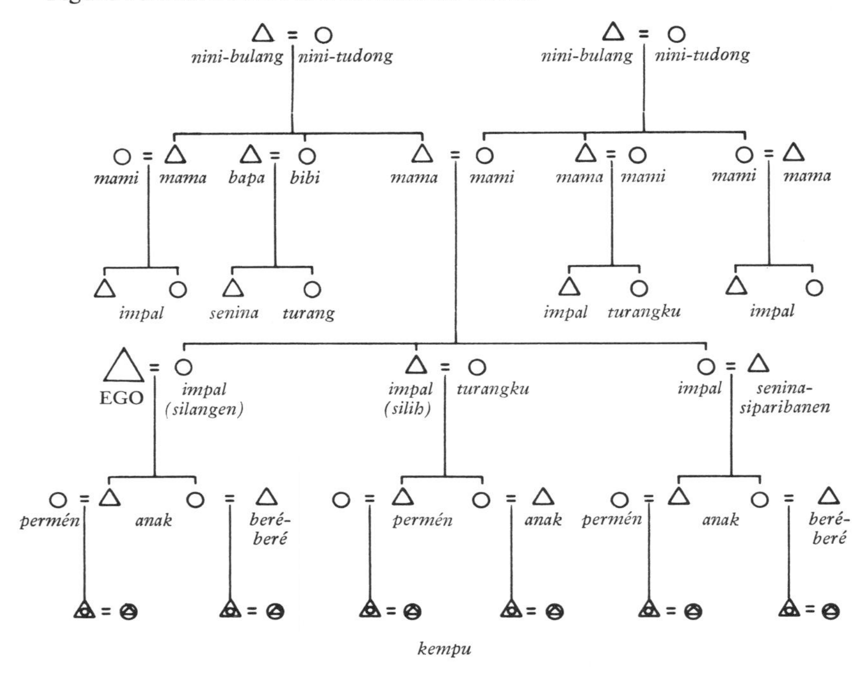

Figure 15. Woman's terms of reference for affines.

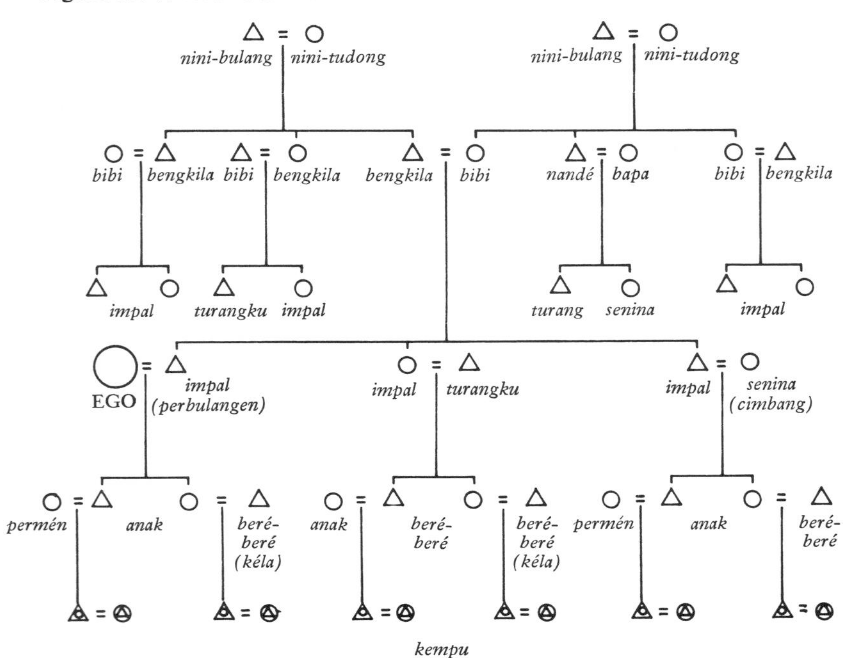

example, the father's eldest brother is sometimes referred to as *bapa tua,* and his youngest brother is sometimes referred to as *bapa nguda,* while his other brothers are *bapa tengah.* These expressions are never used in reference to one's father himself. If one's father is the eldest of a set of brothers, then one has no *bapa tua,* and if one's father is the youngest of a set of brothers, one has no *bapa nguda.* However, if one's father is one of several brothers who are intermediate in birth order in the sibling set, then one may have *bapa tengah.*

These same expressions may be used to distinguish among mother's brothers and father's sisters. Since MZ and FZ are both designated *bibi,* the expression *bibi nguda,* for example, is potentially ambiguous; it may denote mother's youngest sister or father's youngest sister. If the social context of use of the expression does not render the expression unambiguous, it may be clarified by a relative product expression, e.g., *turang bapa,* FZ, or *senina nandė,* MZ.

It is important to note that the qualifications with regard to birth order in the sibling set are applicable only in the context of reference to one's own parents' own siblings. Karo do not distinguish among parents' parallel cousins in this way. Also, the distinctions are made only in the context of indirect reference to the designated kinsman. To use them in direct address would be regarded as impolite; as already noted, Karo avoid mention of differences in degree of relationship where it is not necessary to draw attention to them.

In addition to the terms listed in Table 19, the following expressions sometimes are used. Relatives of the third ascending generation may be called *entė*; those of the fourth ascending generation may be called *entah,* and those of the fifth *empong.* In general, however, all such relatives are addressed or referred to as *nini,* grandparent. This term may be used metaphorically in reference to an aged stranger. There are no special terms for relatives of the third descending generation or below; all such relations are designated *kempu,* grandchild. Where the kinship term itself is not sex specific, as in the case of *nini,* sex of the designated relative may be signified by addition of the expression *bulang* (man's headdress) or *tudong* (woman's headdress). Further, clan names in simplified form may be added to the expression *nini* in reference to a grandmother but not in reference to a grandfather. Thus, a grandmother whose natal clan is Tarigan may be called *nini tigan,* and a grandmother whose natal clan is Ginting may be called *nini iting* or simply *iting.* In some parts of Karoland there is another term, *laki,* for *nini bulang* or grandfather.

As noted in the text, matrilateral parallel cousins are regarded as special kinds of classificatory siblings. Those of the same sex are *senina sepemerén,* those of the opposite sex are *turang sepemerén.* The expression *sepemerén* signifies that their mothers are sisters or classificatory sisters, or more broadly that their mothers belong to the same clan. There is no comparable expression to distinguish paternal parallel cousins from other kinds of classificatory siblings.

Although cross-cousins in general are *impal,* a man's FZD is regarded as a special kind of *impal,* one who is like a sister in that she is not marriageable; she is designated *turang impal.* Conversely, a woman's MBS is her *turang impal,* also. As previously noted (p. 166), a man's MBD also is said to be like his sister, but she is marriageable and is not designated *turang impal* but simply *impal.* Conversely, a woman's FZS is not designated *turang impal* but simply *impal.*

Also as noted in the text, the expressions *senina,* same-sex sibling, and *turang,* opposite-sex sibling, are used idiomatically with the senses "same-sex member of one's own clan" and "opposite-sex member of one's own clan," or "clan brother" and "clan sister." In these uses the terms have no generational signification.

In general, the simple terms given in Table 19 are employed in direct address as well as in indirect reference to the designated relative if he or she is older or generationally senior to ego. The exceptions are that the terms *mami,* WM, and *bengkila,* HF, are not employed in direct address. This is because one is obliged to avoid his or her parent-in-law of the opposite sex, and this includes a prohibition on speaking directly to such relatives. This prohibition is extended to other close *kalimbubu* and *puang kalimbubu* by marriage of a man; similarly, a woman avoids the brothers and classificatory brothers of her HF, the husbands of the sisters and classificatory sisters of her HM, and her HFZH and HFFZDH, all of whom are her *bengkila.*

In ego's generation all junior relatives are addressed by personal name and all senior relatives are called *kaka,* regardless of whether they are kin or affines. In some parts of Karoland, however, as in Kuta Gamber and Liren, brothers-in-law (who are *impal*) use the term *silih* self-reciprocally as a term of direct address. In this generation, *turangku* avoid one another and so the term is not used in direct address, nor does the junior one call the other *kaka.* In general, children, grandchildren and other relatives of their generations are addressed by personal names. The exceptions are that a man does not directly address his SW as a *permèn* or *permain,* nor does a woman directly address her DH as *berèberè* or *kèla,* again because these relatives must avoid one another and may not speak to one another.

It is clear enough that the distribution of most Karo kinship terms beyond their focal denotata is fairly consistent with the division of relatives in general (*kadèkadè*) into three major categories (*senina, anakberu, kalimbubu*). That is, the denotata of many terms are confined exclusively to one or the other of these three categories. (The obvious exceptions are *nini,* grandparent, *bibi,* MZ, FZ, and *impal,* cross-cousin.) As is shown in appendix III, this partial correspondence is a product of Karo rules of kin-class extension, and it is not true that these terms are basically the names of subcategories of the three major categories of relative. The tripartate division of *kadèkadè* and the much more complex division of the same category into numerous more specific kin classes are different but complementary systems of classification.

Because of this complementarity, it is possible for a Karo to deduce the appropriate kin class of another person from his knowledge of their mutual relations as *senina-senina* or *anakberu-kalimbubu,* and this procedure is often used as a shortcut to direct genealogical reckoning of kin-class membership. Thus, for example, two men who have a common *anakberu* may conclude that they must be related as *senina,* that is, as agnates of one kind or another; and so too for those who have the same *berèberè,* mother's clan (also *kalimbubu* by birth). If they know no more about their genealogical and marital relations that, it has to be presumed, resulted in their having a common *anakberu* or *kalimbubu,* they have to be content to regard one another as *senina,* agnates of some (unspecified) kind.

But if they are able to discover what some other members of their lineages or clans call or called one another, then they may be able to compute a more specific kin-class relationship for themselves. That is, in order to discover what specific kinds of *senina* (agnates) they are to one another, they have to have some knowledge of their relative generational status. Thus, for example, if two men discover that they have an *anakberu* in common, they then discuss their various agnates until they find two or more who they know call one another, say, father and son. Then on the basis of their knowledge of what these men call them, they can decide what to call one another. For example, if A calls his agnate father and B calls his agnate grandfather, and these two agnates call one another father and son, A and B may conclude that they are related as *senina* in the more specific sense of same-sex (classificatory) sibling. Of course, they are able to do this by generalizing from their knowledge of the primary senses of the kinship terms and how these are related to one another.

It sometimes happens that, when reckoning kin classification in this way, Karo discover that they are related in more than one way, or they may find that they are unrelated at the lineage or subclan level. (Since the five clans are regarded as related as both the *anakberu* and *kalimbubu* of one another, knowledge of clan affiliation alone is an insufficient guide to more specific kin-class reckoning, though as previously noted, members of the same clan regard one another as *senina* or *turang* in the broad sense of agnate.) Where multiple relationships are discovered and in one way the persons concerned are *senina-senina* but in another *anakberu-kalimbubu,* the *anakberu-kalimbubu* relationship has priority. In this way, boys and girls who meet for the first time (as nowadays is fairly common in towns and cities) maximize their *impal* rather than their possible *turang* relations. Indeed, when they are unable to discover some "meeting point" in their genealogies and have to suppose that they are not related, they call one another *impal.* Since they are not actually MBD-FZS or otherwise closely related as *anakberu-kalimbubu,* they are free to court one another.

Finally, it may be noted that even though two Karo may be fairly closely related and may know their exact genealogical relationship, they may explain to another that they are, say, *bapa* (father) and *anak* (son) because they have a *kalimbubu* by birth in common. Thus, a man may explain that he calls his MFZS *bapa* because that man's *kalimbubu* by birth and his *kalimbubu* by birth are the same. It should not be thought, however, that this implies that their father-son terminological relationship follows from the fact that they have a common *kalimbubu* by birth, or that they intend to assert that all persons who have common *kalimbubu* by birth are related as father-son (it should be evident that this is not true). The fact that they share the same *kalimbubu* by birth follows from the fact that their mothers belong to the same lineage, and their relationship as father-son follows from the fact that one is the cross-cousin (*impal*), and specifically the FZS, of the mother of the other. Karo can and often do explain their relations in this way as well as in terms of *anakberu* and *kalimbubu* relations. When they explain their relations in this latter way, they are emphasizing the ways in which their families, rather than they as individuals, are related; they are not stating general rules of kin-class reckoning.

Appendix III

A Structural Semantic Analysis of the Karo System of Kin Classification

by H. W. Scheffler

The data presented in this study for the Karo system of kin classification are unusually full and detailed, in comparison with the published data on other Indonesian systems of kin classification. It is possible therefore to construct a formal semantic model of the Karo system which has a fair probability of being the correct model, i.e., that model of the system which comes closest to replicating its essential features or, in other words, its structural principles and their interrelations. The analysis presented below is based on the assumptions and procedures explicated in detail in Scheffler and Lounsbury (1971). The data presented by Dr. Singarimbun, especially those concerning the polysemy of the terms, reveal that the assumptions are valid in this instance, and therefore the procedures are applicable.

ANALYSIS

As indicated in Scheffler and Lounsbury (1971:87), the first step in analysis is to establish the focal referent(s) of each term. These are the kintypes that fall within the ranges of the terms when used in their primary senses. Dr. Singarimbun has already isolated these referents for us and presented a list of them in Table 19 (column 2). He has indicated, too, that when used to denote these kintypes the terms may be lexically marked by postfixing the expression *kal,* true or real. That is to say, the use of a kinship term in its primary sense may be signified by this means.

The next step is to establish componential definitions for the terms at their primary ranges of denotation. This step presents only a few special analytical difficulties.

First, it should be noted that the tripartite distinction made in Scheffler and Lounsbury (1971:116-17) between kin, step-kin and affines or in-laws, and posited there as a general feature of systems of kin classification (though one that may be expressed in a variety of ways), appears to be relevant in this instance. So far as we know (from the data presented here), the Karo language features no single-term designation for the category of relatives by blood (kin in the strict sense). Even so, Karo culture does include or posit such a category of relatives. The Karo suppose that they are related by blood to both parents, and it must follow that they suppose they are related by blood to their parents' parents, their parents' siblings, and so on. They do not suppose that they are necessarily related by blood (genealogically) to such relatives as their FZHs (*bengkila*) or their MBWs (*mami*), though of course they may be (since, e.g., MBW may be MMBD). It follows that these terms (*bengkila* and *mami*) do not signify that the designated relative is supposed to be a relative by blood. Neither do they signify that the designated relative is an in-law, i.e., spouse's parent or sibling or, conversely, child's spouse or sibling's spouse. There are other special terms which designate these (or some of these) in-law relationships. Therefore, *mami* and *bengkila* must be special step-kin terms. Most other step-kin types are denoted by consanguineal terms. Indeed, the categories designated by *mami* and *bengkila* have the status of subclasses of the consanguineal categories designated by *mama* (MB) and *bibi* (FZ), respectively.

Note that although MBW and FZH receive special designations, their reciprocals, HZC and WBC, are designated *berébere* and *permén* respectively, i.e., they are merged terminologically with ♂ ZC and ♀ BC. If HZC is a classificatory ♂ ZC, it follows that the reciprocal type of relative, MBW, is a classificatory MB, though a special kind (and not called or referred to as *mama,* presumably because she is a female, not a male, relative). Similarly, if WBC is a classificatory ♀ BC, it follows that the reciprocal type of relative, FZH, is a classificatory FZ, though a special kind (and not called or referred to as *bibi,* presumably because he is a male, not a female, relative). An analogous arrangement occurs in the Siriono system of kin classification (Scheffler and Lounsbury 1971:119-21), where the classifications of FZH as *ari,* grandfather, and of MBW as *ami,* grandmother, are governed at least in part by an extension rule that operates in this system also (see below p. 225).

The special affinal terms also are subclass designations. This becomes apparent when we consider that the reciprocals of *kėla,* DH, are *mama* (WF) and *mami* (WM). That is, WF is a classificatory mother's brother, and WM is a classificatory mother's brother's wife (ultimately also a kind of classificatory mother's brother). The reciprocal of both *mama* and *mami* at their primary ranges of denotation is *berėberė,* ♂ ZC. It must be then that those relatives who are *kėla* are also *berėberė; kėla* is a special designation for that *berėberė* with whom a couple's daughter has established a spouse relationship (as opposed to those *berėberė* who are merely potential spouses for their daughter). This need not imply that a woman is obliged to marry her FZS or some other *berėberė* of her father (and mother); it implies only that, whomever she marries, that man is to be regarded as a special kind of *berėberė* by her parents.

Somewhat similarly, there are special designations for HM, *simetua,* and HF, *ajinta,* and for ♂ SW, *permain,* but no corresponding special designation for ♀ SW. SW for female ego is simply *permen,* a kind of woman's brother's child. Thus, HF, *ajinta,* must be a special kind of *bibi,* FZ. This is shown further by the fact that HM may be referred to or addressed as *bibi* and HF as *bengkila.*

A man's WB and ZH may be designated *silih* or *impal.* This shows that those relatives who are *silih* also are *impal;* it must be that *silih* denotes those *impal* who are the brothers of the woman whom a man has actually married, and, conversely, those *impal* who are actually married male ego's sister – as opposed to those *impal* who are merely cross-cousins or classificatory cross-cousins. Of course, a man is not obliged to marry an *impal,* or any other particular type or kind of kinswoman, and so his WB or ZH is not necessarily a man whom he classified as *impal* prior to his marriage. Even so, as is shown below, one of the extension rules of this system is that WB and ZH as designated kinsmen are to be regarded as structurally equivalent to MBS and FZS, respectively. That is to say, WB is assimilated to the terminological status of MBS and ZH to the status of FZS, but again WB and ZH may be distinguished from other *impal* by the expression *silih.*

It is interesting to note that despite the fact that WB is a *kalimbubu* and ZH is an *anakberu,* the term *silih* is self-reciprocal and may denote either of these relatives. *Silih,* though its use is restricted to males, is comparable to the English expression brother-in-law. Because of its self-reciprocity, it is doubtful that the term has any connotations of social seniority or juniority, i.e., connotations having to do with dominance and submission in social relations.

Éda, ♀ BW, and *beru,* HZ, likewise designate special kinds of *impal,* the *impal* who have married a woman's brother or classificatory brother and, conversely, the sister and classificatory sisters of a woman's husband.

It would seem that the spouse terms are not designations for subclasses of *impal.* As noted above, a man is not obliged to marry an *impal.* It might still be, however, that whomever he marries, he is obliged by the rules of kin-class extension to regard his wife as structurally equivalent to his MBD for purposes of designation of her or her relatives. But, as is shown below, while the extension rules of this system include rules that equate siblings-in-law (as designated relatives) with cross-cousins, they do *not* include a rule that equates spouses with cross-cousins. It would appear, then, that a man's wife is denoted by the expression *impal* if and only if she was his *impal* prior to their marriage. If she was not, she herself is not assimilated to the *impal* category, but her siblings are. Similar considerations apply to the reciprocal relationship, woman's husband.

It seems that *turangku* designates a special subclass of *impal.* Again, as will be shown below, one of the equivalence rules of this system is that male ego's WB as a linking relative is to be regarded as structurally equivalent to female ego's brother. It follows that WBW is structurally equivalent to ♀BW, *impal.*

Finally, the expressions *entė, entah* and *empong* designate special subclasses of classificatory *nini,* grandparent. That is to say, *nini* is extended to relatives of all ascending generations (greater than G+2), but those in G+3 may be distinguished further by the expression *entė,* those in G+4 by the expression *entah,* and those in G+5 by the expression *empong.* There are no corresponding subclass distinctions among the reciprocals in the descending generations.

With these preliminary considerations out of the way, we may proceed to specify componential definitions for the primary senses of Karo kinship terms.

Componential Definitions

The appropriate dimensions of opposition and their relevant values are as follows.

1. Relative (R) *vs.* not a relative (nR). The former category is divisible into kinsmen (K, related by blood), step-kin (SK) and in-laws or affines (A). For a detailed discussion of this division, see Scheffler and Lounsbury (1971:117-17).
2. Lineal (L, direct ascendant or descendant kinsman) *vs.* collateral (C, cognate but not a direct ascendant or descendant). Because true (*kal*) siblings are those relatives who share the same mother *and* father, not merely the same mother *or* father, we may distinguish a special subclass of collateral relatives in ego's own generation, i.e., co-lineal kin or full siblings. This category is represented by the sign Co-1 in the componential definitions below.
3. Generational removal. This is a five-valued dimension, G+2, G+1, G=, G-1, G-2.
4. Parallel (//) *vs.* cross (X). Stated in the most general terms, this is the familiar same- *vs.* opposite-sex opposition. The exact locus of the comparison varies with genealogical context as follows. For co-lineals (siblings), the comparison is between ego and alter (indicated by $//_2$ *vs.* X_2 in the componential definitions). For other alters in G= who are the foci of kin categories (only *impal*) and for alters in G+1, the comparison is between sex of ego's linking parent and the sex of that parent's sibling who is the designated or linking kinsman; conversely, for alters in G-1 the comparison is between sex of ego and the sex of ego's sibling who is the linking kinsman (indicated by ($//_1$ *vs.* X_1 in the componential definitions).

5. Sex of alter: male (♂) *vs.* female (♀).
6. Sex of ego: male (♂E) *vs.* female (♀E).

Using these dimensions and their values, we may specify the primary senses of the principal Karo kin terms as in Table 20.

Although the step-kin categories *mami* and *bengkila* are subclasses of the kin categories *mama* and *bibi,* they may be given componential definitions. The designated relatives are spouses

Table 20

Primary Senses of the Principal Karo Kinship Terms

	Term	Focus	Definition
1.	*nini*	PP	(K · L · G+2 ·)
	nini bulang	FF, MF	(K · L · G+2 · ♂)
	nini tudong	FM, MM	(K · L · G+2 · ♀)
2.	*kempu*	CC	(K · L · G-2 ·)
3.	*bapa*	F	(K · L · G+1 · ♂)
4.	*nandé*	M	(K · L · G+1 · ♀)
5.	*anak*	C	(K · L · G-1 ·)
6.	*mama*	MB	(K · C^1 · G+1 · X_1 · ♂)
7.	*berébere*	♂ZC	(K · C^1 · G-1 · X_1 · ♂E)
8.	*bibi*	FZ, MZ	(K · C^1 · G+1 · · ♀)
9.	*permēn*	♀BC	(K · C^1 · G=1 · X_1 · ♀E)
10.	*senina*	♂B, ♀Z	(K · Co-1 · G= · $//_2$)
11.	*turang*	♂Z, ♀B	(K · Co-1 · G= X_2)
12.	*impal*	FZC, MBC	(K · C^2 · G= · X_1 ·)

of certain of ego's kinsmen or kinswomen. Since the spouse of a female relative must be a man and the spouse of a male relative must be a woman, it follows that the terms may be defined componentially by means of the definitions of the terms that designate the linking kinsmen supplemented by the component Sk, step-kinsman. The presence of the component male (♂) in the definition of the appropriate kin term indicates that the designated step-kinsman is a female, and the presence of the component female (♀) indicates that the designated relative is a male. Thus:

mama, MBW: $(Sk \cdot [K \cdot C^1 \cdot G{+}1 \cdot X_1 \cdot ♂])$
bengkila FZH: $(Sk \cdot [K \cdot C^1 \cdot G{+}1 \cdot X_1 \cdot ♀])$

Definitions of the special affinal or in-law terms may be specified as in Table 21.

Table 21

Primary Senses of Karo In-law Terms

Term	Focus	Definition
1. *simetua*	HM	(A · G+1 · ♀ · ♀E)
2. *ajinta*	HF	(A · G+1 · ♂ · ♀E)
3. *kȇla*	DH	(A · G-1 · ♂)
4. *permain*	♂SW	(A · G-1 · ♀ · ♂E)
5. *silih*	WB, ♂ZH	(A · G-1 · ♂ · ♂E)
6. *ȇda*	♀BW	(A · G= · ♀ · ♀E · KSp)
7. *beru*	HZ	(A · G= · ♀ · ♀E · SpK)

Sibling Subclasses

It remains only to take note of the several special classificatory sibling subclasses. One such subclass is lexically marked by the expression *sepemerȇn.* This subclass consists of ego's matrilateral parallel cousins, and the category is extended to include those more distant kintypes which reduce to sibling types and do so through the matrilateral parallel cousin types (see below, "Extension Rules"). The principal *sepemerèn* classificatory siblings may be defined componentially as (K · C^2 · G= · // · U), where the sign "U" stands for uterine relationship, that is, relationship through female consanguineals only. Of course, MFBDC is not a uterine relative, but the definition applies to the focal types of the category, to the principal or primary *sepemerèn* relatives, not to the broader category of *sepemerèn* relatives that is generated by the extension rules of the system.

The two self-reciprocal categories *senina siparibanen* (WZH) and *cimbang* (HBW) may be regarded as "co-spouse" categories. Both are sibling (or classificatory sibling) subclasses; this is evident from the fact that WZH must, by the equivalence rules of this system, reduce to ♂B, and HBW must reduce to ♀Z.

Extension (Equivalence) Rules

The next step in analysis is to isolate and specify the rules whereby Karo kinship terms are extended from their primary to other denotata. These rules specify the conceptual operations whereby the broad, extended senses and ranges of the terms are derived from their narrow primary senses (and ranges). In this system, as in many others, the extended senses of the terms are derived from their primary senses by neutralization or suspension, in specifiable genealogical contexts, of certain conceptual distinctions made at the level of the primary senses. An extension rule may be expressed analytically in either of two ways: (1) in the form of a simple verbal statement specifying the conceptual distinction that is neutralized and the relevant context(s), or (2) in a formula written in kintype notation and specifying a limited genealogical structural equivalence between two or more specified kintypes as linking or as designated kin. Such a formula is just a convenient means of expressing a semantic neutralization rule.

It would take too much space to describe here the process by which the rules stated below were isolated and tested for their ability to generate the full ranges of Karo kin terms from their primary denotata. In what follows I simply present the rules and give some examples of how they work.

One further preliminary observation is essential. In general, the foci of kin terms are invariant to the extension rules; no rules are posited which would operate on these kintypes. The foci of subclasses, however, are reducible to the foci of the principal classes to which these subclasses belong (see also Scheffler and Lounsbury 1971:105-106). Thus, for example, *bibi* is a special subclass of *nandė,* mother; the foci of *bibi* are MZ and FZ. All other kintypes classified as *bibi* must be reducible to the kintype M, the focus of the principal class of which *bibi* is a special subclass.

One of the extension rules of this system is the same-sex sibling merging rule, or in other words, a rule of neutralization of the distinction between lineal kin and parallel collateral kin. The appropriate formulaic expression of this rule is:

1. Same-sex sibling merging rule:
   (♂B. . . → ♂ . . .) ≡ (. . . ♂B → . . . ♂) and
   (♀Z. . . → ♀ . . .) ≡ (. . . ♀Z → . . . ♀),
   i.e., let anyone's sibling of the same sex, when as a linking relative, be regarded as structurally equivalent to that person himself or herself; conversely, let a linking relative's sibling of the same sex be regarded as structurally equivalent to that linking relative himself or herself.

This rule accounts (formally) for the facts that FB is designated *bapa,* the same as father, and FFB is designated *nini,* the same as FF.

Note, however, that grandparents' opposite-sex siblings also are designated *nini,* the same as grandparents' same-sex siblings. This may be accounted for by supposing that, for purposes of designation of G+2 kin, the opposition between cross and parallel collaterals is neutralized, G+2 cross collateral kin are treated as though they were parallel collaterals and, thus, identified terminologically with lineal G+2 kin via the same-sex sibling merging rule. This is rule no. 2, the cross-parallel neutralization rule:

2. The cross-parallel neutralization rule:
   ($PPSb_x$. → $PPSb_{//}$.) ≡ (.♀ $Sb_x CC$ → .♀ $Sb_{//}CC$)

i.e., let anyone's parent's parent's sibling of the opposite sex, when as a designated relative, be regarded as structurally equivalent to that person's parent's parent's sibling of the same sex when as a designated relative; conversely, let the child's child of ego's sibling of the opposite sex be regarded as structurally equivalent to the child's child of ego's sibling of the same sex.

Another rule neutralizes the distinction between co-lineal kin and other collaterals of the first degree, or in other words between full and half-siblings:

3. (PC → Sb), self-reciprocal:

Thus, for example, ♂FS is to be regarded as structurally equivalent to ♂B and, therefore, is designated *senina.* Further, the rules so far stated account for the classification of parallel cousins as though they were siblings. To illustrate this: FBC is to be regarded as structurally equivalent to FC via rule no. 1, and via rule no. 3, FC is equivalent to sibling. More distant kin-types such as FFBSC also reduce to sibling types by the same rules:

FFBSC, by rule no. 1 → FFSC,
FFSC, by rule no. 3 → FBC,
FBC, by rule no. 1 → FC,
FC, by rule no. 3 → Sb.

The fourth rule neutralizes the distinction between parents and step-parents and, conversely, between own children and step-children:

4. The step-kin merging rule:
(FW → M) ≡ (HC → C) and (MH → F) ≡ (WC → C).

This rule accounts for the fact that MH is designated *bapa,* father, and also, when taken in conjunction with rule no. 1, for many other extensions of kin terms as well. For example, FBW is designated *nandė*, mother. This designation is determined as follows:

FBW, by rule no. 1 → FW,
FW, by rule no. 4 → M.

The fifth rule neutralizes the distinction between lineal kin who are more than two generations removed from ego and those who are only two generations removed:

5. The grandparent rule:
   (.⚥PPP → .⚥PP) ≡ (CCC. – CC.),
   i.e., let ego's parent's parent's parent be regarded as structurally equivalent to ego's parent's parent; conversely, let anyone's child's child's child as a designated relative be regarded as structurally equivalent to that persons own child's child as a designated relative.

Thus, for example, FFF is to be regarded as structurally equivalent to FF and, therefore, is designated as *nini.* If one wishes to be precise about the generational status of the designated relative, FFF may be designated *entė* rather than *nini.*

So far, the rules posited for the extensions of Karo kin terms are not unusual; the same rules (or rules very much like them) are found in many other systems of kin classification. The sixth rule, however, is a fairly unusual one, though it is not by any means unique or peculiar to the Karo system. This is a rule of the type described elsewhere (Scheffler and Lounsbury 1971:35-36, 112-114) as a spouse-equation rule of kin-class extension. The need to posit such a rule for this system and the precise specification of the rule in this instance are evident from the following considerations.

Note that both FFBD and FMBD are classified as *bibi.* However, FFBDC are classified as *impal,* while FMBDC are classified as siblings. Also, although not indicated in Table 19, FFBDH is classified as *bengkila* and FMBDH is classified as *bapa.* It is clear from this that FFBD is identified with FZ and FMBD with MZ. The classification of FFBD as equivalent to FZ is readily accounted for via the extension rules already noted:

FFBD, by rule no. 1 → FFD,
FFD, by rule no. 3 → FZ, therefore *bibi.*

It follows that FFBDH is equivalent to FZH and that FFBDC are equivalent to FZC. However, the kintype FMBD is invariant to the rules so far posited; none of the rules applies in this instance.

Therefore, it is necessary to posit a further rule. In discovering the form this rule should take, we may begin by positing a rule and its corollary which will account for the particular reduction required, i.e., the reduction of the kintype FMBD to the kintype MZ. It should be more or less obvious that the appropriate rule (or part of it) is:

6. The spouse-equation rule:
(. . . ♂MBD → . . . ♂WZ) ≡ (♀FZS . . . → ♀ZH . . .),
i.e., let a male linking relative's mother's brother's daughter be regarded as structurally equivalent to that man's wife's sister; conversely, let a woman's father's sister's son, when as a linking relative, be regarded as structurally equivalent to that woman's sister's husband, when as a linking relative.

The more general rule (♂MBD → ♂WZ), etc., should not be posited here, for although ♂MBD and WZ are both *impal,* ♂MBD is one of the foci of *impal;* we should not posit any rules that would be applicable to the focal types as such (though we may posit rules that operate on the same kintypes in contexts other than as designated kin). Also, it should be clear that we should not posit the rule (. . . ♂MBD → . . . ♂W), etc., for this would have the effect of directly equating FMBD with FW, who is *nandė* rather than *bibi.* By rule no. 6, the reduction of the kintype FMBD is as follows:

FMBD, by rule no. 6 → FWZ,
FWZ, by rule no. 4 → MZ, therefore *bibi.*

The rule (no. 6) stated above is only a part of the spouse-equation rule. To account for the fact that MFZS is classified as *bapa* and ♂MBDC as *anak,* we have also to posit the rule

(. . . ♀FZS → . . . ♀HB) ≡ (♂MBD . . . → ♂WZ . . .).

It should be virtually self-evident that this rule and the one stated above are merely specific instances of the more general rule that may be stated as follows: Let any man's MBD be regarded as structurally equivalent to that man's WZ in all contexts other than male ego's MBD as a designated kinswoman; conversely, let any woman's FZS be regarded as structurally equivalent to her HB in all contexts other than female ego's FZS as a designated kinsman.

For reasons noted below (see "Comment"), it seems appropriate to regard this rule as a corollary of the spouse-equation rule rather than as the main part of that rule. The main or principal component of the rule in this system (see also Scheffler and Lounsbury 1971:199-210, on the Kachin and Haka Chin system) would appear to be

(WF → MB) ≡ (♂DH → ♂ZS).

This rule accounts for the fact that WF is termed *mama,* the same as MB, and the directionality of the rule is necessitated by the fact that MB is the true or proper *mama, mama kal.*

In addition to this rule and the corollary that has been noted already, we must posit still further corollaries to it, i.e., logically equivalent restatements of the rule in yet other genealogical contexts, and in relation to other kintypes. A full statement of these corollaries is presented in Table 21 but one may be noted here. One of the corollaries of the spouse-equation rule is

(.♂WZ. → .♂MBD.) ≡ (.♀HB. → .♀FZS.),

i.e., let male ego's WZ as a designated relative be regarded as structurally equivalent to male ego's MBD as a designated kinswoman; conversely, let female ego's HB as a designated relative be regarded as structurally equivalent to female ego's FZS as a designated kinsman. This accounts for the fact that WZ and HB are designated *impal,* though they are not the true or proper *impal.* The fairly strict context restrictions on the rule are necessitated by the fact that, if the rule were not so restricted, a number of analytical difficulties would arise. Thus, for example, although it is true that WZC are classified as *anak,* the same as one's own children, it cannot be that WZ is structurally equivalent to ♂MBD when WZ is considered as a linking kinswoman. If this were so, WZC would have to be regarded, for purposes of reckoning kin-class membership, as equivalent to MBDC; if this were true, the spouse-equation rule itself would then be applicable, taking us back to WZC. This circularity may be avoided by restricting the relevant corollary of the spouse-equation rule as above and by supposing that the reduction of WZC proceeds in this way:

WZC, by rule no. 1 → WC,
WC, by rule no. 4 → C, therefore *anak.*

In addition to these corollaries, there are also two auxiliaries to the spouse-equation rule. These deal with equivalences that are not logically entailed by the spouse-equation rule itself, and so they cannot be described as corollaries of that rule. It seems appropriate, however, to describe them as auxiliaries to that rule because they are conceptually related to it, even if not logically implied by it.

Note that in this system ♂FZDC is classified as *berèberè,* as though equivalent to ♂ZC. Also, female ego classifies FZDC as *berèberè,* as though equivalent to ♂ZC. Conversely, MMBS is classified as *mama,* as though structurally equivalent to MB. Similarly, ♀MBSC is classified as *permēn,* the same as ♀BC and, conversely, FFZD is classified as *bibi,* apparently as though structurally equivalent to FZ, while FFZS is classified as *beng-kila.* Interestingly enough FFZDH is classified as *bengkila,* too, so that in this instance a kinswoman's brother and her husband are both designated by the same term. None of the rules so far posited accounts for these equivalences. Also, we have yet to account for the reduction of MBW to MB and of FZH to FZ, which reductions are required by the fact that *mami* is a sub-class of *mama* and *bengkila* is a subclass of *bibi.*

If we take into account the fact that ♂FZD and ♀MBS are designatable as *turang impal,* cross-cousins who are like opposite-sex siblings, we may account for some of these equations by positing the next rule.

7. First spouse-equation rule auxiliary:
   (♂FZD . . . → ♂Z . . .) ≡ (. . . ♀MBS → . . . ♀B)
   (♀MBS . . . → ♀B . . .) ≡ (. . . ♂FZD → . . . ♂Z).

In other words, a man's FZD is to be regarded as structurally equivalent to his sister in all contexts other than male ego's FZD as a designated kinswoman; conversely, a woman's MBS is to be regarded as structurally to her brother in all contexts other than female ego's MBS as a designated kinsman. Even these restrictions are lifted, however, insofar as ♂FZD and ♀MBS may be designated *turang impal,* that is, as *impal* who are like opposite-sex siblings. Of course, this rule accounts for the fact that FFZDC, as well as FFZSC, and MMBSC, as well as MMBDC, are classified as *impal.*

To account for the subclass statuses of *mami* and *bengkila,* we must posit yet another auxiliary of the spouse-equation rule.

8. Second spouse-equation rule auxiliary:
   (.♂WB . . . → .♀B . . .) ≡ (. . . ♂ZH. → . . . ♂Z.)
   (.♀HZ . . . → .♂Z . . .) ≡ (. . . ♀BW. → . . . ♀B.).

In other words, when reckoning the classification of persons to whom he or she is related through an opposite-sex sibling-in-law, let ego take the place of his or her spouse and treat that opposite-sex sibling-in-law as though he or she were a same-sex sibling of the opposite sex of ego, etc. By this rule, WBC are reckoned as structurally equivalent to ♀ZC. Conversely, MBW is reckoned as structurally equivalent to MB (though designated by the subclass label *mami*) and FZH is reckoned as equivalent to FZ (though designated by the subclass label *bengkila*). This rule, in conjunction with one of the corollaries of the spouse-equation rule, accounts for the classification of ♀FZDC as *berěberě*, because ♀FZD as a linking kinswoman is structurally equivalent to HZ as a linking relative; thus, ♀FZDC is equivalent to HZC, and HZC is equivalent to ♂ZC. Similarly, a man's MBSC is equivalent to WBC, and WBC is equivalent to ♀BC.

Of course, this auxiliary of the spouse-equation rule implies that a man's WBW and, conversely, his ZHZ should be designated *impal*. Instead, they are designated *turangku*. However, as noted above, there is no difficulty here because the need for this rule and other considerations suggest that *turangku* may be regarded as a subclass of *impal*. Because WZH and HBW are classified as special kinds of siblings, we must suppose that an additional rule of this system is:

9. The co-spouse rule:
   (WH → ♂B) and (HW → ♀Z),
   i.e., let a man's WH be regarded as structurally equivalent to his brother (self-reciprocal), and let a woman's HW be regarded as structurally equivalent to her sister (self-reciprocal).

At first glance this rule may seem a bit odd, for in most instances a woman's HW would be that woman herself and a man's WH would be that man himself. Note, however, that in the case of a polygynous marriage a woman's HW is another woman, and to all appearances each wife must regard the other as a classificatory sister. Of course, polyandry is not a feature of this society, and so two men cannot be married to the same woman at the same time. However, a man may marry the wife of a deceased brother or classificatory brother, in which case the successive husbands of a woman would be brothers or classificatory brothers of one another. Also, those kinswomen whom a man may marry are potential wives for his brothers, and those kinsmen whom a woman may marry are potential husbands for her sisters. Thus, it might be supposed for purposes of classification, that whomever a marriageable kinswoman of ego does marry, that man is to be regarded as male ego's brother, and whomever a marriageable kinsman marries, that woman is to be regarded as female ego's sister.

These rules are necessary and sufficient to account for all of the simple (non-metaphorical) extensions of Karo kinship terms. The validity of this claim will not be demonstrated here by means of a "proof table" such as that presented in Scheffler and Lounsbury (1971:128-30) for the Siriono system of kin classification. By following the procedures indicated there, the reader may demonstrate for himself, if he so desires, that these rules are sufficient to do the job. He may determine for himself, by attempting to formulate a more economical set of such rules, that the rules posited here are necessary as well as sufficient to do the job of accounting (formally) for the assignment of terms to the various types of kin, step-kin and affines. It may be useful to note that there is no need to order the extension rules of this system, although there is such a need in the case of the Siriono system (cf. Scheffler and Lounsbury 1971:126). Because there is no order among the rules, certain relatives may be designated by more than one term. A man's WZ, for example, may be designated as *impal* (via one of the corollaries of the spouse-equation rule) or as *silangen* (W, via the same-sex sibling merging rule).

COMMENT

It was noted above that, in this system, the principal component of the spouse-equation rule would appear to be (WF → MB) ≡ (♂DH → ♂ZS), etc., rather than the rule equating a man's MBD with his WZ in all genealogical contexts other than male ego's MBD as a designated kinswoman. The choice seems appropriate for the following reasons.

In Scheffler and Lounsbury (1971), it was noted that the MBD-FZS – spouse-equation rule of kin-class extension

> is sometimes associated with the right of a man to claim his MBD in marriage (though in some cases the claim is restricted to one man from each sibling set), and sometimes with the right of a man to claim a ZS as a DH. At this point we cannot say that the existence of such rights provides the necessary and sufficient conditions for the institutionalization of the MBD-FZS – spouse-equation rule. It may be that the rule occurs in the absence of such rights, or that the rights occur in some societies without receiving expression in the associated systems of kin classification. The available ethnographies, though often suggestive, do not provide unequivocal evidence on these points, so we cannot fairly argue that the rule of kin classification is uniformly associated with such rightful claims of men over their MBDs or their ZSs; we can only say that we know of no clear-cut negative instances (p. 220).

It seems reasonably certain from Dr. Singarimbun's account of the Karo case that this is a negative instance. From Dr. Singarimbun's account of Karo marriage rules, it is clear that a man is not obliged to marry a MBD (or classificatory MBD) in preference to a woman of some other kintype or category; nor do men have rightful claims over their MBDs as wives, or over their ZSs as DHs. The closest that Karo come to recognizing such rightful marital claims is in a woman's *moral* obligation to her brother to encourage one of her sons to consider proposing to one of her BDs. The girl, for her part, is not jurally obliged to accept the proposal; it is always emphasized that she has the right to refuse any proposal, whether it emanates from her FZS or not. Of course, a girl's parents may attempt to persuade her to accept a particular proposal, but to all appearances they are not jurally obliged to persuade her to accept the proposal of a FZS any more than they are obliged to persuade her to accept the proposal of some other kinsman or non-kinsman. While they are obliged not to casually dismiss or refuse a proposal made by their daughter's FZS, neither should they casually dismiss or refuse a proposal made by some other kinsman or non-kinsman. In short, although Karo value the "perpetuation" of interfamilial marital alliances – such that the sons of men who are WB-ZH are themselves WB-ZH – they are not under any jural constraints in this respect (except for the rules that prohibit marriages that would confuse established *kalimbubu-anakberu* relations).

But even if Karo are not jurally obliged to perpetuate established interfamily alliances (and thereby the whole network of *senina, kalimbubu* and *anakberu* relations entailed by them), we are not necessarily left without an explanation for their use of the MBD-FZS – spouse-equation rule of kin-class extension. (Of course, even if such an explanation were not readily apparent, we would still have to accept the fact that the rule is part of the Karo system of kin classification; the evidence for the existence of that rule is different from the evidence for any explanation of its occurrence in that system.) A possible explanation in this instance is that *a man's WF is assimilated to the right- and duty-status of a MB.*

As we have seen, a man's principal *mama* is his MB (*mama kal*), and his WF, for all his social importance or significance, is merely a classificatory *mama.* That is to say, a man's WF is ascribed the terminological status of his MB. Of course, we are not entitled to assume, on the basis of the terminological evidence alone, that this ascription of terminological status must be associated with, much less rest on, reflect or express, a concommitant ascription to WF of the (or some part of the) right- and duty-status of MB. After all, we know of many instances (in other societies) in which certain relatives are attributed the terminological statuses of other (closer) relatives but without also being ascribed the right- and duty-statuses of those other (closer) relatives (see Scheffler and Lounsbury 1971:152-53). In this instance, however, there are reasons to suppose that WF *is* ascribed the right- and duty-status of MB (or some significant part, at least, of that status).

Dr. Singarimbun reports (p. 153) that the Karo express considerable concern about the fact that, when a man marries a woman other than a MBD (or another immediate *kalimbubu*), his duties to his WF will necessarily conflict with his duties to his MB; he will associate more closely with his WF, and will become socially isolated from his MB, at least to some extent. It is only when one's primary and immediate *kalimbubu* by birth and one's primary and immediate *kalimbubu* by marriage are one and the same persons that this social separation is avoided. All of this implies, of course, that a man's duties to his WF are at least closely similar to his duties to his MB; otherwise, there would be no necessary conflict of duties.

Thus, regardless of whom a man marries, his social relations with his WF are like his social relations with his MB, at least in their right-and-duty content. Now, if it were the situation here that a man had a rightful claim over his ZS as DH, we might reasonably suppose that the assimilation of WF to the terminological and jural status of MB is based on, reflects, or expresses that rightful claim. But, of course, no such rightful claim is acknowledged in Karo adat. It should be recalled, however, that in Karo society, each and every marriage creates a *kalimbubu-anakberu* relation between two families, the family of origin and the family of procreation of the female spouse in that marriage. It follows from this that a man's family of procreation must stand in the same kind of social relationship to his wife's family of origin as his own family of origin stands to his mother's family of origin. It may be more appropriate, however, to say that a man's family of procreation must stand in the same sort of social relationship to both his wife's family of origin and his MB's family of procreation. This is because, for a young man of marriageable age, it is highly probable that this MB has taken the place of his MF as his most prominent living principal *kalimbubu* by birth. Thus, again, regardless of whom a man marries, his social relations with his WF are like his social relations with his MB, at least in their right-and-duty content. His WF is the head of his family of *kalimbubu* by marriage, just as his MB is the head of his family of *kalimbubu* by birth (having "replaced" his MF in that status).

It may be, then, that the Karo use of the MBD-FZS – spouse-equation rule of kin-class extension is the means by which the Karo accommodate the classification of kin to the system of interfamilial alliance. This is not to suggest that this is the only means by which that accommodation might have been achieved, but it is a perfectly rational, logical "solution" to the "problem" (if it necessarily is one) of accommodating one socially significant system of classification to another; and it can hardly be denied that it must simplify life both cognitively and pragmatically to have these two systems so accommodated to one another, both in the genealogical and marital relations they organize conceptually and in the social relations they order normatively.

They are *not* so close, however, that in the end the Karo have been forced to "reduce" one system to the other. The two systems of classification remain conceptually distinct; the system of kin classification is not simply an elaboration of the other system of classification; and the accommodation of the structure of the system of kin classification to the structure of the system of classification based on interfamilial alliance is anything but complete. It is only insofar as the classification of kin and inlaws is governed by the spouse-equation rule that the system of kin classification is accommodated to the system of classification based on interfamilial alliance. It should be virtually self-evident that the definitions of the primary senses of the terms are not notably, if at all, shaped by considerations of keeping *senina, kalimbubu* and *anakberu* terminologically distinct from one another. Moreover, most of the other extension rules of this system are not in the least peculiar to it or even to that class of systems of kin classification which feature MBD-FZS – spouse-equation rules of kin-class extension.

If this is the appropriate explanation of why the Karo employ a spouse-equation rule of kin-class extension, it is of course not an explanation of the Karo *system* of kin classification. It is merely an explanation (and perhaps only a partial explanation) of *only one* feature of that system.

Comparative Observations

Although the published data on a few other Indonesian systems of kin classification are not as full as those provided here on the Karo system, they are sufficient to confirm that other systems with much the same structural features exist in this area. For two others in particular – the systems of kin classification of the Manggarai and Endeh districts of Flores Island – Needham (1966b, 1968) has proposed an interpretation that differs in a number of important respects from the model presented here for the Karo system. Since Needham's interpretation of the Manggarai and Endeh data could conceivably be placed on the Karo system, and the model presented here for the Karo system could be extended to the Manggarai and Endeh systems, we should briefly consider the possible merits of

Needham's interpretation. Before considering its possible relevance to the Karo case, however, we should ask how well it accounts for the Manggarai and Endeh data.

Needham's interpretation of the Manggarai and Endeh systems is that these are "two-section systems" or "symmetric prescriptive alliance systems" of social classification. However, as he notes, in both societies MBD-FZS marriage is favored and FZD-MBS marriage is proscribed; also, there are reports of "asymmetrical" intergroup marital alliance. As Needham interprets the situation, the rule of marriage (or one of the rules of marriage) is "asymmetrical." Needham concludes that in both instances (as in some others, e.g., Garo) we have to deal with societies in which the people "order their social lives by the categories of a two-section terminology" yet practice "asymmetric prescriptive alliance," or in other words, "apply their terms of social classification in an asymmetric fashion" (Needham 1966b:154-55; 1968:329). The possibility of such an arrangement is contrary to the assumptions (about certain necessary connections between terminological form and other social forms) that have guided Needham's previous analyses and interpretations of many other "relationship terminologies." Thus, Needham is forced to jettison most of the sociological baggage of his theory of "prescriptive alliance systems of social classification" and to argue that there is no necessary connection between terminology (system of kin classification) and any features of social structure, certainly not insofar as "two-section systems" of classification are concerned.

It is important to realize that, in abandoning most of his sociological claims for the type "symmetric prescriptive alliance system of social classification," Needham has in effect deprived the expression itself of virtually all meaning, and certainly of any reference to presumed distinctive structural features. Application of the designation is made to depend wholly and solely on the presence of some (not clearly specified) set of terminological equations and distinctions of kintypes, and the structural principles which presumably govern these equations and distinctions are not specified. They are not specified because, although the social structural features previously alleged to account for these terminological equations and distinctions are now regarded as non-essential features of such systems of classification, no other structural principles have been specified to replace them. In short, it is semantically vacuous to assert, as Needham does, that a particular system is the terminology of a symmetric prescriptive alliance system of social classification simply because it features certain terminological equations and distinctions of kintypes. To describe the system in this way, and on these grounds, tells us nothing about its inherent structure.

So the first major difficulty with Needham's description of the Manggarai and Endeh systems is that the description is devoid of any semantic content. Therefore, it is difficult to see how the description and the analysis on which it is based can reasonably be described as "structural" (cf. Scheffler and Lounsbury 1971:136-37).

Another defect in Needham's interpretation is that it is based on the assumption that the terms of these systems are not kinship terms, i.e., they do not designate genealogically-defined categories, and do not have primary genealogical denotata from which their broader ranges are derived by means of genealogical (and perhaps other kinds of) rules of terminological extension. Dr. Singarimbun's data establish beyond a reasonable doubt that this assumption is not valid in the Karo case, and data gathered in the field by Needham himself may be analyzed to show that the assumption is invalid for the Endeh system, too. I refer here to data provided by Needham (1968:315) on the use of Endeh kinship terms in relative-product expressions, and on the ways in which at least some of the terms may be lexically marked when used to denote non-lineal relatives who may be designated by the same unmodified terms as are certain lineal relatives. These data clearly indicate that the terms are polysemous, that their structurally primary denotata are certain kintypes, and that they are extended to relatives of other types (of course, they may be extended metaphorically to non-relatives as well). (See Scheffler and Lounsbury 1971 and Scheffler 1972 for extensive discussion of the reasoning on which these assertions are based.)

Further still, it is not at all obvious that the Endeh system should be classified as a "two-section system," even if one accepts Needham's criteria. The data on the Endeh system show some signs of serious inconsistency with Needham's "two-section system" model. Some of these are noted by Needham, others are not. For example. Needham's (1968) discussion of Van Suchtelen's data takes no account of the reported classifications of second cousins, though these classifications are listed in Needham's table (1968:308). In these data we find the following (for male ego except where noted):

weta:	Z, FBD, FZD, FFBDD, FFZSD, FFZDD
nasa:	♀FZS, ♀FFBDS, ♀FFZSS, ♀FFZDS
èdja:	FZS, FFBDS, FFZSS, FFZDS, ZH, WB
ipa:	♀FZD, ♀FFBDD, ♀FFZSD, ♀FFZDD

To this Needham (1968:315) adds: *nasa,* ♂MBD, and *èdja,* ♂MBS, on the basis of his own inquiries in the field in 1955. Now, in a genuine "two-section system" FFZDC would be classified as "siblings" by either sex of ego, and FFZSC would be classified as "cross-cousins," also by either sex of ego. While this pattern is partially present here, it should be clear that there is a much stronger tendency to classify both FFZDC and FFZSC as cross-cousins, exactly as in the Karo system. Indeed, the only apparent counterindication is that ♂FFZDD is here classified as ♂Z, but this classification is not in fact inconsistent with the possibility that terminological extensions in this system are governed by much the same rules as in the Karo system, especially the spouse-equation rule and its auxiliaries. The obvious difference between the Endeh and Karo systems is that, in the Endeh system, ♂FZD is identified with ♂Z not only as a linking relative but also as a designated relative. Thus, ♂FFZDD is identified with FZD, as in the Karo system, but the Endeh identification of ♂FZD with ♂Z as a designated relative implies that FFZDD also is classified as sister. Van Suchtelen's report that ♀FZSC is classified as *aneh,* ♂ZC, is consistent with this interpretation (cf. Needham 1968:320-21; see also Scheffler and Lounsbury 1971:210-14 for comment on the Manggarai data).

We are forced to conclude that Needham's observations on the Manggarai and Endeh systems can provide no guidance in understanding the Karo system of kin classification, but that the model presented here for the Karo system is, with minor modifications, extendable to the Manggarai and Endeh systems.

References

Abbreviations

AA - American Anthropologist. Menasha, Wisconsin.
BIJD. - Bijdragen tot de taal-, Land- en Volkenkunde van Nederlandsch-Indië. Den Haag.
TIJD - Tijdschrift voor Indische Taal-, Land en Volkenkunde. Batavia.

Bruner, Edward M.
1959 Kinship organization among the urban Batak of Sumatra. Transactions of the New York Academy of Sciences 22:118-25.

Cole, Fay-Cooper
1945 The peoples of Malaysia. New York: D. van Nostrand.

Dumont, Louis
1968 Marriage alliance. *In* International Encyclopedia of Social Sciences, vol. 10:19-23. New York: The Macmillan Co.

Duyvendak, J. Ph.
1940 Inleiding tot de ethnologie van de Indische archipel. Batavia: J. B. Wolter's

Fischer, H. Th.
1935 De aanverwantschap bij enige volken van de Ne Nederlands-Indische Archipel. Mensch en Maatshappij 11:285-97, 365-78.
1936 Het asymmetrisch cross-cousin-huwelijk in Nederlandsch-Indië. Tijd. 76:359-72.

Fortes, Meyer
1953 The structure of unilineal descent groups. AA 55:17-41.
1969 Kinship and the social order. Chicago: Aldine Publishing Co.

Geddes, W. R.
1957 Nine Dayak nights. Melbourne: Oxford University Press.

Goody, J. ed.
1958 The developmental cycle in domestic groups. Cambridge Papers in Social Anthropology, No. 1. Cambridge: Cambridge University Press.

Heine-Geldern, Robert
1935 The archaeology and art of Sumatra. Weiner Beiträge zur Kulturgeschichte und Linguistik, 3.

Hurgronje, C. Snouck
1906 The Achehnese, vol. 1. Translated by A. W. S. O'Sullivan. Leiden: E. J. Brill.

Joustra, M.
1902 Mededeelingen omtrent en opmerkingen naar aanleiding van het Pek Oewaloeh of het doodenfeest der Merga Sembiring. Tijd. 45:541-56.
1903 Eene verklaring van den naam van het Sembiringsche doodenfeest. Tijd. 46:472-5.
1904 Karo-Bataksche vertellingen. Verhandelingen van het Bataviaasch Genootschap van Kunsten en Wetenschappen, deel 56, la stuk. Batavia: Albrecht.
1907 Karo-Bataksch Woordenboek. Leiden, E. J. Brill.
1918 Korte mededeeling in zake het Sembiringsche doodenfeest. Bijd. 74:618-9.
1926 Batakspiegel. Leiden: S. C. van Doesburgh.

Keuning, J.
1948 Verwantschaprecht en volksordening, huwelijksrecht en erfrecht in het Koeriagebied van Tapanoeli. Leiden: Eduard Ijdo.
1958 The Toba Batak, formerly and now. Translated by Claire Holt. New York: Modern Indonesia Project, Southeast Asia Program, Department of Far Eastern Studies, Cornell University.

Koentjaraningrat
1967 Tjelapar: a village in South Central Java. *In* Koentjaraningrat, ed., villages in Indonesia. Ithaca, New York: Cornell University Press, pp. 244-80.

Kunstadter, Peter
1966 Residential and social organization of the Lawa of northern Thailand. Southwestern Journal of Anthropology 22:61-84.

Kunstadter, Peter, et al.
1963 Demographic variability and preferential marriage patterns. American Journal of Physical Anthropology 22:511-19.

Leach, E. R.
1945 Jingphaw kinship terminology. Journal of the Royal Anthropological Institute 75:59-72. Reprinted in E. R. Leach, Rethinking Anthropology. London: Athlone Press.
1958 Concerning Trobriand clans and the kinship category tabu. *In* J. Goody, ed., The developmental cycle in domestic groups. Cambridge Papers in Social Anthropology, No. 1:120-45. Cambridge: Cambridge University Press.

Lévi-Strauss, Claude
1966 The future of kinship studies. Proceedings of the Royal Anthropological Institute for 1965: 13-22.
1969 The elementary structures of kinship. Translated from the French 2nd ed. 1967 (1st ed. 1949) by J. H. Bell, J. R. von Sturmer, and R. Needham, ed. London: Eyre and Spottiswoode.

Loeb, E. M.
1935 Sumatra: its history and people. Wiener Beiträge zur Kulturgeschichte und Linguistik, 3.

Maybury-Lewis, David P.
1965 Prescriptive marriage systems. Southwestern Journal of Anthropology 21:207-30.

Nasoetion, Masdoelhak Hamonangan
1943 De plaats van de vrouw in de Bataksche maatschappij. Utrecht: Kemink en Zoon.

Needham, Rodney
1962 Structure and sentiment: a test case in social anthropology. Chicago: The University of Chicago Press.
1966a Review of J. C. Vergouwen's The social organisation and customary law of the Toba-Batak of North Sumatra. AA 68:1265-8.
1966b Terminology and alliance: 1 - Garo, Manggarai. Sociologus 16:141-57.
1968 Endeh: terminology, alliance, and analysis. Bijd 124:305-35.
1971 Introduction. *In* Rethinking kinship and marriage, R. Needham, ed., pp. xiii-cxvii. London: Tavistock Publications.

Neumann, J. H.
1926 Bijdrage tot de geschiedenis der Karo-Batakstammen, I. Bijd. 82:1-36.
1927 Bijdrage tot de geschiedenis der Karo-Batakstammen, II. Bijd. 83:162-80.
1930 Poestaka Ginting. Tijd. 70:1-146.
1951 Karo-Bataks - Nederlands Woordenboek. (Lembaga Kebudajaan Indonesia). Medan: Varekamp and Co.

Pelzer, K. J.
1945 Pioneer settlement in the Asiatic Tropics. New York: Institute of Pacific Relations.

Peters, Emrys
1945 The proliferation of segments in the lineage of the Bedouin in Cyrenaica. Journal of the Royal Anthropological Institute 90:29-53.

Ronkel, P. S. van
1918 Drawidische volksnamen op Sumatra. Bijd. 74:263-6.

Scheffler, Harold W.
1972 Kinship semantics. *In* B. J. Siegel, ed., Annual review of Anthropology, vol. 1, 1972, pp. 309-28.

Scheffler, Harold W. and Lounsbury, Floyd G.
1971 A study in structural semantics: the Sirionо kinship system. Englewood Cliffs, N.J.: Prentice-Hall Inc.

Tamboen, P.
1952 Adat-Istiadat Karo. Djakarta: Balai Pustaka.

Ter Haar, B.
1948 Adat law in Indonesia. Translated and edited with an introduction by E. Adamson Hoebel and A. Arthur Schiller. New York: Institute of Pacific Relations.

Tideman, J.
1935 Review of Loeb, 1935. Mensch en Maatachappij 11:381-2.
1936 Hindoe-invloed in Noordelijk Batakland. Amsterdam: Uitgaven van het Bataksch Instituut, No. 23.

Tugby, Donald J.
1958 Social structure and social organization in Upper Mandailing, Sumatra. Unpublished Ph.D. thesis, The Australian National University.

Vergouwen, J. C.
1964 The social organisation and customary law of the Toba-Batak of Northern Sumatra. (Trans. from the 1933 Dutch edition by Jeune Scott-Kimball.) Koninklijk Instituut voor Taal-, Land- en Volkenkunde. Trans. Series, No. 7. The Hague: Martinus Nijhoff.

Wagner, F. A.
1959 Indonesia: the art of an island group. Translated by A. E. Keep. London: Methuen.

Wouden, F. Van
1968 Types of social structure in eastern Indonesia. (Trans. by R. Needham from the 1935 Dutch ed.) Koninklijk Instituut voor Taal-, Land- en Volkenkunde. Trans. Series, No. 11. The Hague: Martinus Nijhoff.

Ypes, W. K. H.
1932 Bijdrage tot de kennis van de stamverwantschap, de inheemsche rechtsgemeenschappen en het grondenrecht der Toba- en Dairibataks. 's Gravenhage: Martinus Nijhoff.

Index